The Ernst & Young Information Management Series

Development Effectiveness

Strategies for IS Organizational Transition

Also from Ernst & Young

The Ernst & Young Guide to Total Cost Management
The Complete Guide to Special Event Management
The Ernst & Young Guide to Raising Capital
The Ernst & Young Guide to Expanding in the Global Market
The Ernst & Young Resource Guide to Global Markets
Understanding and Using Financial Data: An Ernst & Young Guide for Attorneys
The Ernst & Young Business Plan Guide, Second Edition
Managing Information Strategically
(*The Ernst & Young Information Management Series*)
Mergers & Acquisitions, Second Edition
The Ernst & Young Almanac and Guide to U.S. Business Cities
The Name of the Game: The Business of Sports

Forthcoming from Ernst & Young

Privatization: Investing in Infrastructures Around the World
The Ernst & Young Guide to Financing for Growth

The Ernst & Young Information Management Series

Development Effectiveness

Strategies for IS Organizational Transition

By Vaughan Merlyn
Ernst & Young Center for Information Technology & Strategy℠

John Parkinson
Ernst & Young Center for Information Systems Planning & Delivery

With Bob Phillips and Roy Youngman

John Wiley & Sons, Inc.
New York • Brisbane • Chichester • Singapore • Toronto

This text is printed on acid-free paper.

Published by John Wiley & Sons, Inc.

Library of Congress Cataloging in Publication Data

Merlyn, Vaughan.
Development effectiveness : strategies for IS organizational transition / by Vaughan Merlyn [and] John Parkinson : with Bob Phillips and Roy Youngman.
p. cm. — (Ernst & Young information management series)
Includes bibliographical references.
ISBN 0-471-58954-3
1. Management information systems. 2. Information resources management. 3. Organizational effectiveness. 4. Total quality management. I. Parkinson, John, 1950- . II. Phillips, Bob. III. Youngman, Roy. IV. Title. V. Series.
HD30.213.M47 1994
658.4′038′011—dc20 93-604

Printed in the United States of America
10 9 8 7 6 5 4 3

It must be considered that
there is nothing more difficult to carry out
nor more doubtful of success
nor more dangerous to handle
than to bring about a new order of things.

Niccolo Machiavelli
The Prince

The productivity of people requires continuous learning,
as the Japanese have taught us. It requires adoption in the West
of the specific Japanese Zen concept where one learns to do better
what one already does well.

Peter Drucker

No one knows what they want until you give them
what they ask for.

Jerry Weinberg

If you want to understand something, try to change it.

Walter Fenno Dearborn

This one is from John for Marianne,
and from Vaughan for Gillian and Louise.

Contents

Preface

Although the application of information technology (IT) to the solution of business problems is still in its relative infancy (less than 50 years old) in comparison with many other aspects of business and organization management, it has already assumed a central role in enterprise effectiveness and the pursuit of competitive positions. There is, therefore, great pressure on information systems (IS) professionals to move the process of developing information systems away from the category of "craft" and toward that of an engineering discipline that can provide low cost, rapidly developed, and effective business systems to meet complex, changing enterprise needs.

At the same time, the enabling technologies available to support these new developments, both for the development process itself and for the target application environment, continue to evolve rapidly. Making use of the new technologies requires a constant updating of skills and a careful evaluation of relevant experience in a work force reduced by demographic factors that cannot be countered by any simple short-term actions. As a final constraint, investment capital for new systems and new technologies is increasingly scarce. New developments therefore have to be justified more thoroughly than ever, and new information systems must be much more effective in use in order to be acceptable. Responding to all of these issues poses *the* major challenge for IS organizations over the coming decade.

Historically, the IS organization has responded with more (and usually more expensive) technology at the expense of establishing a sound infrastructure for development and by largely ignoring the need to manage individual and organizational change in a constantly changing business and technical environment. Even if business could continue to afford such an approach, it has not worked well. Information systems still take too long to develop, are often delivered late, cost too much, and provide too little business benefit. A significantly better process is needed and needed soon, but whatever replaces our past and present efforts must learn from their shortcomings and from previous attempts at improvement.

Any new process must also accommodate the results, however poor we may now think them, of the last two or more generations of development efforts. These produced the information systems that run our businesses today, systems that cannot be replaced overnight.

We must seek out a process that recognizes the importance of managing change in an acceptable fashion, so that organizations and individuals are not overwhelmed. At the same time, the new process must deliver improvements in quality and performance quickly enough that an increasingly skeptical enterprise will allow the IS organization time to put its complete house in order.

Most IS organizations will not achieve the necessary transformation in outlook and approach without some, perhaps a great deal of, external help. This book sets out an approach to improving the effectiveness of the IS organization that is a useful blend of insights from a variety of theoretical viewpoints and practical experience of making these changes work in real-world situations. It is not a complete or guaranteed answer for anyone, but it should be a sufficient starting point for the IS organization that knows it needs to become more effective and is wondering where and how to begin, or how to accelerate improvement initiatives already under way.

We have divided the book into three parts. In *Part I*, we identify and describe the factors that have created the present situation for the IS organization, consider what can be learned from past efforts, and set an agenda for the sustained high performance IS organization we wish to create.

In *Part II*, we examine the key issues of organizational change management, organizational design, and measurement related to a successful transition from the current state of most IS organizations to the desired high-effectiveness future state.

In *Part III*, we describe a model process for planning and managing the required transition.

Acknowledgments

Acknowledgments are due to the large number of people who have made key contributions to this book. Bob Phillips and Roy Youngman, our colleagues in Ernst & Young's U.S. National Office, started out with us as authors and made important contributions before other commitments and demands for their considerable talents diverted them. Mary Silva Doctor, Charles Gold, Sheila Smith, and Rick Swanborg at the Center for Information Technology and Strategy contributed generously, inspired by the participating sponsor companies of the IS Leadership Multi-Client Research Program. Thanks to Kent Boesdorfer, Mark Hefner, and Joyce Olson of Ernst & Young's Organizational Change Management group for helping us appreciate the complexities of cultural change. This book is the richer for their ideas and insights.

The many colleagues at the firm's two research centers in Boston and Las Colinas, a number of our line consulting partners, as well as several patient executives at some of our consulting clients who read and reviewed parts of the manuscript, gave generously of their time and experience to question our ideas and assertions. Their comments and suggestions added greatly to the content of our work. We have borrowed freely from our discussions with all of them. Any errors in presentation or understanding are, naturally, ours, not theirs.

We also gratefully acknowledge the support and encouragement received from our partners throughout Ernst & Young's U.S. Management Consulting practice—in particular: Alan Stanford, national director of Information Technology Consulting; Dale Wartluft, national director of Systems Planning and Delivery; Blaine Hurst, formerly director of the Center for Information Technology Planning and Delivery, and now Chief Information Officer with Boston Chicken; and Bud Mathaisel, director of the Center for Information Technology and Strategy[SM].

Special thanks to Jennifer Burgin, Pauli Morin, and Janet Santry for their help with reference material and graphics.

Finally, thanks to Jon Zonderman, who helped us structure and merge our written ideas, and to our editor Susan Barry of John Wiley & Sons, Inc.

Vaughan Merlyn
Boston, 1993

John Parkinson
Dallas, 1993

Authors' Note

Those who believe the challenges of effective development are all technological, and that the solutions lie in new technologies, will be disappointed in this book's light treatment of technology. This is, however, deliberate. There are many excellent sources of material about new and emerging technolgies. We believe that it is the process and people implications of new technology that are typically short changed, both by IS management, and by the literature. We have therefore chosen to focus this book on these aspects.

PART I

The Current State of IS Development and Pointers for the Future

Chapter 1 discusses how the changes taking place in business create new demands and expectations from information systems (IS). Here we analyze the implications of these changes for IS developers and show why improving software development is an important business issue. By analyzing past experiences with development automation, we show why the results have been so disappointing, and why achieving an effective development environment demands significant management attention. From these past automation experiences the lessons to be learned are extracted, both from the successes and from the failures.

Chapter 2 explores how the best IS organizations are approaching systems development, from the perspectives of people, process, technology, and infrastructure. It offers a look at how "best practices" are working, and where they are falling short.

In Chapter 3 we begin to paint a picture of a desired future-state vision for IS and describe the characteristics and behaviors that we would expect to find in a highly productive IS development organization.

1

How We Got Here—Information Systems Development and Attempts to Improve Performance

In the 40 or so years that computers have been used to support business, the technology has come a very long way. Yet businesses are still, by and large, ineffective in the use of this technology. The information systems (IS) organization faces a number of challenges, most of which have been around for years. Many attempts have been and are being made by IS developers to improve the way they work. But most of these initiatives have failed or have fallen into disrepute. What lessons can be learned from these efforts, and where can both IS and business managers look for better solutions?

Issues for Business Managers

There are many challenges facing businesses and organizations today. The growing size, complexity, and diversity of global markets, the increasingly rapid pace of product development and deployment, the shrinking of product life cycles, and (for the foreseeable future at least) the restriction of available investment and working capital all put intense competitive pressure on business managers.

Customers are becoming much more focused on service quality as a means of differentiation in markets where products may not be well differentiated. Regulators throughout the world are placing increasingly complex and costly reporting and control demands of all kinds on businesses. New issues and concerns, such as time to market, reskilling an aging workforce, and the environment, arise and must be addressed.

Reacting to all of these competitive pressures simultaneously is far from easy. For this reason, and because of the need to react to the inevitable unforeseen changes in the business environment—what Bob Horton, CEO of The British Petroleum Company p.l.c. called "the management of surprise"[1]—business managers and executives today are faced with unprecedented demands.

Not only must they deploy available assets effectively, they must also cope with continuous efforts aimed at cost reduction and quality improvement. Not only must they expand markets and product lines, they must also target more effectively and manage risk in new and changing markets. Not only must they find, develop and retain people with the key managerial and technical skills that keep their products and services innovative, they must also anticipate future shifts in demand (or fashion) and be prepared to react to them.

Faced with these pressures to remain competitive and profitable, senior managers are increasingly coming to realize that the only truly defensible competitive advantage is the ability to react more quickly and to effectively manage change.

Better Information

A key factor in the ability of managers to respond more quickly and manage change in today's business environment is the acquisition of better information. That means having in-depth knowledge about the business and its resources, products, customers and markets. To establish and maintain the necessary knowledge, enterprises are increasingly turning to a generally neglected asset—information about their customers, potential customers, suppliers, competitors' and potential competitors' products and services, and how these come together—as a way to support their continuing growth objectives. No matter what kind of enterprise is involved, the emphasis is changing from a traditional functional focus (manufacturing, distribution, or finance, for instance) to one of effective information management, with the information organized around a structure similar to that shown in Figure 1.1.

This shift in emphasis has quickly led to the realization that the required information is often present, but not usually in a form that can be used effectively. All too often, some key information is absent altogether.

The lessons to be learned from the Management Information Systems (MIS) developments of the last 20 years are important.

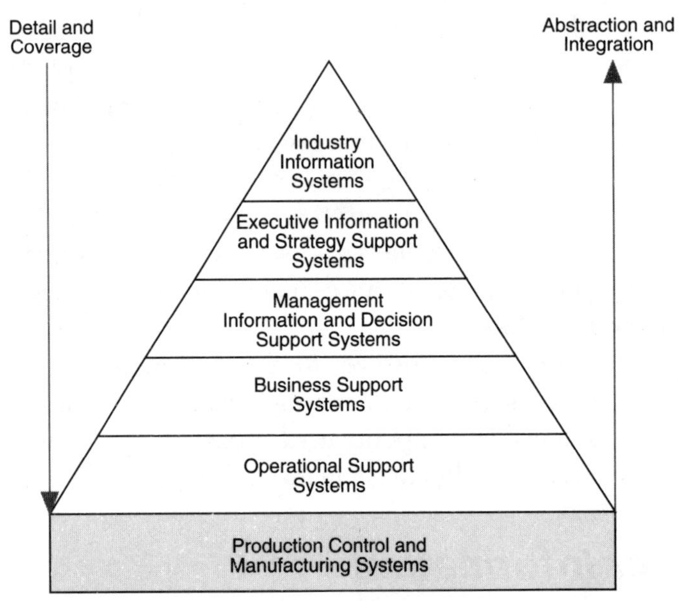

Figure 1.1 *A Classification Structure for Information Systems in a Typical Enterprise*

A note on the word *enterprise* is in order. Although the vast majority of organizations that will benefit from efforts to increase the effectiveness of their systems department are commercial businesses, in today's world virtually every large entity depends on information systems and, hence, information system development—from national to provincial or state and even local government; international organizations such as the United Nations and the European Community; and nonprofit organizations such as universities, foundations or community service organizations. To make sure that you—and we—do not fall into the pattern of using *corporation* to denote organizations that can benefit from systems development, we will frequently refer to the enterprise, enterprise-wide systems, and enterprise-wide information.

Although it is well known that technology is required to support effective management processes (and in some instances to shape or enable these processes), technology alone is not enough. Rather, it is also essential to overhaul organizational structures, to constantly revisit and challenge business assumptions, and to articulate widely and effectively the policies and principles that determine the way a business operates.

Without information, managers and staff cannot be sure that their efforts are directed toward the business's objectives or that their efforts are effective. Even when an effective MIS is in place, business processes do not stand still, and the MIS that supports them must move with them. Without all of these factors working together correctly, technology can seldom achieve its true potential in supporting an information-based organization.

Organization theorists and business strategists are supporting this move to the information-based company. Many organizations are today beginning to remove the layers of management that exist only to move information from one level of the organization to another. It is proposed[2] that these functions exist only because enterprise information systems are inadequate.

Much of the thinking behind the drive to innovate or redesign business processes assumes that information technology will be a key form of leverage (along with improved staff capabilities and better organizational design) in the redesigned business process.[3] Equally, management by fact and empowered work groups and individuals, both increasingly common themes in the latest wave of thinking on sustainable quality practices, require the free flow of accurate, timely, and relevant information within the enterprise.

Consequences for IS Developers

There is little doubt that information systems will be asked to play an increasingly central role in the successful enterprises of the twenty-first century. If they are to do so, the providers of these information systems must be in a position to respond rapidly and effectively to the changing needs they support. It will no longer be sufficient to offer multiyear development time frames or disjoint data bases in response to information systems requirements.

When a new system is needed it is needed *now*, not in 2 years' time when the need will have changed. The IS development function has to become effective in meeting this challenge, or it will be threatened with replacement either internally (end-user computing and insourcing) or externally (outsourcing).[4]

To meet these needs, an IS department must transform itself from an organization that prides itself on its technical prowess to one that is integrated into the enterprise and prides itself on servicing its "customers"; from an organization that seeks design or programming elegance to one that seeks effective, user-friendly solutions to business problems; from an organization that looks and acts like a cost center to one that looks and acts like a partner in the creation of sustainable business value.

This is not going to be easy. Traditionally IS expenditure has grown ahead of actual corporate growth. From essentially zero in the 1950s, the proportion of gross income devoted to IS-related budgets is now typically 3% to 5% in most organizations, and as high as 20% in some.[5] This growth pattern cannot continue for much longer. There is good evidence[6] that in 1990 the total spent on information systems (hardware, software, and services) in the United States and Europe went down, in real terms, for the first time in about 20 years. In 1991 it went down further (probably about 10% in real terms) as the economic downturn in Western economies took hold. In preliminary data for 1992 the decrease looks to have continued, perhaps to as much as 30%. In the wake of this sudden reversal, even previously "recession proof" businesses, such as IBM and Digital Equipment, have been sent reeling.

This trend could easily continue. As margins are squeezed, businesses seek to reduce overhead costs, and IS is almost always seen as an overhead. Consequently, there will be fewer resources to meet a continuing demand. Such new investment as there is will probably go first toward operational support, and not necessarily to the development area.

There will also be fewer people available. Again, since the

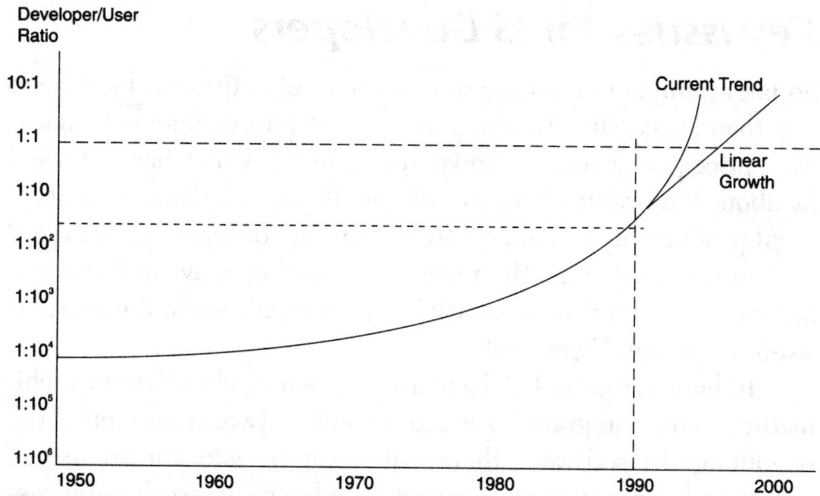

Figure 1.2 *Growth Trends in the Developer/User Ratio for Information Systems*

1950s, the developer/user ratio[7] shown in Figure 1.2 has moved from a very comfortable 1:10,000 to an uncomfortable 1:50 today, and this trend is continuing. Before the end of the century it will need to be at least 1:1 if nothing happens to change the productivity of the development process or to constrain user demand. This is clearly an impossible scenario, unless the demand for professionally developed information systems suddenly disappears, which is extremely unlikely.

Even if businesses created millions of new jobs for developers, demographics will also work against filling them. There will be fewer people in the prime IS employment age groups between now and about 2015.[8] Everyone will be competing for the smaller pool of technological talent, so costs will rise. The IS organization will be caught in a classic vice—required to deliver much more with markedly less in available capital and skilled resources. "End-user" computing will meet an increasing part of this demand, but not all information systems can be built by end users. Professional developers must also become much more productive and effective.

Key Issues for IS Developers

So far, attempts to increase development effectiveness have been less than successful. In comparison with improvements in hardware price performance, shown in Figure 1.3, which has increased by about ten orders of magnitude[9] in 40 years, software development productivity has improved by only one order of magnitude.[10]

At the same time, the range of technologies available for use in new information systems will broaden significantly, if not explosively, as seen in Figure 1.4.

In hardware, the PC, local area networks, client/server architectures and integrated service digital networks are only the beginning. In software, there will soon be widespread use of expert systems, computer-supported cooperative work, multimedia, cooperative processing, object-based development and neural networks.

New technologies will continue to appear—despite the lack of knowledge about how to make effective use of what is already

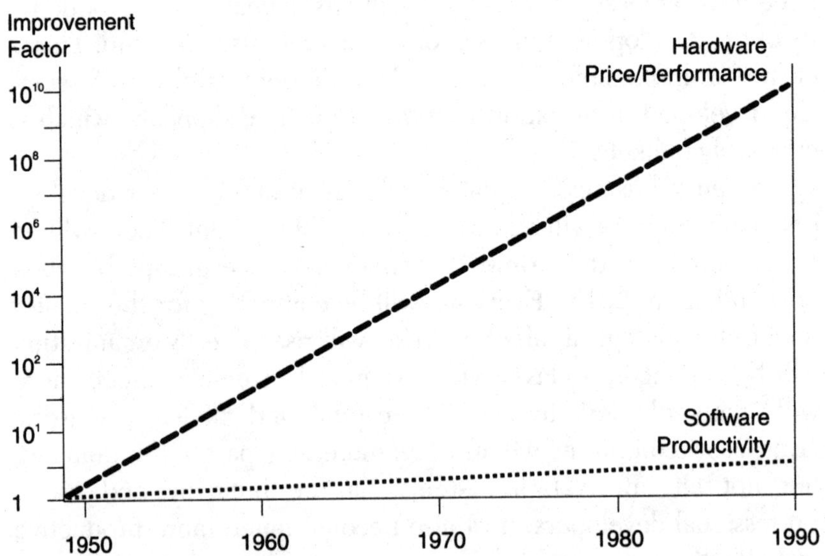

***Figure 1.3** Improvements in Hardware Price Performance as Compared with Software Development Productivity*

available. Selecting appropriate technologies for key information system developments will become increasingly important as the range of options expands.

In contrast to all the new technological wonders, however, businesses also need to be able to maximize the return on the investments made in the past. There is no real likelihood of their being allowed to throw away all existing systems, however bad they are, and start again. At best, there may be a progressive reengineering of current systems into a better form for future use and support.

Managing the investment in existing systems is an important issue to which we shall return a number of times. The 80 to 100 billion lines of existing COBOL code (and the 20 to 30 billion lines of everything else) will not go away soon.[11] As a measure of just how bad this problem is, consider that current commercial information systems represent a huge investment—probably about $2.7 trillion in current values,[12] as

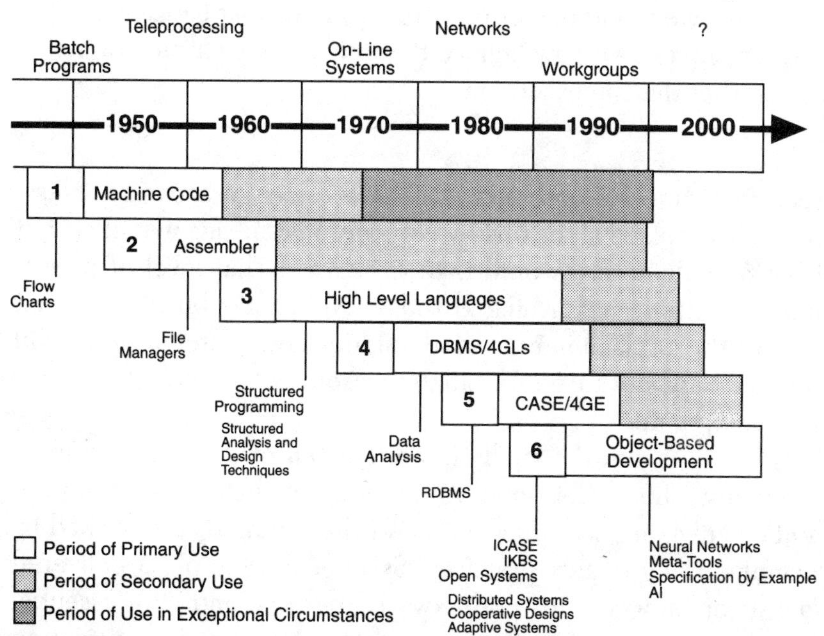

Figure 1.4 *Trends in Increasing Complexity in Software Development Technologies*

Systems outliving their usefulness

There are some truly extreme cases of systems that have outlived their usefulness. One large Scottish financial institution is using the very latest IBM mainframe computers to run an accounts payable application written 17 years ago. Their state-of-the-art hardware emulates an IBM 1401! Everyone who was associated with the original development has left the business. The documentation is rudimentary, and it is impossible to make any changes to the code, because no one understands it anymore. But the application works, and there has never been time to redevelop it. On the principle that "if it isn't broken, don't try to fix it" the organization just keeps on going and hopes nothing goes wrong.

We used to think that this was an isolated example, which we often used in presentations to illustrate the extremes of old systems. Instead, in almost every audience we found one or two organizations that had similar examples. We now believe that this is a typical situation rather than an exception.

seen in Figure 1.5, although it is hard to get an accurate assessment. To replace all of this by conventional means would cost at least $4 trillion and would take decades.[13] That level of investment is simply not available today. Nor could businesses wait during the replacement period for the new systems—that will not get built because all available resources are being used for redevelopment.

There is also the vitally important but often neglected issue of quality. The IS developer's reputation for quality is often poor and even when good, does not meet the standards established by manufacturing quality practices. Systems are too often delivered late, over budget, with undiscovered defects, and with essential functions missing or working incorrectly. No amount of attention

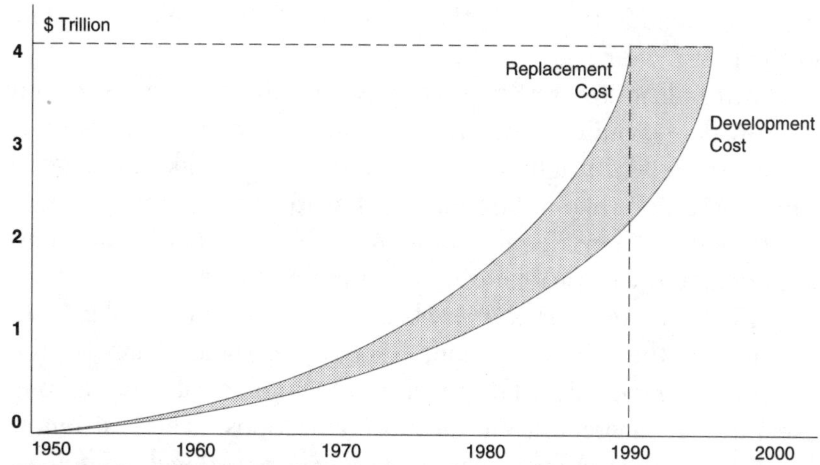

Figure 1.5 *Cost to Develop Compared with Cost to Replace for All Installed Information Systems*

to detail or control procedures seems to be able to affect this problem significantly. It is simply no good doing things fast if they are also done wrong.

This situation can all be summarized fairly simply:

Effective management needs better information.

Better information for the enterprise depends on better information systems.

Better information systems requires better information systems development.

Better Information Systems Development

An IS department has to be able to develop high-quality information systems, rapidly and at a reasonable cost, and then maintain or evolve them cheaply and effectively. Why doesn't this happen already? In fact, is the criticism of IS development fair in the first place?

After all, systems of increasing complexity and sophistication actually do get built, used, and maintained. The IS organization is usually staffed by bright, enthusiastic people who like to do good work and do not like to be thought of as fools or incompetents. If the IS development dilemma is going to be solved, it is important to understand why problems exist in the first place.

First the good news. It is clear that not all the problems are internal to the IS department. One key problem area is the general ignorance of and disinterest in technological issues among executive management in most organizations. This extremely common phenomenon can be called *"Executive Technophobia."* As a result, senior management is poor at articulating its requirements in a comprehensible manner and even poorer at understanding the consequences of the solutions offered by IS developers. IS managers are therefore left with little understanding of business priorities or of the problems and issues that their customers in the business would most like to have addressed.

Now for the bad news. For too long, organizations have been managed in spite of their information systems, rather than because of them. As two of our colleagues at the Center for Information Technology and Strategy℠ have observed in a recent book:

> *Some argue that information is simply a collection of data, that if you take a stream of financial data and put it on a page, you have given a person information. . . . Information is not just data collected; rather, it is data collected, organized, ordered and imbued with meaning and context. Information must inform, while data has no such mandate. Information must be bounded, while data can be limitless. In order for data to become useful to a decision maker as information, it must be presented in such a way that he or she can relate to it and act upon it. . . . Many early attempts to create management information systems failed because the attempts organized data into forms that were meaningful to computer programmers and data organizers, but didn't enable managers to pose questions regarding the data, to relate to it, or to manipulate the data to acquire information.*[14]

This is where the true human cost of software lies. Not with the 10 or 20 or 100 people who developed the system in the first place, but with the hundreds of business users who then have to use it. Remember the developer/user ratio?

Most of these problems could be tolerated if the information systems that were eventually delivered worked effectively and did what their users wanted. All too often, however, they fail to do one or both of these (Figure 1.6), and a substantial proportion are never delivered at all.

Systems that have been sold by their developers with the promise that they will improve business processes often make performance worse, introducing or failing to detect errors and slowing down business operations to an unacceptable degree. Inevitably, users lack confidence in the new systems and are reluctant to give up their old ways of doing things. All too often they run both old and new systems in parallel, further eroding the promised efficiency gains, introducing additional errors in coordination and accuracy, and creating subsequent costly requirements for correction.

This phenomenon became so common that research was undertaken to find out why a system as delivered did so little of

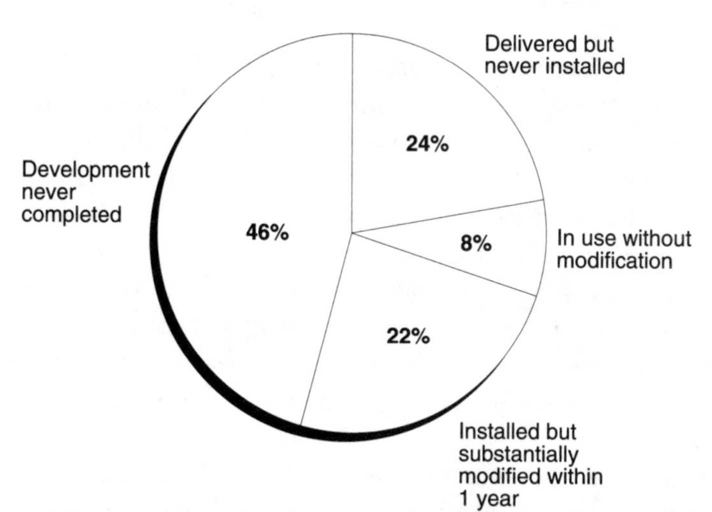

Figure 1.6 *Delivery and Subsequent Modification Statistics for Software Development Projects*

Systems That Make Things Worse

We once saw a computerized customer information system introduced by a consumer finance company for its customer services division. The system replaced three separate manually maintained customer files with one integrated customer data base. All the 100 or so customer service staff, who spent most of their time answering telephone queries, had on-line terminals to the new data base.

Unfortunately, at the end-of-month inquiry peak (combining inquiries from customers with weekly repayments and those with monthly repayments) traffic increased so much that the system response time slumped to more than 2 minutes (from about 15 to 20 seconds), more than doubling the length of a customer call. The customer services staff got so fed up with this that they all began to keep their own sets of files for their most common callers. Within a short time the old three-file system had been replaced by a 100+ file system, and chaos ensued.

what was expected and required. Several studies, carried out in a variety of development environments in the United States and Europe[15] during the second half of the 1970s and the early 1980s, showed clearly that the problem lay principally in the area of ***requirements analysis*** and ***specification***.

More than 60% of the defects and errors reported in information systems after they have been installed can be traced back to this source (Figure 1.7).[16] Enhancing the understanding of users' requirements is clearly an area that has to be addressed if sustainable improvements in productivity and quality are to be achieved.

Gaining an adequate understanding of requirements is not easy. Analysts and users often speak quite different languages, but

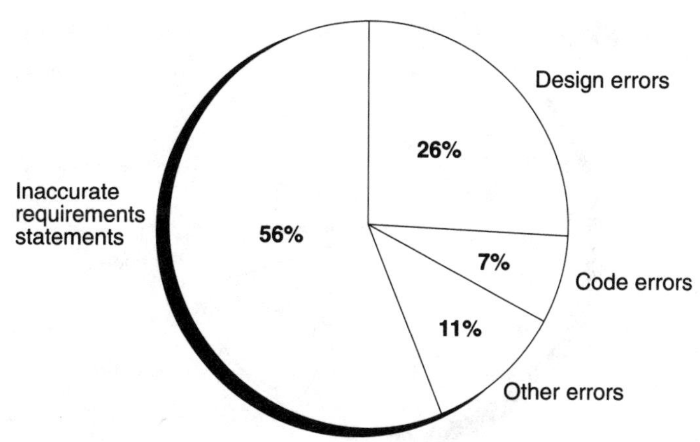

Figure 1.7 *Sources of Postimplementation Defects in Information Systems*

with approximately the same vocabulary. Miscommunication, for which opportunities abound, occurs mostly without conscious realization. The marketing department's view of a credit card is quite different from that of the customer service department, and both are different from that of the systems analyst, even though all involved use credit cards.

The research of the 1970s and 1980s also looked at the comparative cost of correcting errors at various stages of the development life cycle. The results showed that in terms of the effort required (a good but by no means perfect cost comparison), it was always cheapest to fix errors as close to their origin as possible. Delaying correction into the next phase of the life cycle increased the cost by a factor of at least 10 and sometimes as much as 100. This pattern of increased cost was made worse by further delays until, postimplementation, a fix could cost 1,000 times as much as it would have during analysis.

Yet most support effort (up to 80% in some installations, as shown in Figure 1.8) was actually being spent to do just that—fix errors introduced during analysis but not discovered until sometime after the system had been implemented.[17]

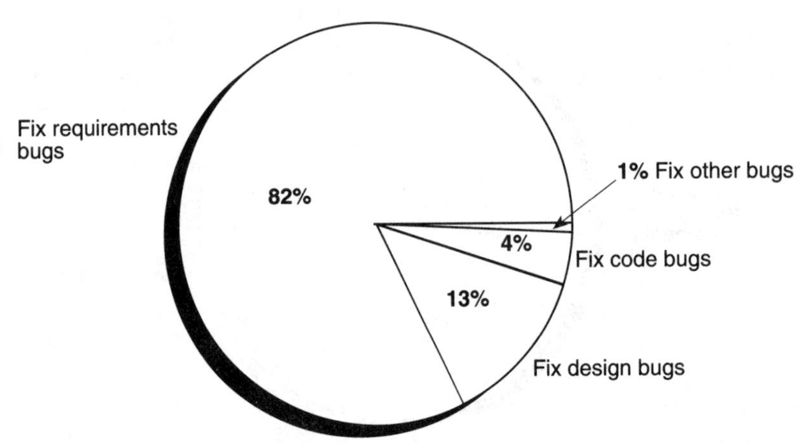

Figure 1.8 *Effort Expended in Correcting Postimplementation Defects by Source of Defect*

Wrong People, Wrong Specs

One part of the requirements problem stems from the way the IS industry expects its "analysts" to behave. Advertisements for systems analysts all too often emphasize the technical skills (data base, programming background, technical environment) required, rather than the business awareness, problem solving, and communication skills that are really essential to the analysis process.

It is not surprising that analysts recruited, trained, and promoted on the basis of these technical skills try to use them when doing their jobs. Unfortunately, the attempt often leads to a kind of "technological tunnel vision"—identifying the solution to every problem in terms of an information system—and to incomprehension on the user's part.

Users have reacted by increasingly ignoring the corporate information systems department and branching out on their own. This has become much easier since relatively inexpensive personal computers and software packages have transformed the cost of getting started in information technology (IT).

As a result, tens of millions of PCs have invaded user departments in all sorts of guises, creating both a "Tower of Babel" of information and a surplus of "information fiefdoms."

PCs in the IS Department

One international credit card company proudly stated that it had recently installed more than 10,000 PCs in user departments around the world. When the CIO was asked how many PCs there were in the IS department for the use of the system development group (a staff of several hundred), he did not know. It turned out that the group had just 13—used for word processing by the senior managers' secretaries. When asked how many PCs they planned to install in the next year, he readily admitted to another 2,000 or so—for user applications. How many for the IS groups? Just 10, for financial reporting and budgets.

This profusion of PCs also led to the archetypal scene in corporate data processing in the 1980s: the business user, sitting at a PC, typing information into a spreadsheet from a computer printed report produced by the organization's central data processing facility.

Why do they do it? Because once the data is in the spreadsheet it is *theirs*, and they personally can do the things *they* want to do with it, right there and then when *they* want to do it—not just the things some remote data processing department has decided they can do in a week's or a month's time. Business users have become used to the PC's response time, relative simplicity, and ease of use. They do not want to go back to slow, unfriendly and never-quite-right mainframe applications that always seemed to separate a user from his or her data.

Gratifying though this may be for individual users, from a corporate perspective it can become disastrous. There is often massive duplication of information, loss of control over accuracy and reliability of content, and waste of resources. Equally, however, the proliferation of PCs has broadened the base of people in an organization who expect information technology to work and to help them in their jobs. These expectations are difficult to reconcile with the traditional, slow-motion approach to IS developments from which major systems projects frequently suffer.

Strangely enough, the proliferation of PCs has not extended to the IS Department to anything like the same degree. Although terminals are common, PCs are often relegated to secretarial staff, for use with word processing and spreadsheets. This reluctance to adopt the personal computer is difficult to explain. Nevertheless, it is a real factor in holding back improvements in staff productivity in IS organizations. PCs bring all sorts of cheap productivity tools within the reach of the individual developer, and PC-to-mainframe communications work comparatively simply and reliably.

IS Development Track Record

Considered from within the IS development process, the main problem with the effectiveness of systems development seems to be staff productivity. Those few people—and there are still disappointingly few of them—who collect statistics on the programming process have shown that an "average" programmer, using a modern on-line development environment, can write 400 or so lines of compiled and unit tested COBOL or similar code per 8-hour working day—that is 50 lines per hour, or 50 hours for an "average" 2,500-line program.[18] Yet when a development project is viewed as a whole, the average output of the programmers involved, calculated as the total lines of code in the finished application divided by the number of staff days to produce it, turns out to be only about 120 lines of code per day—15 lines per hour, or 167 hours per average program.

An obvious question is, "Where did the 280 missing lines go?" Perhaps the most likely explanation is that the application code gets rewritten anywhere between two and ten times during the coding and testing process, mostly during system and acceptance testing—the first time that the business users get to really see it and to complain about what it does or does not do.

This might be called the "requirements discovery during testing" scenario. Each finished application is therefore "developed" several times before it can be delivered in an acceptable form. This redesign/recode/retest process is enormously wasteful of time and effort. It is also complex to manage—to the extent that the continual reworking is itself a major source of error and defect creation.

Nevertheless, past development improvement efforts have looked at programming productivity as a good place to start improving development effectiveness. In the traditional development life cycle shown in Figure 1.9, the phases carried out by programmers account for most of the resources involved in producing a finished application.

In the late 1960s, relatively large productivity gains had already been achieved in programming productivity, so it was known that programmer productivity could be improved by better tools, and programming seemed a reasonable place to start the drive for further improvements. As might be expected in a technology-driven industry, the first attempts to improve productivity made extensive use of additional technology. During the early

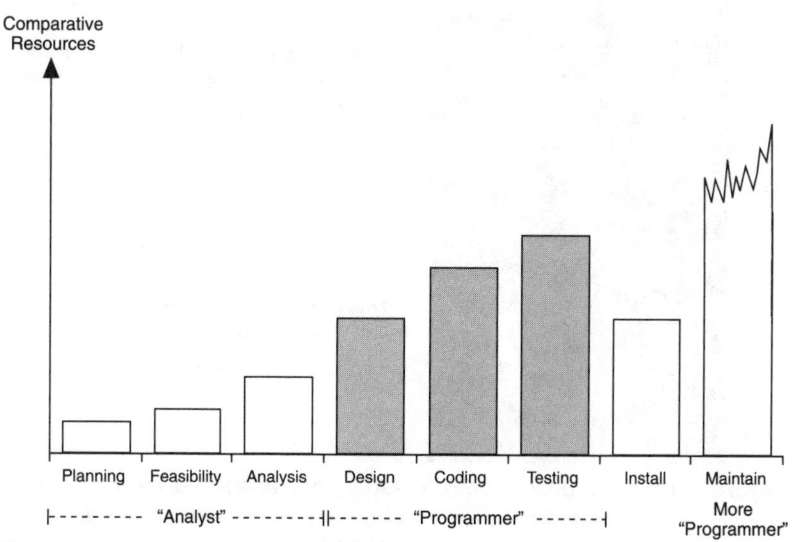

Figure 1.9 *Relative Effort by Stage in the IS Development Process*

1970s programmers were given online computer terminals and new software tools, all aimed at reducing the time needed to develop a working program. More and more of the programming in an application was taken out of their hands altogether. Soon a working application could be made up from 65% supplied functions and only 35% application code, as seen in Figure 1.10.[19]

The result? Mostly, no significant change in overall productivity or, at best, marginal improvement. Furthermore, the capital cost of development centers soared as more dedicated resources were required for development support. Bigger machines—even machines dedicated to development work—seemed to be the only solution. Of course, with hardware price-performance improving all the time, the cost of this extra capac-

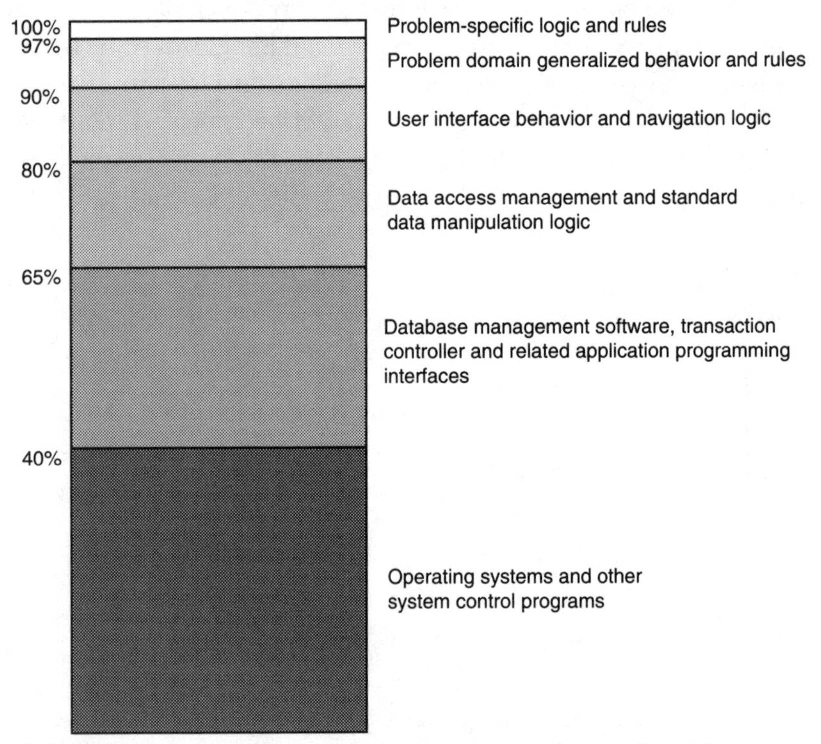

Figure 1.10 *Proportions of Executable Code Image Attributable to Application Component Sources*

ity was declining, even though the actual cost of the development center never seemed to drop in real terms.

All the new software productivity tools cost money as well. So did the training needed to use them. And although most programmers learned to use the new tools quickly, they were not quite so productive initially and tended to make mistakes, and because everyone was new to the tools the mistakes were not always noticed quickly, and so on.

High-Level Languages: From 3GLs to 4GLs

The second round of productivity improvement initiatives, beginning in the mid-1970s, was also technology-based, but attacked the problem from a different angle. Traditional programming languages like COBOL required large numbers of statements to describe the actions required by a program. COBOL and the other third-generation languages (so-called 3GLs) predated data base management systems (DBMS) and transaction managers, so the languages had not been designed to make use of these new software capabilities and tools. Making everything work together was complex and often difficult to do well.

It seemed reasonable, therefore, that programs written in a language that allowed a program to be defined in fewer statements could be written more quickly. Moreover, fewer statements, especially in a simple syntax, would tend to contain fewer errors, thus simplifying testing and correction of the programs. The solution? A new generation of "very high level" languages offering a reduction of 5 or even 10 times in the number of lines of code needed to write a program. Many of these products were introduced by the major DBMS vendors, allowing tight coupling to the data management functions and teleprocessing software already in place.

IS organizations were asked to embark on another round of investment in tools, training, learning-curve productivity losses, and correcting early development errors. By this time, however, fewer businesses were willing to jump into the new technology in the same way they had embraced on-line program development, and the new 4GLs were slow to take off, despite being heralded as the "final solution" to the IS productivity problem.

Potential adopters were right to be cautious. Early 4GLs had severe performance problems, in some cases being 20 or more times less efficient in their use of computer resources than the equivalent COBOL program. There were a number of major project disasters, widely publicized, indicating that all was not as wonderful as the vendors had promised. It seemed that developing acceptable information systems with 4GLs was no easier than it had been with conventional methods, and introduced new risks. The 4GL just let the development team create rubbish that much faster, and dreadfully inefficient rubbish at that.

The magic 4GL solution had burst its bubble, and the languages were no longer seen as a panacea. Instead, they were used in information centers to satisfy simple query and report generation needs and for small departmental data base applications. In this role 4GLs have been moderately successful, since a large proportion of IS development work is of this type, and real gains in productivity have been achieved, as shown in Figure 1.11.[20]

Attempts to promote 4GLs as end-user tools have been less successful, and rightly so, since virtually all current products, vendor claims notwithstanding, are aimed at trained programmers. This does not mean that users cannot master them, just that any who have done so could probably have mastered a conventional programming language as well.

As expected, the bill for the hardware to develop and run applications in 4GLs continued to rise. Few sites found a reduction in machine resources as a result of the new tools, as seen in Figure 1.12.[21] Most saw a modest increase in requirements, some a huge increase.

4GL applications were also harder to tune, as most of the system functions were buried out of sight of the programmers. Solving this problem required some programmers to become specialists in the database management system used by the lan-

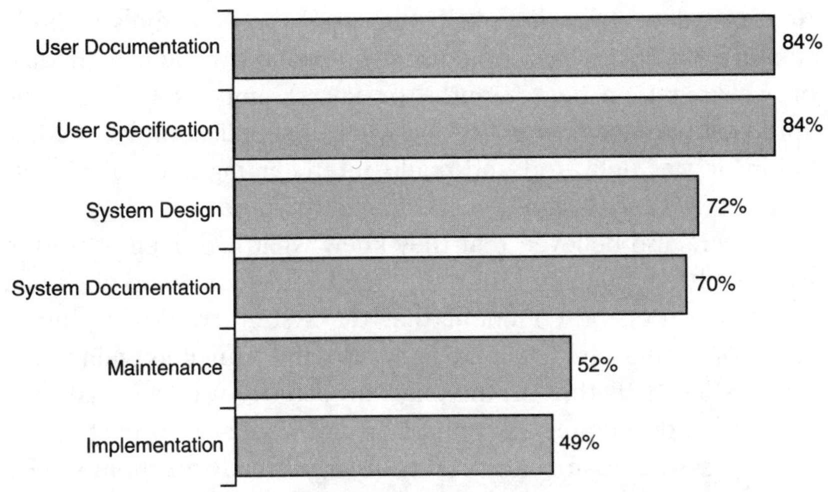

Figure 1.11 *Comparative Productivity Improvement Attributable to the Use of Fourth Generation Languages*

guage—more training costs, learning-curve effects, and errors in the first systems developed for the poor users to live with.

4GLs also did nothing to ensure that the information systems that were developed were the ones really needed by the business. IS departments tried to improve their chances of getting things

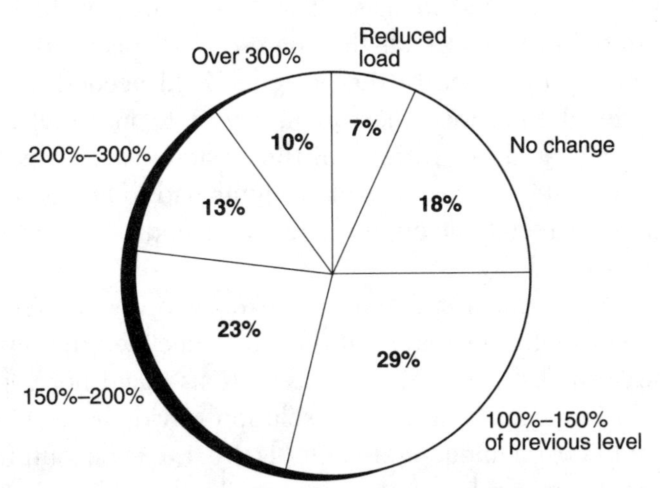

Figure 1.12 *Comparative Processing Requirements of Applications Developed Using Fourth Generation Languages*

right by adopting an approach that used the 4GL tools to build simple prototypes. This could usually be done very quickly (in days or weeks rather than months or years), and users liked the approach because they got to see what the application looked like before it was delivered and could intercept many requirements specification and design defects at an early stage.

Users also believed that they knew what had been agreed to by way of functionality (after all, they had seen it "working") and could therefore be confident that the system would be understandable and useful to them. They also, unfortunately, gained the impression that the prototyping procedure was all that was involved in developing an application and went away expecting the finished system to appear in a day or so, all ready for them to use. They were, of course, invariably disappointed.

The Problems with a Lot of Lira

Moving into an unplanned business situation can generate unforeseen requirements for information systems. An insurance company that wanted to buy a new subsidiary in Italy discovered that the number of digits required to account for business in lira was greater than its systems could manage. The IS organization took 3 months to discover all the (hard-coded) places that a change to the size of the currency field needed to be made. It then took more than a year to make all the changes and to retest all the systems successfully. Meanwhile, the two sets of accounts had to be consolidated manually at huge clerical cost and with a great many errors.

In a similar situation, a broker who was offered a line of motor insurance, also in Italy, declined the business for the same reason—his systems could not cope with lira. The IS manager's solution (divide everything by 1,000 on input and multiply by 1,000 on output) might have worked, but was vetoed by the auditors!

Having designed the application's external view, often not much more than the user interface, the IS developers now had to figure out how to make the application software support it in an efficient fashion. In most cases this took just as long as ever. In some cases it took considerably longer, as the user interface was now effectively fixed (in the business users' minds), and could not be modified to solve internal design problems. Users ended up waiting not days but weeks or months for their prototypes to be finished and delivered.

Even then, the systems often did not work properly. The users were still left wondering what they had to do to get an information system that worked the way they did and which made life easier rather than more difficult.

Rapid Development for Mortgage Processing

An overseas bank with an established presence in London wholesale money markets wanted to enter the UK home loans market and needed to build an information system to support this new business. The organization's market "window of opportunity" was small—less than 6 months. The system had to link closely to existing money market systems so that the bank could be competitive on rates.

Rather than develop the system conventionally (which would have taken too long) or buy a package (which would be difficult to link in with existing systems), the bank modeled the requirements of the new system using a CASE tool, modeled the interface to existing systems (already documented using the tool), and developed the resulting design in a 4GL.

The result—the system was up and running in less than 20 elapsed weeks, and the bank's mortgage business was under way. Since then, new facilities have been added at regular intervals, but virtually no changes to the original design have been needed.

Better User Requirements Definition

As noted earlier, many IS failures are due to a misunderstanding of the user's requirements by the analyst, or the inability of users to communicate those requirements, and a resulting misspecification of the system when requirements were written to form the basis of a programming specification. It turns out that many of these misunderstandings stem from difficulties with an ambiguous requirements specification language (English or its equivalent) and a resulting lack of rigor in the specification process. Bridging this gap in understanding was not going to be easy. Analysts could not spend long periods of time watching what was going on and deducing the business rules and procedural logic from their observations. In the first place, the users would not put up with it. And how could anyone be sure that the analyst had seen everything that went on? A more rigorous and, at the same time, efficient approach was required.

Early attempts to introduce rigor followed the 4GL approach. Languages were developed for the specification of problems and their solutions. Although these worked to an extent, they were too difficult for most analysts to learn and to use reliably in practical situations. What they did show, however, was that generating a rigorous written specification was a difficult and error-prone process. A better method was needed.

One early approach was the replacement of some of the words with diagrams. Diagrams offered a neutral "language" that could be used intuitively by both analysts and users and considerable rigor could be built into the diagramming process. Several different diagramming standards were developed for modeling business functions and processes during the early and middle 1970s, and most were tried out.

As experience accumulated, the best diagramming techniques were identified and refined, and the methods, by now generally called *structured analysis and design methods*, were formally documented and published by their authors. As a result, a number of diagram-based approaches became well established and began to be used in major development projects.

It was at this point that a few practical problems with the approach became apparent. To use the methods effectively, analysts and designers needed to be trained and to practice the key techniques (generating more expense, learning curve problems, and early errors). To model a real application also required a great many diagrams, sometimes hundreds of them. Relationships between diagrams were complex, with changes in one having an impact on many others. Keeping track of the required changes became increasingly difficult (and therefore error prone) as the projects progressed.

Creating the diagrams was also a problem—not the initial creation, which both analyst and user usually enjoyed (or at least coped with), but the subsequent amendment (erase, redraw, erase, redraw . . .) process. Pencil and paper are a difficult medium to update—especially when moving a box on a sheet of paper may involve redrawing 12 or 15 boxes and 40 lines—and both users and analysts soon became bored and frustrated with the activity.

As a result, users of the diagramming techniques tended to work toward avoiding changes rather than getting the diagrams right. Both analysts and users became expert at fudging issues of business processing in order to avoid lengthy and unreliable change procedures. Therefore, much of the rigor of the diagram-based techniques was lost.

Quality assurance and review were also a problem. We have had to carry out this sort of quality assurance procedure on a number of occasions—and have as a result coined the "thirty-errors rule."

Every set of diagrams from a real project using manual structured methods contains at least thirty errors.

We have *never* seen an exception to this rule in more than 10 years of looking at dozens of examples in many industries and market sectors.

Nevertheless, the structured approach was a big step forward, if only because it served to prove that diagrams could, in fact, work, that attempting to incorporate rigor was actually worthwhile, and that just modeling business processes was not enough.

The "Thirty Errors" Rule in Action

A key government development project, one of the largest non-military information systems developments in the world, used manual structured methods as its primary quality control mechanism. The project also devoted a large percentage of its resources (something like 40 percent of total staff time) to quality reviews and quality assurance procedures. In the process of looking at Computer Assisted Systems Engineering tools for a later stage of the project, we were involved in a review of the applicability of such tools to the organization's environment. The project manager explained their approach and claimed with some pride that the specifications that had been developed were error free. To prove it, he selected a volume at random from the more than 50 linear feet of requirements specification documents and opened it at a random page. There, right in front of us on a data flow diagram, was an obvious error.

Structure and Standards

In the late 1960s and early 1970s the development of data base management systems led some method developers to look at ways of modeling information systems in terms of the way that data was structured, rather than just describing what was done with it. It soon became apparent that if this "data analysis" was done on a formal basis, the resulting model was remarkably robust, even when substantial changes were made in the actual processing of the kinds of information that had been modeled.

The formal representation process used a "relational" algebra to generate a mathematically defined logical model of the relationships between sets of business information. This form of *relational* analysis soon became established as the standard approach to data modeling. Data bases designed from relational models were easier to develop and maintain than those resulting from purely physical or process oriented analysis and design methods.

Unfortunately, relational data analysis in the real world is a complex and demanding process, and not all that easy to learn to do well (and so there are significant training and learning curve problems). Once again, diagrams were adopted as a means of simplifying and presenting the results of data analysis and refined for use in the structured analysis and design processes.

Now, by comparing the models of how data was to be processed with the models of data relationships, it was possible to incorporate considerable rigor into a specification and to provide for a degree of consistency and completeness checking that had been impossible before the introduction of structured methods. Of course, while the methods were paper-based, carrying out these checks was a laborious and time-consuming process and remained error prone. But it was, nevertheless, a big step forward.

It should be clear by now that in order to cope with all these new approaches and techniques, development staff need to spend most of their time either away on training courses or at home, reading user manuals. They also need a safe way to practice what they have learned so as to become familiar with the practical aspects of the methods and techniques that somehow do not seem to be taught in training courses. It takes several weeks, perhaps months, of training and practice to become proficient in a structured method,[22] and because few projects actually use all the techniques taught, staff often need refresher training as well.

While all this is happening, development and maintenance activities still have to carry on. Few organizations have the luxury of starting with a clean systems slate, so newly trained staff are often diverted onto existing projects that are not using structured methods. Under time pressure, the rigor of the structured approach can easily get lost in the rush to finish the requirements definition or the design phase of a project that is running late. Bad habits quickly reassert themselves, and the expensive methods documentation gathers dust on the shelves.

Data Modeling as a Guide to Better Business Procedures

One of the authors well remembers facilitating a session with a product manager from a large retail bank and the project manager of the IS team that was building an information system to support a new type of checking account. It was clear that the two were not communicating until we started to draw some simple diagrams showing how customers, accounts, and credit cards related to each other. In a half hour of intensive data analysis we achieved more than they had managed in the previous 6 weeks of work. Both user and project manager went from a state of mutual frustration to, if not harmony, at least a clear appreciation of the requirement and of the limitations of the technology that would be used to satisfy it.

On another occasion, working with a merchant bank on a corporate finance application, we discovered that it was possible for a client to be both a borrower and a lender in the same transaction. A quick check of the bank's current data base showed one occasion on which this had happened (a parent company had paid the bank a fee to borrow money from one of its own subsidiaries as part of a consortium finance deal). The possibility had never occurred to the designers of the bank's old systems, but the data analysis clearly showed it—and pointed to a design requirement that might otherwise have been missed.

The easiest alternative to adopting a structured approach is to adopt a set of standards instead. Of course, standards are really a *supplement* to structured methods, not an alternative. However, it is common to hear data processing managers say, "We don't need to adopt a methodology—we already have a set of standards that does everything we need."

Good standards have several functions in the development process, none of which replace a structured approach. Standards tell analysts and designers how to make certain kinds of decisions that would otherwise be arbitrary, and they can help to enforce installation-specific rules. To be effective, however, standards must be flexible, providing a broad framework of good ideas and "best practice" but allowing room for innovation.

Standards writers are often reluctant to admit the need for this flexibility, however, and many sets of standards are highly prescriptive, without actually being at all comprehensive. This tendency leads not to development within common standards, but to rote standardization. Such standardization means changing or constraining the business to suit rigid inflexible systems, not building systems flexible enough to evolve along with the needs of the business.

By the early 1980s the information systems development "business" was in considerable difficulty. Backlogs of unsatisfied development requests were still increasing,[23] as seen in Figure 1.13, and users were turning more and more to increasingly

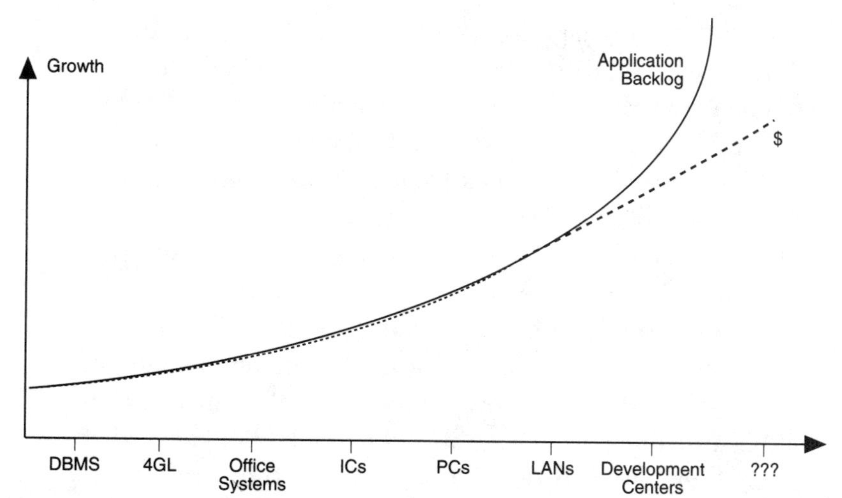

Figure 1.13 *Comparative Growth Rates for Visible Applications Backlog and IS Expenditure*

Reengineering—A Tool for Clearing Out the Rubbish

An insurance company, faced with the need to redevelop an old and ill-documented suite of applications programs, believed that the task was so large that it could not be completed by its own staff and was considering spending more than $35 million to replace the application with purchased software in the form of a package. The old application consisted of around 4,000 COBOL programs, using a mixture of VSAM and IMS data bases. More than 6.5 million lines of largely undocumented code were involved, and the application (managing life insurance products) was complex. The company estimated that more than 600 staff-years would be required for a conventional redevelopment project, costing $40 million to $70 million, lasting at least 5 years, and carrying a high risk of failure. No wonder it was considering buying a package.

Instead, the IS department spent 6 months developing a data architecture for the company's life insurance business, and mapping each of the 4,000 programs to this architecture. To do so it used available CASE tools to document the use of data represented by the COBOL data division of each program. It also conducted an audit of the use of the outputs from each program. The total cost was about 6 staff-years, or $1 million.

What did the development team find? Approximately 2,800 of the programs could be eliminated by better design and an improved data base. The application had evolved far ahead of its documentation, and in several instances processing absurdities had arisen because one part of the support team did not know what another part had done. For instance, there was a 20-program batch run that contained seven sorts of the same file of data—two of the sort sequences (of more than 7 million records) were identical.

What did the company do? Using the data architecture as a basis, it began a phased conversion of the remaining 1,200 programs to use a DB2 (relational) data base. The conversion was largely tool assisted, using a code generator for the production of new application code. Within 18 months all of the application had been converted to the new environment. The total redevelopment cost, including tools and training, was less than $12 million.

One would think that, faced with such a singular success, the rest of the company's IS organization would be racing to adopt the same approach. Not so. The auto division, faced with almost the identical task, was unconvinced that a conversion was possible, and is still considering buying a package. It is, however, also evaluating CASE tools. As might be expected, the tools being considered are not those used by the team that rebuilt the application for the life business.

powerful and inexpensive microcomputers for short-term "computing" solutions that all too often became permanent. 4GLs had for the most part failed to live up to expectations, and structured methods were likewise proving harder to bring into use, and harder to yield benefits from, than had been promised.

At the same time, new development requirements continued to appear. Office automation, expert systems, new networks, communications, and processing architectures were on the horizon. Yet management was increasingly reluctant to continue to pour money into IT when they had so little apparent benefit to show for past investments.

The typical IS department had for 20 years been offering miracle solutions—"silver bullets"—to productivity and quality problems, solutions that repeatedly required "just one more" round of investment. Most of these solutions did indeed work to some extent, but none of them was the universal solution that had been promised. Every time a solution appeared, either the technology failed in some (usually unpredictable and often "people-related") way or a new set of problems arrived, requiring yet more investment to solve.

The introduction of structured and semiformal development methods and a more rigorous approach to requirements specification had, however, shown some real promise. Experiences in real-time systems development had proved that formal specification procedures, although difficult to learn and laborious to operate, did improve the quality of the delivered system. Clearly, a formal analysis and design structure was a good idea—it was just too difficult for most analysts and programmers, let alone users, to come to grips with and still maintain a reasonable level of productivity. It seemed that in commercial data processing systems, productivity and quality in systems development were mutually exclusive objectives.

Enter Computer Aided Systems Engineering (CASE), in particular, and a wide range of development support tools in general. By automating aspects of the development process it should be possible to attack both the productivity and the quality issues at the same time: productivity by replacing manual tasks with tech-

A CASE for Accounting

One of the perpetual complications of securities, foreign exchange, and commodity trading is the reconciliation, after the event, of the trader's and accounting system's views of any particular transaction—in particular, its profitability and contribution to the trader's earnings. Some considerable time may expire between the initial record of the trade and the terms attached to it, its actual settlement and the attached terms, and the entry of the trade into the business's accounting system. During any of the intervening periods, many things can happen that change the terms of the transaction, possibly fundamentally.

Designing a system that not only records and balances out these differences but also enables managers to estimate what the different book positions actually represent is far from easy, but this is essential to maintain control and to provide adequate audit trails.

Modeling the requirement on a CASE tool allowed one specialist systems house to develop a basic system that could be easily customized to support many different trading environments. In the process of demonstrating the system to potential buyers, the systems house sales force became adept at using the model to prove that the software could be adapted readily to the needs of individual businesses. As a result, more than one customer adopted the same approach—using the model to explain to their staff why the amount they thought they had earned in bonuses was always more than they were actually paid!

nology, which IS has done extensively elsewhere, but not so extensively to itself; quality, by using the technology to prevent or detect errors before they enter the delivered systems.

This all sounds too good to be true, and, of course, it is. In the next chapter, we look at some tasks that development support tools and their associated processes have been developed to do, and begin to evaluate how far these capabilities go in building effective development efforts.

Notes

1. Quoted from an interview on BBC television's "The Money Programme."

2. The topic of redesigning the enterprise to eliminate information handling management functions has been written about for more than a decade. For a sample of the available material, see: William H. Davidow and Michael S. Malone, *The Virtual Corporation*, (Harper Business Books, 1992), and Michael Scott Morton, *The Corporation of the 1990s*, (Oxford University Press, 1991).

3. Thomas H. Davenport, *Process Innovation: Reengineering Work Through Information Technology*, (Boston: Harvard Business School Press, 1993).

4. While outsourcing—handing over the management and resources of the IS function to an external organization via a form of long-term service contract—has become popular in the early 1990s, the "insourcing" alternative has received less discussion. With one form of insourcing, a third party is hired to manage and improve the IS function for a shorter period (still typically 3 to 5 years) and then to reinstate IS as an improved and effective internal function of the enterprise.

5. Information gathered from the Ernst & Young IS Leadership Multi-Client Research Program supports the diversity of size and definition in IS budgets—and highlights the difficulties associated with deciding just how much the enterprise spends on information technology.

6. Based on a number of Organization for Economic Cooperation and Development (OECD) publications and industry size sources. There is no single source that accurately reflects the total expenditure on all IS-related areas (hardware, software, services, direct internal costs, and indirect internal costs). In particular, it is very difficult to estimate the internal costs related to IS but not represented by the IS budget.

7. The developer/user ratio is an interesting statistic that we first saw quoted in a conference paper in the late 1970s. No attribution was given for the 1:10,000 figure, but the arithmetic, based on estimates for the number of developers and the number of people making direct use of the systems they develop, seems reasonable. The current figure is based on data from the financial services industry, one of the most information-intensive business areas. Over all industries, a current ratio of about 1:100 is likely.

8. Data from the World Health Organization's annual population estimates and projections. The demographics of Western industrialized societies have been widely published for more than 20 years. The results of socioeconomic and fertility choices post-1946 have provided us with a classic boom and bust model of population size and cohort distribution. Population estimates are notoriously inaccurate, however, and other factors (immigration and new ethnic mixes) continue to make prediction an uncertain business.

9. Based on the cost of fabricating a processor capable of 1 million instructions per second (MIPS). In reality, there are many additional variables involved in estimating comparative price performance for complete systems. The two-by-two-by-four rule (power doubles and prices halve every 4 years) is as good a heuristic as any. This is an extension of "Moore's Law," first proposed by Dr. Gordon Moore of Intel Corporation in the early 1970s. Moore proposed that the storage density of random access memory (RAM) chips doubled every two years (the "two-by-two" rule). By the mid 1980s, the rule had been modified to reflect an ability to quadruple density every three years (the "three-by-four" rule). Add in the reducing price factor and recent advances in wafer manufacturing processes to get the "two-by-two-by-four" rule.

10. Based on the hours required to develop a fully tested 1,000-line pro-

gram. Again, there are many more variables involved in the real world of development and a comparatively small amount of reliable data.

11. This very widely quoted figure is really a "best guess" based on the length of time COBOL has been available (c. 25 years) and the data from those few organizations that have actually counted how much source code they have. Although by no means "right," the number is sufficiently large to be truly indicative of the nature of the problem represented by legacy systems.

12. This figure is arrived at by multiplying the estimated number of lines of source code by the estimated average number of hours needed to deliver a line of code and by the average cost per hour over the 25 years or so that the development took. As such, it is probably something of an underestimate (proportionally more code was written in the last half/quarter/tenth/etc. of the period, when costs were higher but productivity was better).

13. Estimated by using today's average cost and productivity figures for technology-assisted 3GL development of predominantly on-line information systems.

14. Quoted with permission from *Managing Information Strategically* by our colleagues James McGee and Laurence Prusak of Ernst & Young's Center for Information Technology and Strategy[SM]. (New York: John Wiley & Sons, 1993).

15. Based on information derived from research undertaken by (then) AT&T's Bell Laboratories on internal AT&T information system development projects during the late 1970s. The original findings were confirmed in a separate study by the IBM SHARE group in Europe in the early 1980s.

16. See note 15.

17. See note 15.

18. There are a wide variety of figures quoted for unit productivity in programming. These numbers come from one of the author's own records for a long series of development projects between 1979 and 1983. They have the advantage of a consistent measurement approach, consistent team membership, and consistent technology. These performance figures are *better* than those from most other sources.

19. We have been collecting data on the structure of the "executable image" (the object code that actually runs on the computer) for a wide range of execution platforms and application types over a period of several years. While there are wide variations in actual values, the trend toward a smaller "developed" proportion of the object code is clear and accelerating.

20. Information based on a study of 4GL usage in large European IS development organizations, published by Inbucon in 1986.

21. See note 20.

22. See Gregory H. Boone, Vaughan P. Merlyn and Roger E. Dobratz, *The Second Annual Report on CASE* (Bellevue, WA: CASE Research Corporation, 1990). Now available from Ernst & Young.

23. Based on estimates for unsatisfied application requirements in large U.S. corporations, published by Gartner Group in 1988. Additional confirmation from a survey of large IS development organizations in the United Kingdom and Europe undertaken by Ernst & Young for the Scottish Development Agency's "Invest in Scotland" initiative in 1991.

2

Leading Practices—and Where They Still Fall Short

> Given more than 40 years of experience in developing and maintaining information systems within organizations, it should at least be possible to describe a set of "leading practices," which together set a baseline standard for today's information systems development performance. Even if this set turns out to be less than is needed for a truly effective IS organization, it is at least an initial target for those seeking to improve.

Today's most effective information systems (IS) organizations have a number of attributes in common, even though they may differ considerably in the details of how they make these attributes work for them.

- There is a comprehensive, consistent framework and approach to the definition of information systems development and maintenance processes. All IS staff know this framework and approach, and they all use it.

- Within the common framework, there are well-understood ways to customize the methods and processes that are actually used, according to the objectives and needs of individual projects.

- There is recognition of the need for, and provision of, a range of appropriate techniques and tools that can vary between projects (again according to objectives and requirements) and that changes over time.

- IS organization management recognizes the need for, and encourages the development of, a productivity-enhancing infrastructure, working environment, and culture.

- All IS staff are objectively assessed as to their capabilities, and there is a conscious and visible effort both to match current capabilities to the required work and to develop and extend staff skills and experience.

It is possible, therefore, to look at current leading practices in terms of process, techniques and tools, environment and culture, and staff capabilities, and to develop a "best of the current state" baseline. By identifying areas where current leading practices still fall short of what is needed, we can look at what an IS organization needs in order to be truly "world class."

Development Processes Today: What the Best Are Already Doing

In many, perhaps most, effective IS organizations, the development process is derived from a form of information engineering (IE). Although there is a common and justified belief that IE is not sufficient to meet all of the needs of "real world" IS development and maintenance, it is still a good place to start. The underlying principles of IE are:

- A focus on the economies to be realized from a sharing of business data
- Visible and effective business sponsorship for the work of the IS organization
- Involvement of an information system's customers ("users") throughout the development process
- Accelerated development and delivery through the use of development support technology and prototypes
- IS development planning aligned as far as possible with the business's strategy

Because most organizations use purchased software as well as custom-developed information systems, leading IS organizations have extended the basic IE approach (which largely assumes that new requirements will be met by developing new solutions from scratch) to include a formal process for the identification, acquisition, and installation of third-party application products. In many instances, this process has to interrelate with the custom-development process to enable effective modification or extension of a baseline package to meet detailed business needs. An understanding of the sets of information that drive both processes is key to ensuring that they can be used together without duplication of work or gaps in required work products.

Virtually all IS organizations spend the majority of their resources on the upkeep and enhancement of current information systems—often called *legacy systems* to indicate their age and poor state of maintainability. After struggling for many years with the issue of an effective maintenance process, leading IS organizations are now making limited use of reengineering technologies and processes to improve the enhancement and extension of existing systems. Although technologies in this area have lagged behind development support technologies in both coverage and capability, significant improvements in the quality of legacy systems and the data they hold are being realized in areas where support is available and effective.

Leading IS organizations have done much to accelerate the delivery of high-quality information systems. Streamlining processes to eliminate unnecessary work and promote reuse of existing components has been necessary in developing the efficient managed work flow environments that are the goal of those seeking sustained high performance and quality levels. Underlying this investment in acceleration is a willingness to measure the IS development and maintenance processes so that they can be objectively assessed and improved.

Beginning in the 1980s, a steady stream of new development support technology, most notably CASE and other tools, was developed. As more tools become available, infrastructure issues and the need for a development technology architecture have been recognized as additional critical success factors. Those organizations that have done best with adopting and using CASE and similar tools have concentrated on learning how to use a few tools effectively, rather than trying out every new tool that comes along.

Also, the effectiveness of development support technology must be measured if the often significant investment in tools is to be justified.

Leading IS organizations recognize that they need to tailor their general approaches to the specific needs of projects. Customization and flexibility in use allow each project to be designed with only the work required to create the deliverables selected to meet project objectives. Although all projects of the same type are sufficiently similar to permit comparison, no project need suffer in effectiveness from the inclusion of non-value-added tasks.

The leading IS organizations all manage projects well. Seminal research[1] in the United States and Europe in the 1980s showed that, of all the factors effecting the outcome of a project, only the capability of the project manager was a consistent determinant of success. Leading organizations have generally progressed beyond the application of general project management principles to their development and maintenance processes. They have developed or adopted integrated project and program management processes that are specifically adapted to the characteristics that distinguish the development, delivery and maintenance of information systems. Recognition that the development of high quality information systems in a short time with limited resources requires a different form of project management approach is one of the initial keys to Development Effectiveness.

Processes Today: What Is Still Missing

Although leading IS organizations have made great strides in establishing and using standard processes for development and, to a lesser extent, maintenance, some aspects of a truly effective process are still missing.

Both anecdotal and research evidence[2] from the mid-1980s onward calls into doubt the more extravagant claims of both software and information engineering with regard to the elimination of defects resulting from misstated requirements. In particular, the following inferences seem likely:

- It is effectively impossible to achieve defect-free requirements specifications prior to building the prototype of a system. In addition, the time required to improve a requirements specification by removing additional defects increases geometrically with the number of defects so far found. In practice, this means that versions of requirements specifications after the third or fourth iteration do not improve enough to justify the additional effort required to accomplish them. The optimum process seems to be at most three rapid iterations for requirements capture, followed by the development of a prototype to be used as the basis for subsequent improvement. In addition, the first iteration should be as rapid as possible. Trying to get too much done on the first pass also seems to be counterproductive, although it may be possible to proceed directly to a prototype if the first iteration goes well enough.

- Even when requirements are well specified, information systems that meet them cannot be successfully implemented, because the underlying business processes are often unchanged, or changed only minimally. However, reengineering business processes is usually not seen as the province of IS developers, and it is difficult to synchronize the new process design with information system requirements based on the old process.

- The elapsed time from original requirements specification until business requirements are expected to change is alarmingly short (perhaps as little as 6 months). Because even the best development processes typically take two to three times as long as this to deliver a working information system, changes will be inevitable.

- It is often practically impossible to get effective input from business users and managers on which to base the analysis of business requirements. Furthermore, critical knowledge may not be available from standard documentation or available users. No requirements analysis process can guarantee to identify the absence of something when no one knows it is missing. Using independent (i.e., nonuser) business subject matter experts can help to identify omissions through a review process based on knowledge of similar situations (comparison by analogy), but still cannot guarantee completeness.
- Even when sufficient inputs are available, business users are often unable to adequately review the form of the specification required by the IS organization for accuracy, consistency, and completeness. Users specify their requirements in a particular form and language. Requirements analysts must translate this into a more formal language that can drive system design and construction. The results can be difficult for users to understand and verify as correct and complete.

The solution to these issues does not seem to lie with more analysis effort, or with better requirements analysis processes, although these would clearly help; some improvement opportunities are examined in the next section. Rather, an overall accelerated development process based on cheap and quick-to-build, high-quality prototypes seems to provide a better solution.[3] Business users have proven adept at surfacing defects during participative testing and early use of new software.[4] Accelerated delivery processes deliver software to business users that can be tried out, modified on the basis of experience, and, hence, rapidly improved to meet changing requirements.

Improved Requirements Analysis Processes Can Help

Improvements in requirements analysis processes have centered on five areas:

- **Identifying and securing the participation of informed sources of requirements** (both people and documentation). In many instances this is difficult, because the best sources are usually those running the business, and their availability for intensive participation in requirements definition processes (however accelerated) remains problematic. Substituting less well-informed participants can work successfully, but the process is slower and more prone to specification defects.
- **Rapid consensus formation using facilitated workshops** to surface and gain agreement on business requirements and solution options. Workshops can be rapid and effective mechanisms for identifying and documenting requirements, but they are resource intensive and require specialized skills (in facilitation and in the business subject matter under investigation) to be successful. When any of the key success factors for a workshop are absent (as they often are), effectiveness is reduced and the risks of defective or incomplete specifications are increased.
- **The use of prebuilt generic models and specific solution examples to refine initial requirements**. Specification by example allows business users to surface requirements by contrast with an existing model or solution. Behavioral research[5] indicates that this process is several times as effective as structured discovery in confirming requirements, but that participants can suffer from the "what you see is what you want" syndrome.

Independent subject matter expertise is required to guard against this behavior. In addition, the example must be a good one in the first place.

- **Process redesign as a fundamental part of the business solution**, prior to designing new information systems support. Unless information systems are designed to support the right business processes, they will fail to satisfy business users' real requirements because these requirements are dependent on a process change. Reimplementing poor business processes with better support technology seldom satisfies user requirements, no matter how well specified.
- **Model-driven development**, using CASE or Object-Oriented Analysis tools to collect and organize requirements information into models that can be used to drive the design and construction stages of the life cycle. This was the great promise of the 1980s, but only the latest generation of tools has developed to the point where it is even partly feasible. Some of today's tools can be used to support a model-driven approach, but still lack many of the capabilities needed to make the approach simple and reliable in all situations.

The lesson here is that good requirements analysis is extremely difficult to do. Without the right level of participation by the right sources of requirements, the right discovery and analysis processes, good subject matter experts, good analysts and good tools, it is unlikely to work well. Even with all of these factors in place, it is not a guaranteed or risk-free process, because no one can guarantee that all the required communication processes will work effectively—nor detect when they have failed.

Because there is no guarantee that requirements will be specified exactly correctly, systems professionals must accept that there will be a degree of rework in design and construction and must plan for it. The alternative—freezing the specification in a form known to be deficient and then building a solution that matches something no one actually wants, a practice common in the 1970s—is no longer a generally acceptable approach.

It is this known need to be able to incorporate changes to requirements in the design and construction phases that focuses the necessity for version control and configuration management processes and tools. If the design never changed, individual components could be built, from which a system could be assembled without concern for versions. A single configuration model would also suffice. Knowing that changes will occur, however, means planning for and establishing effective version and configuration controls before they are needed.

Focus on Teams

Selecting the right team members and team leaders is known to be an important part of creating a high-performance organization. Yet IS development processes have little to say about how to do this. Even when role definitions are provided and used, there is little guidance on what types of people do well in specific roles and what types do badly. Once again, IS organizations have traditionally used an overly simple assumption—that all IS staff are essentially the same—even though IS managers know that this assumption is invalid.

A significant minority[6] of IS organizations have begun to use behavioral assessment testing in an attempt to address these issues, and there is some evidence of success in roles for which a specific behavioral profile is known to help or hinder performance. In our own experience, however, behavioral assessment makes relatively little difference to the successful formation of a team. Better approaches are needed.

Even when effective teams are constructed, IS organizations do not have team-focused management processes, nor do most organizations train their project managers in "people management" skills. This is a serious omission. Most project managers progress to their jobs through demonstrating technical skills rather than people skills, yet there is good evidence to suggest that people skills predominate in the management of high-performing teams.

Effective processes are a key ingredient in sustained high performance, when supported by appropriate technologies in the form of developer support tools. In the next section, we examine the leading types of tools and their contribution to development effectiveness.

Tools Today: What the Best Are Using

Development support tools are not new. Tools of various kinds have existed since the days when assembly-language programming replaced machine-level coding. Until the middle of the 1980s, however, tools were mostly aimed at individual tasks, with little thought for coordination. Thus, development support technology was a collection of useful single tools, mainly aimed at coding tasks. With the advent of CASE, Object Oriented Development, and Client-Server tools, however, the prominence of the role of tools in influencing productivity and quality has risen sharply. There are now many different kinds of tools and we will look at them in a smaller number of convenient groups.

Workbenches

"Workbenches" were among the earliest collections of tools to be developed under the "CASE" banner. Many kinds of workbench tools have been developed, and workbenches now form the second largest group (there are now at least 150[7] products) of available commercial tools. Workbenches fall into a number of classifications, according to the following broad criteria:

- **Methods and Approaches Supported**. Workbenches that support only one method (process) or life cycle model are of little use if the IS organization does not use that particular method, or a method based on that particular model. On the other hand, a tool that is tightly coupled to a single approach can concentrate on implementing one set of model building rules efficiently.

- **Richness of the Underlying Life Cycle Model**. One of the keys to effective use of a CASE tool is the number of "object types" supported. Although the user's methodology will (or at least should) determine the number of things about which information needs to be gathered and stored during planning, analysis, or design, not all of these are necessarily supported by any particular CASE tool.

- **Applications Areas Supported**. Workbenches are usually aimed at only one of the two main application areas of information technology:

  Commercial data processing (both interactive, transaction oriented, and batch processing)

  Real-time processing (Command, Control and Communications Information [C^3I], process control, embedded systems, etc.)

  The third main area, *scientific computing*, is hardly addressed at all, although a few workstation-based tools are beginning to appear.

- **Range of Techniques Supported**. Modern structured methods (including IE and object oriented development) require the use of a large number of related techniques to complete a development project. The extent to which a workbench supports the complete range, or even a minimum subset, varies considerably.

- **Approach to Multiuser Support.** Because projects of a size worth worrying about need to be developed by teams, not individuals, some provision must be made for sharing information within a team of co-workers and between teams. This requirement leads to issues of version control, configuration management, and ownership of work.

No current workbench provides complete facilities in all of these areas, but the best of the available products do address all the major areas of concern and are developing toward solutions in the critical, but difficult, areas of rigorous specification of requirements, quality management, change control, and automatic generation of executable code from requirements definition.

Work Flow Managers, Process Managers, and Integrated Project Support Environments

Many of the activities and tools used by a development project provide significant amounts of useful information, either about the conduct and progress of the project itself or about the situation or enterprise in which the project is taking place. Much of this information could be of use to other projects or to other areas within the enterprise. However, because it is not central to the development process it is easily lost or deliberately discarded. Given the number of times that a project team "reinvents the wheel," especially when setting up and estimating the resources required for a project, there is a clear incentive to capture, organize, and retain this "spin-off" data, provided that it can be done at a reasonable cost and without delaying the project itself.

The technical problems faced by early programming support environments (PSEs) showed that the development of automated tools to support cooperative work was much more difficult than developing tools for the support of the development process itself. Key problems were:

- **The need to support multiple users working on the same things at the same time.** This was the essence of the project support problem, as virtually all project teams consisted of more than one person. Without this facility it was not possible to provide effective configuration management of work products.

- **Management of change and version control**. During a project, most of the things managed by a PSE were developed through a sequence of versions. Changes were requested and incorporated at various stages, not always to the "latest" version.

- **Granularity of the information model**. The first two requirements meant that PSE developers were forced to provide a detailed information model and to build their repository in such a way that version control could be implemented for each instance of the model's contents. A complete information model may require several hundred different types of content, and generate millions of instances for the version-control system to manage.

- **Scale**. Large projects, in terms of duration and team size, could not always be avoided. They typically generated a host of problems beyond those of small or medium-scale developments. In particular, large projects experienced considerable "personnel drift," both in team composition and in individual roles and responsibilities. They also typically experienced a good deal of requirements drift as well, so large scale version control and configuration management became even more important.

It soon became apparent to PSE developers that support of the programming team was only one part of the overall management environment. Efforts were directed to extending the support capability to the complete project life cycle from requirements definition to deliverable installation, resulting in the integrated project support environment (IPSE) concept.

IPSEs and other development support tools can be seen as complementary developments, with the IPSE providing a management framework into which individual development support tools can be slotted for specific tasks. With the increasing interest in process management tools and the move toward generic work flow managers as enablers of improved business process effectiveness, the application of similar work flow management ideas to IS development and maintenance is also growing among leading organizations. Because few development support tools actually address any process management issues in a significant fashion, the IPSE concept has much to offer. For this reason IPSEs are beginning to appear in support of large-scale commercial developments, mostly in Japan and Europe, less so in the United States.[8]

Application and Code Generators

Probably the largest and most diverse group of development support tools are application and code generators. Although problems of definition make it difficult to say just how large the group really is, a good guess would be about 400[9] products, excluding dozens of tools that generate applications only for single-user microcomputers. Application and code generation tools are based on one or more of the following approaches:

- Very high-level programming languages, in many cases an extension of an established 4GL and an associated data base management system
- Prototyping and rapid development tools, for the development of relatively simple applications that can make use of existing corporate data bases
- User interface (especially Graphical User Interface [GUI]) development tools linked to event-driven code and data base generators for client/server application architectures
- Information center (IC) or end-user computing (EUC) support, including the development on microcomputers of applications that can link to corporate data bases

- Automatic code generation from application design specifications, removing the need for most or all manual coding
- Object oriented programming languages and development tools

The increasingly rapid adoption of client/server technology as an environment for mission-critical business systems has given a significant boost to the subset of application and code generation tools that work in, or can be easily converted to, this environment.[10] As the basis for generating environment-independent applications, these tools are well matched to the hardware manufacturers' attempts to insulate the application developer and user from the physical architecture of the machine on which the application is to run.

Application Area Specific Tools

The major application packages developed by software vendors during the 1960s and 1970s were attractive to their purchasers because they solved common core operational application development problems in a standardized way and removed the need for maintenance of key applications such as financial ledgers and payroll. Their disadvantage for users was that they were too standardized, and it was difficult to tailor them to the individual requirements of different organizations. Vendors addressed this need by developing customization facilities, based on a large number of options, from which users could select those that best met their requirements. Any customization beyond this had to be done by conventional development of add-on facilities.

Redevelopment Engineering

For about 25 years, most large-scale IS departments have been building up a portfolio of applications that are badly designed, poorly integrated, and expensive to maintain. They represent an enormous investment in development resources and contain an enormous volume of essential data. Indeed, some application data bases are now so large and so essential to the continuing operation of the businesses that own them that they simply cannot be shut down for the length of time it would take to transfer them to a new data base technology. It is all their operators can do to keep them backed up and secure.

There is a widely perceived need to redevelop core operational systems on better design principles and to integrate currently separated data sets. But the resources to do this just do not exist. Organizations have to go on living with what they have for the next decade at least. It would be nice if something could be done to clean up the worst of these current applications without having to go to the expense of replacing them.

Tools that address these problems should arguably be the most interesting area to most IS departments. There is evidence[11] that up to 80% of IS resources are consumed by work on currently installed applications, and that the older an application is, the more expensive it is to maintain. Documentation gets progressively further out of step with the code, and the probability that each new change will introduce an undetected error grows exponentially.

Many applications were originally coded before structured design was introduced and, hence, are poorly structured. Even programs that start in a well-structured form tend to "drift" toward convoluted code as time passes and successive generations of programmers work on them. Code-mapping tools are not difficult to build, and several exist. Recoding tools are also available, improving on the processing maps, and removing unexecuted or redundant code.

Taking the next step—analyzing and improving program data structures—is a good deal harder, because the tools need to examine all usage that is made of data, not just the usage by a single program, if they are to ensure integrity and consistency. Tools that can do some of the required analysis and modification are beginning to appear, especially for environments where there is already a DBMS, or at least a data dictionary, in use by the program.

The final step in reengineering—selecting an existing set of programs and automatically redesigning them to satisfy a new requirements specification—is still a long way off. Even the best current technology (products that include embedded expert system technology to allow them to behave "intelligently") is some way from solving this problem, although it does make manual approaches feasible by automating and linking many of the individual steps required.

An interesting subset of these tools is aimed primarily at documenting the application from the code that currently runs it. From source code, data base descriptions, COBOL source libraries, and Job Control Language procedures, they generate program specifications. For badly documented or undocumented systems, this can be an important first step in regaining control of an application.

Verification, Validation, and Testing

When an application has been developed, the developers must demonstrate that it performs the tasks for which it was designed accurately, reliably, and with adequate performance. Once apparently error-free programs are obtained, testing concentrates on demonstrating that the application functions work correctly. This process invariably shows up additional defects, which have to be corrected and retested: an extremely time consuming and resource-intensive procedure. As a result, testing usually concentrates on what is expected to happen; tests designed to ensure that the application behaves correctly when the unexpected happens are omitted.

It is a truism that anyone can design a system that works well if its users never make any errors. In the real world, such perfection is rare. Applications must be able to react correctly to a wide range of unexpected conditions and to recover reliably from a wide range of errors. Testing is not usually performed to check that all these circumstances have been provided for. A further complication arises from the fact that testing seldom exercises all of the code in a program, so it is not possible to know exactly what the code does under all circumstances.

A number of attempts have been made to build tools that assist with this process, both in the commercial and real-time application development areas. The main types of tools that have resulted so far include the following:

- **Test Harnesses**. These provide a framework for consistent testing of sections of an application, using prespecified sets of function tests. The results can be recorded in a test data base for later analysis and to pinpoint errors or problems.
- **Test Data Set Generators**. With the increased use of data modeling techniques in requirements analysis, it is now possible to generate test data sets using data element definitions derived from the requirements modeling process.
- **Static Code Analyzers**. These tools analyze and report on all the possible execution paths of a program, by tracing through the code, and can detect a wide range of structure anomalies.
- **Dynamic Code Analyzers.** These tools generate execution frequencies for code paths and report on changes to variables and data elements during execution of the program code.
- **Sensitivity Analyzers**. These tools check the accuracy of the arithmetic carried out by programs, especially integer arithmetic where rounding errors or overflow can occur, and floating point arithmetic where the precision with which numeric values are represented can cause huge variations in the results of complex calculations.

In most cases, a combination of these tools will improve the chances that a delivered application performs the tasks expected of it correctly and reliably. One thing all tools in this category have in common is that they generate very large amounts of information about the structure of an application. The skill then lies in interpreting this information and in using it to detect and rectify subtle logic and structure errors.

At one time it may have been sufficient to test an application as far as resources allowed, and trust that any undetected errors would not cause a disaster. Errors that did turn up after installation simply contributed to the application maintenance load. In the future it will be necessary to take a much more rigorous and methodical view of the testing and verification process. It will also be essential to document all testing activity and to maintain comprehensive records of what was done, and the results, so as to demonstrate that all reasonable actions were taken to establish that an application was error free and matched its specification.

Project Management

Although good project management is probably *the* key determinant of a successful outcome to a software development project, few tools of any type provide much useful project management support and few specialized project management tools are based on the repository concept, as development support tools generally are.

A project management tool should, ideally, support the preparation and maintenance of the following plans:

- A **Work Plan**, setting out the work steps, tasks, and activities that will make up the project, specifying work dependencies, preferred activity sequences (where this is possible), and the estimates of the resources (people, technology, and supplies) required to complete the plan. To make life easier for the project manager, this capability should link closely to a process management or work flow management tool.

- A **Resource Plan**, matching available resources to the requirements of the work plan to generate a **Project Schedule.**

- A **Quality Management Plan**, specifying how deliverables are to be quality assured, assigning responsibilities to team members, and adjusting the project schedule as required.
- A **Risk Management Plan,** identifying and specifying risks that are associated with the project and how they will be addressed. The project schedule will again need to be modified to accommodate additional actions resulting from the risk management plan.
- A **Project Budget**, identifying the total monetary cost and expected cash flow for the project.

These six plans form the basis for the initial definition of a project. Once the project is under way, the project manager's tools should:

Provide a means of recording actual resource expenditure against estimates at the appropriate level of activity detail (which may vary from stage to stage of the project). It should also be possible to aggregate effort around work products and deliverables.

Generate reports on progress to date, current status, and work remaining to completion.

Record significant events during the project and relate them to any required changes in the project schedule or other project plans.

Maintain an index and cross reference to all project documentation.

Maintain a list of open issues that are unresolved at any stage of the project as a prompt to work still to be completed.

In this way, a project history data base can be built up and used to modify or review the estimation and control processes employed by the project manager. To do this properly requires a model of a "project" that defines the information sets that will be collected and manipulated.

Unfortunately, few project management tools actually provide these facilities. Instead, a number of tools for the management of software development projects, principally for the definition and monitoring of work breakdown structures (WBS), are available. To date, none of these tools really addresses the project management requirements of the new generation of tool-supported development methods such as IE.

Miscellaneous Tools

There are a number of tools that do not fit easily into any of the basic categories. Partly this is because they are highly specialized, or very new and not yet established. In part, it is because development support technology is a fast-growing area, and it is not always clear what should be included and what left out. It will probably be some considerable time before the boundaries stabilize (for instance, design and construction tools are increasingly offering testing and source code reengineering capabilities).

Tools Today: What Is Still Missing

In reviewing the range of leading development tools today, there are a few clear pointers to a realistic (perhaps overly pessimistic) expectation of what can actually be achieved:

- There are many similar tools in most of the categories listed. Potential users often find it difficult to distinguish between individual tools and, hence, to choose the tools most appropriate for meeting their requirements. This difficulty is exacerbated by widespread confusion between definitions for tools, techniques, and methods.
- The market is still highly diversified, with no clearly dominant vendors. There is also likely to be consider-

able consolidation between existing vendors over the years; and this is already beginning to happen.

- The emphasis remains on workbenches for analysis and design, with a growing appreciation of the need for code and data base generators.

This situation leaves both existing and potential development tool users with a number of significant problems:

- Even the best-integrated tool sets provide insufficient coverage of the complete life cycle to be used, without additional nonintegrated tools. Tool kits are therefore needed, and considerable effort is required to make the tools within a kit work together. (See Figure 2.1.)
- Users of development support tools are insufficiently trained in necessary usage skills and are unprepared for the changes that the technology produces in the development processes they are used to. Hence, IS organizations cannot make the most of the potential benefits to be derived from using the tools.
- Few tools are as good as their vendors claim, and potential users are being put off by stories of oversold capability and poorly met expectations. In this negative atmosphere, success stories are often ignored or discounted and valuable lessons are being lost.
- There are few signs of standards emerging for interworking between tools. Proprietary standards may be a step in the right direction but can cover only a portion of the total development marketplace.

As a consequence of these problems:

- Take-up of development support tools has been slow, with relatively few tools in use on any given site and most usage still experimental.
- Benefits, if any, are slow to appear and difficult to quantify. As a result, expansion from initial use to widespread

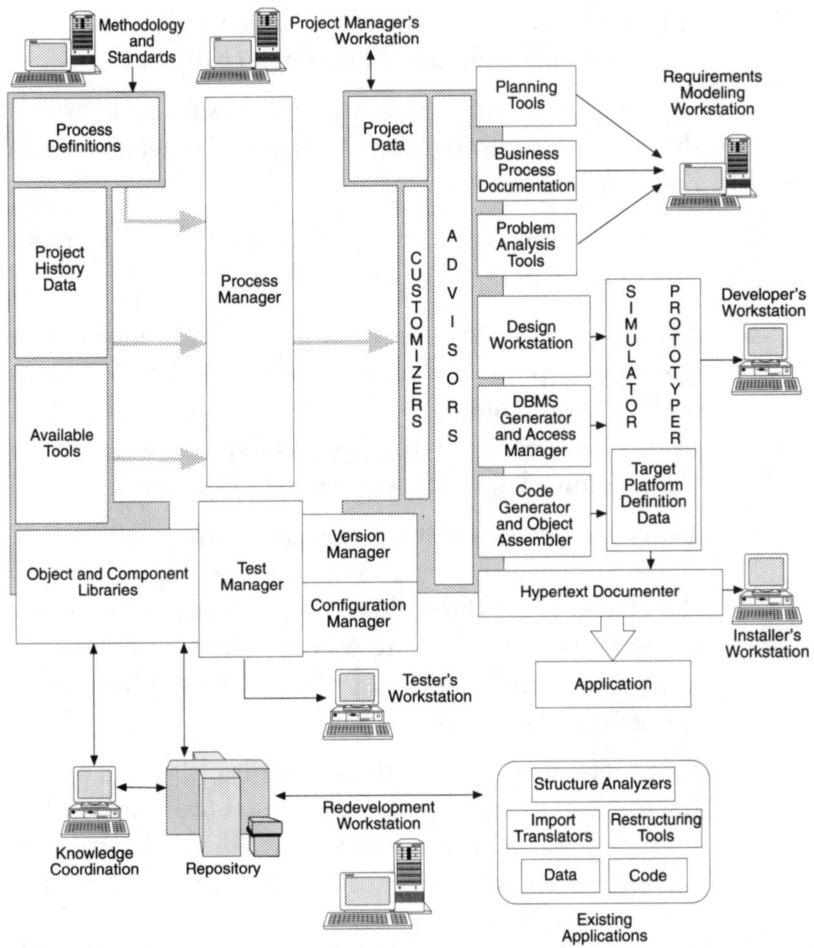

Figure 2.1 *Components of the Complete Developer's Tool Kit*

availability is slow or does not occur, because it cannot be justified.

- Toolbox or tool kit approaches predominate, and much effort is expended on interoperability issues and on addressing areas where there are no available tools.
- Confusion remains, particularly at the levels of management that need to support widespread adoption of sophisticated development support tools.

There are, however, outstanding examples of just how successful organizations can be when using development support tools. Why, then, do so few actually achieve this level of success?

Because there are gaps in the current capabilities of development support tools, and because most tool areas are still emerging technologies, it is important to distinguish between:

- The *strategic* decision to migrate toward an automated development environment for information systems, and
- The *tactical* selection of a set of tools with which to begin the migration process.

In essence, this means that the set of tools in use will change and grow during the initial implementation and afterward. These changes will be driven by the introduction of new capabilities, improved ways of working, and more cost-effective technologies.

It is clear that despite the interest and attention focused on tool development it is not possible to put a complete set of tools together today. Among the plethora of current development tool offerings, there are a number of key tools missing or not sufficiently well developed to meet user needs. The following list is not complete, but it serves to highlight key areas for improvement and major opportunities for tool vendors seeking to fill the gaps.

Standards

One concern that has dogged creators of development tools, as it has most areas of IS development, is standards for the construction and interworking of tools. There would be considerable advantages to common definitions for the design of key tool elements, particularly:

- *The structure and content of the information model for the repository*. This is a basic issue for interoperability.
- *The form and mode of interaction options for the user interface*. Although GUIs have become almost mandatory, they are not the best solution for all forms of

interaction. Nevertheless, if all tools used approximately the same user interfaces, moving from one tool to another would be much easier.

- *The validation and verification rules for objects and models.* If the rules are not the same everywhere, how can anyone be sure that the results of applying them are equivalent?

A definition of the interface between tools and their hardware platforms would also allow users to move a tool from one platform to another as requirements, or technology, changed. So far, few developers have been prepared to publish the internal structure of their repository, making standardization difficult. Even the interchange of information between tools using published export/import standards has often been difficult to achieve because the objects they manage are defined differently. From a user's point of view, this lack of standards is a disincentive to invest heavily in any one tool, inasmuch as there is no guarantee of long-term viability and no clear way to move to an alternative tool should this become necessary.

The Repository

Without a repository, the whole structure built around the toolbox will be less effective and may not be technically possible at an economic price. So far, all that is known is that building a working repository is very difficult. Initial attempts at an enterprise-wide repository technology have all failed.

Tool builders are now concentrating on project-level repositories, and initial products will probably be based on a proprietary information model. What developers have to go on so far does not yet cover all the toolbox environment requirements. Because there will almost certainly be no early de facto standard, most tool developers are waiting to see more of the details of emerging products and technologies before embarking on a new round of developments to produce more tightly integrated or interoperable tool sets.

Other Missing Pieces

In addition to a repository, there are a number of other areas where tools are not yet available or, if available, do not match rapidly changing needs. These include the following:

- **Data Base Generation Aids**. The process of generating an efficient data base design using SQL data definition language (DDL) remains specialized, complex, and prone to error. A tool to automate the majority of the steps required, based on an analysis of an application's design, would assist this process.

- **Test Case Generation**. With a standard requirements definition and solution design approach, using models plus effective development support tools, it should be possible to generate a test plan and a set of test cases automatically from the requirements model and design specification for an application. Coupled to testing and verification tools and target environment profiles, this would allow virtually automatic testing of applications. Such capability would greatly reduce the effort required to plan and carry out the testing process, and improve the reliability of testing. With an integrated version control system for predefined design components, it will not be necessary to test parts of an application that have not been changed.

- **Conversion and Reengineering**. Only about 50% of large installations currently use any sort of DBMS for their core operational systems. Whether or not applications using this data are reengineered, there is a huge amount of data to be converted from current files and data bases to make it useful to applications in the new CASE-based environment. This conversion process is a major headache for data administrators, many of whom have hundreds of gigabytes of on-line storage to manage. While the conversion process is going on, the tools should also be able to help "clean up" the data base design by generating a normalized, logical model of the data from the current physical design and by advising on the new physical design.

- **Software Configuration Management.** The basic tools for software configuration management and version control during development have been available for a long time. Yet somehow, source code library managers' "make" utilities and the like have failed to solve the problem of creating and managing large volumes of reusable code among large numbers of developers. Standard architectural approaches are going to make this problem both easier—more of the code will be provided by system services that cannot be altered by the designer or programmer—and worse—reusability requirements will increase. Code "versions" will also have to exist for different system environments to allow full cooperative processing designs. Tools in this area are getting better, but have a long way to go to fully solve the problem.

- **Common Tools in All Environments**. Developers do not really want to have to learn a different set of tools for each environment in which they must work. Common User Access (CUA) standards for tools are just as important as they are for application software. Most tools, however, pre-date the CUA concept and do not match this ideal. Nor does it seem likely that a common tool interface can be achieved soon.

Our toolbox model at least offers a clear framework for providing the right tool for the job, so long as the tool exists. For a while, however, developers must be prepared to continually change and upgrade their tool kits as new and improved tools become available.

Infrastructure Today: What the Best Have Invested In

Tools by themselves do not create sustained high performance, even when they make high levels of performance possible. Developers must have a technical, process, and organizational environment within which they can make effective and efficient use of their tools. As the early CASE and other graphically-based development support tools were introduced, vendors tried to provide this environment using mainframe technology, with which developers were already familiar. The advent of the personal computer (PC) and of high function workstations essentially rendered these attempts futile. Research[12] into the costs of development infrastructure indicates that an on-line development capability costs an IS organization about $25,000 to $30,000 per year per "seat"[13] to own and operate. Providing comparable capabilities on linked workstations costs up to an initial $25,000 to $30,000 per seat, plus perhaps $10,000 per year per seat subsequently. For a large development and maintenance organization, the change can represent a substantial savings, totaling several million dollars a year. In addition, a well designed and operated PC or workstation-based infrastructure can provide significant performance and service-level improvements. As a result, leading IS organizations have moved a long way toward a development environment that is based on linked groups of workstations or PCs with gateways to a host or network platform.[14]

Another key feature of leading IS organizations is the extent to which customers are involved in the development process and the forms this involvement takes. Rather than treating customers just as sources of information during requirements analysis, leading organizations involve them throughout the development process in a variety of roles, from business sponsor to tester. In organizations where customers have been involved in this way for some time, customers may also be managers for part or all of development and enhancement projects. The IS organizations that have achieved these high levels of customer involvement have used a variety of approaches to make the customer partnership work. Among the most effective of these approaches are:

- Physically locating the development work in the customer's environment
- Co-staffing and co-training project teams
- Working with customers to understand the best way to quantify the business case for an information system and then measure the delivery of business benefits
- Marketing, to both IS colleagues and customers, the successes of collaborative development

Perhaps the most important lesson to be learned from successes in involving customers is that such involvement does not happen by itself. It must be worked at over a considerable period of time, and in a sense, the job is never done. As the individuals involved (on both sides) change, the benefits of involvement must be resold and the processes of effective involvement relearned.

Despite the continuing difficulties associated with the availability of a commercial repository technology, leading IS organizations have begun to implement a more limited form of repository supporting the reuse of information systems components. Although the opportunities associated with the successful adoption of reuse strategies are significant (no other strategy, except purchasing packages and using them unmodified, offers so great a boost to productivity and quality), the technical problems involved are very difficult to overcome. Leading IS organizations have identified where real, albeit limited, benefits can be achieved and have concentrated on harvesting these while learning more about the requirements for an effective enterprise-wide repository.

As local area networks have replaced host-connected terminals as the primary infrastructure technology, leading IS organizations have begun to exploit the capability of the infrastructure to deliver a range of performance support services to developers.

Performance support covers all forms of education, training, coaching, and reference material that can assist a development or maintenance team member in the course of a project. Research in the development of "help" systems[15] has shown that people will use assistance only if it is available at the time they need it. If it takes more than a few minutes to get to a source of help, most people will attempt to do without it, usually to the detriment of the task that is giving them a problem. Traditional forms of help—printed documentation or "asking an expert"—often fail this immediate availability criterion. Infrastructure-based delivery systems can go a long way toward making sure that the right help is available to everyone whenever it is needed. Most such systems today supply only a form of "passive" help, which the user must notice is needed and then ask for. The technologies that are available can potentially be developed to be more proactive in making appropriate help accessible whenever needed.

In concert with the idea that good project management makes more of a difference to a successful project outcome than any other single factor, leading organizations are also investing in infrastructure to support the project manager. Much of this investment is aimed at making measurement easy and accurate. Historically, the costs of data collection for control purposes have been high—perhaps 5% to 7% of the project cost.[16] As a result, data collection has been minimal, often below the level that allows for effective diagnosis of problems and their early solution. Leading IS organizations have invested in infrastructure that decreases the cost of collection while simultaneously improving both granularity and accuracy of the data being collected.

Perhaps the most distinguishing attribute of successful IS development organizations has been the realization that *infrastructure is not just about technology*. Instead, it must include or integrate with many aspects of process, organization, culture, and environment. Without this realization, many fine technology efforts have failed to achieve their potential or simply failed altogether. We return to the theme of a broader-based understanding of infrastructure and how to implement it in Chapter 9.

Infrastructure Today: What Is Still Not Working

The single biggest problem faced by those IS organizations that are investing in an effective infrastructure has not been cost justification (which is hard enough), but rather gaining access to the time and capital needed to create the infrastructure in the first place. Traditional IS development technology has typically been in place for a number of years and was built up incrementally as a part of an enterprise's overall IS infrastructure. Although an IS organization is charged for its use of the technology, this use is marginal and the technology provided specifically for the IS organization has generally been of comparatively low cost (terminals, printers, and communications switches).

With the need for an extensive upgrade to this environment with powerful workstations and local area networks, the sudden jump in the cost of technology exclusively for the use of the IS organization has caused many enterprises to balk. Even those who may agree that the investment should take place cannot always afford it.

The situation is not improved by the second biggest problem faced by infrastructure developers. Because many components are necessary to construct a successful development support environment, a major systems integration effort is required to make the infrastructure effective. Few IS organizations have the skills available to do this quickly and effectively, and there is a steep learning curve for those who seek to develop the skills from scratch.

Many of the hardware and software technologies involved are evolving rapidly, and few can be acquired in a preintegrated form. Development support infrastructure is thus a dynamic, ever-changing integration challenge that few IS organizations are well equipped to meet.

The third problem area concerns the failure of the PC or workstation environment to duplicate the exact behavior of the target platforms on which information systems will be installed.

Although differences with traditional host environments are narrowing, they remain. This requires that the IS organization retain some development capability on the target platform and reduces the full potential of savings resulting from the move to the development workstation. As the range of new target technologies increases, the ability of development workstation-based tools to keep pace will determine the continuing success of workstation development environments.

The fourth problem area, as we mentioned in the preceding section, is the temptation to treat infrastructure as a technology-only issue. Ignoring process and people issues makes the problems look smaller, but does not help to solve them.

Resources Today: How the Best Treat Their Staff

Perhaps the last (but certainly not the least important) area to be recognized as key to the creation of a highly effective information systems development and maintenance capability, the active management of staff as a key resource has come to prominence only in the past few years. In many cases this has been prompted by the unprecedented levels of change forced on the IS organization and its customers by technology and economic recession. The recognition that organizational design and organizational change management are essential success factors in business process redesign has spread to the IS organization rather slowly. However, leading IS organizations are reevaluating their organizational structures and human resource management practices in a number of significant ways.

1. There is a recognition that at least a proportion of IS staff must have a wider—and harder to acquire—skills mix than has usually been required. This mix must include both business and technical skills, and these

skills must be kept current through both practical use and continuing education.

2. To create these "hybrid" skills, IS organizations need to pursue a "multi-track" model of career development, wherein staff have the opportunity to progress in several different ways, focusing on business, technical, or combined skills growth. This approach recognizes explicitly that not all staff are equally able to acquire all necessary competencies, and that measurement and reward systems must be designed to reflect individual growth rather than normative (grade-based) career models.

3. To promote the recognition and adoption of this new organizational structure and culture, leading organizations are also overhauling their hiring, compensation, and recognition systems to reinforce the changes they are trying to make. Staff are being recruited from a more diverse range of educational and experiential backgrounds, and induction processes are being recast to provide a broader range of initial training and experience. Ongoing assessment and coaching form a large part of the capabilities development process.

4. To promote the accelerators available from continuous improvement and component reuse, IS organizations are creating a "build a better mousetrap" culture, in which recognition goes to those who can build effective solutions based on existing ideas, models, or components. This is a significant move away from the culture of "not invented here," "start with a clean sheet of paper," and "creativity over delivery" that has plagued the IS organization in the past.

Organizations that have moved some way in these directions have not had an easy time; even positive changes are to some degree resisted, and not everyone in IS sees these changes as positive. Most of the "early adopters," however, are beginning to see results. They are creating a culture and environment where individual and team learning can occur. In this culture mistakes are still made, but they are more obvious, less penalized, and there is a high degree of confidence that they will be effectively detected and corrected.

Resources Today: Challenges Remain To Be Met

Just as the IS organization and the technology it uses have grown and changed rapidly to create a broad and diverse industry, so have the people who work in IS become a broad and diverse group. Many IS staff members attained their current positions via skills and experience that are increasingly irrelevant to the problems of the IS organization of the present. Although many of these people recognize the situation, few are pleased at the prospect of having to learn new skills, effectively setting them on a par with newer, younger, and less expensive entrants to the IS profession. Maintaining their morale, knowledge, and experience, which are essential to continuing maintenance of existing systems, while changing their skills, expectations, and ability to make a contribution, is a major challenge. IS organizations cannot do without these staff members, but equally cannot let them stay the way they are if necessary changes are to occur. Selling the new career model to those who do not want to fit into or understand it remains a significant problem.

Nor does the IS profession have a breathing space in which to allow the changes to "take." Continuing investment in technology research and changes in business environments will maintain or increase the pace of change with which all organizations have to deal. Expectations that change will slow because no one can cope with it may appear reassuring, but there is little evidence that they are being met. Creating an organizational culture tolerant of high levels of change over an extended period of time is an ambitious goal that few enterprises have been even partly successful in reaching.

As high levels of technical and organizational change continue, one of the major continuing challenges will be to maintain an appropriate level of technical and business skills among IS staff. The losses in effectiveness experienced during the learning curve associated with new types of problems, new solution approaches, and new technologies severely depress the benefits associated with change. If the investment required to become effective is high, as it almost always is today, and the time available to recoup that investment through deployment of new capabilities is short, as the accelerating pace of change seems to ensure that it will be, the IS organization increasingly finds itself unable to maintain a portfolio of required skills and abilities.

Falling too far behind the leading edge may place an organization in a position from which it cannot recover. Simply imposing more stress on IS staff will cause dysfunctional behavior or departure for easier pastures. In the medium term, solving the reskilling problem may be the single greatest competitive advantage that IS can bring to the enterprises it supports.

Conclusion: No One Is the Best at Everything—And There Are No Easy Answers

One lesson to be learned early in the search for best practices in leading IS organizations is that no organization exhibits best practices in every area. In collateral Ernst & Young research with the American Quality Foundation[17] on Total Quality practices, we have found that appropriate "best practice" depends not only on what an organization does, but also on where that organization stands in a kind of "maturity spectrum."

What works well for an organization just getting started in creating an effective IS process and infrastructure will not be appropriate for organizations who have already made some progress towards the IS effectiveness objective. Perhaps more important, practices that work well only after years of painful and sustained effort cannot be successfully adopted by organizations that have not yet made the effort to traverse the intermediate stages of development effectiveness.

Although this may be an obvious point—crawling must precede walking, and walking precede running—the practices of leading organizations are too often touted as examples of success without reference to the effort and time it took to create the practices and to make them successful. It may be tempting for organizations, faced with the need to change dramatically in order to survive, to adopt leading practices as a means to avoid the intermediate steps. However, in our experience this seldom (perhaps never) works and almost always creates more problems than it solves.

In a joint research effort with the Society for Information Management, Ernst & Young has begun to identify, characterize, and measure the effect of existing leading practices for improving quality and productivity in the IS development process. Figure 2.2 summarizes the initial results[18] based on data from 39 study participants. It is clear from the results of this research that a number of leading practices are under investigation or in use, but only a few are showing significant impacts on performance and quality. Of those that are, only one of the top five is directly attributable to technology (the use of workstations to support development on the desk top) and only one other is technology enabled—the use of prototyping. The other three are concerned with issues of organization (cross-functional teams) or process (joint application design and business process reengineering).

In contrast, note that much of this chapter deals with issues related to the use of technology. In a sense, this is symptomatic of the IS organization's fundamental problem. IS staff are technophiles. It is hard for them to accommodate the additional

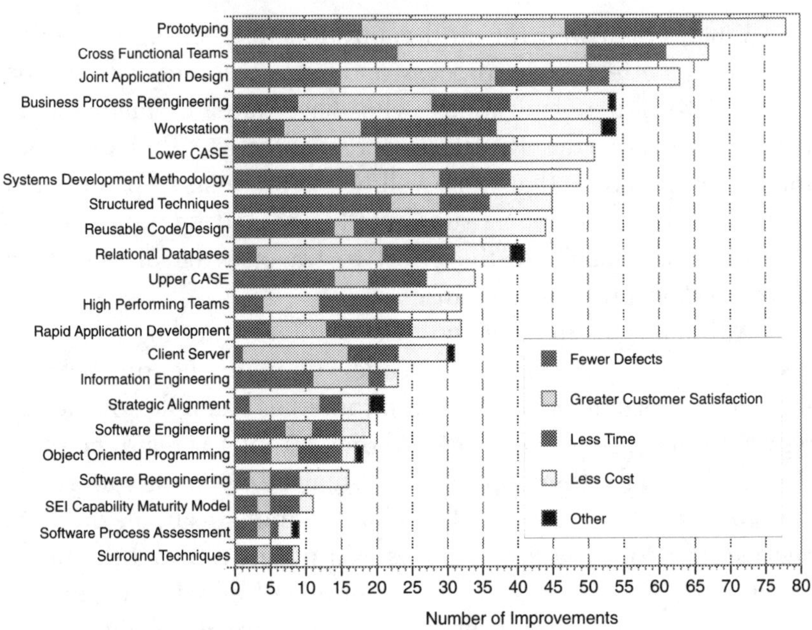

Figure 2.2 *Leading Practices and their Effects*

dimensions (processes and people) required for a balanced and successful organization that can learn and grow. Making the transition to such an organization is a big change, and most of the rest of this book is concerned with successfully making that change.

Notes

1. Two sources of research in particular are relevant. The first, undertaken by the Butler Cox Foundation in 1988 and published as a research report to Foundation members, looked at success determinants in more than 200 software projects. The second, undertaken as a part of the Management in the 1990s program at the Massachusetts Institute of Technology (MIT), considered similar determinants in projects being undertaken by the program's sponsors. Both reached essentially the same conclusion.

2. Based on work by one of the authors on the differences in requirements-related defects discovered after delivery of an application, compared to the requirements analysis effort. Source data from a consistent series of development projects covering over 3000 programs developed between 1979 and 1985. Additional material from *American Programmer*.

3. Barbara Bouldin, *Agents of Change* (Englewood Cliffs, NJ: Yourdon Press, 1989); Dorine C. Andrews, *Fusion* (Englewood Cliffs, NJ: Yourdon Press, 1993).

4. Glenford J. Myers, *The Art of Software Testing* (New York: John Wiley & Sons, 1979); Gerald M. Wienberg, *Quality Software Management* (New York: Dorset House Publishing, 1992 and 1993): Vol. 1, *Systems Thinking*; Vol. 2, *First Order Measurement.*

5. There are several sources for behavioral data of this kind. We have used data from the Human Sciences Advanced Technology Laboratory of Loughborough University in the United Kingdom, which collaborated with us on a number of projects in user-centered design.

6. Actually, we may be doing a disservice to the IS profession. The comment is based on conversations with a number of people who administer these tests and reflects their impressions on coverage (who actually uses the test) and impact (what they do with the results).

7. Based on internal Ernst & Young product tracking data.

8. See note 7.

9. See note 7.

10. *Application Development Management* conference papers (Chicago: Gartner Group, June 1993).

11. Forester Research published data, (London: 1987 through 1990). See also note 11 in Chapter 1.

12. Based on material published by Gartner Group in a series of research reports between 1988 and 1993.

13. A "seat" represents a person in some stage of the software development process. As the process progresses, the person occupying the seat may change, but only a single seat is provided.

14. Extracted from "Leading Practices Report 1.1: A Summary of Leading Practices Within the Systems Delivery Process." A report of a joint project of Ernst & Young and the Society for Information Management. Available from the Ernst & Young Center for Information Technology and Strategy^{SM}, 1993.

15. Based on personal correspondence with the research team at the Human Sciences Advanced Technology Laboratory at Loughborough University (United Kingdom: 1989 to 1992).

16. Bob Grady's two books [Robert B. Grady, *Practical Software Metrics for Project Management* (Englewood Cliffs, NJ: Prentice-Hall, 1992) and Robert B. Grady and Deborah L. Casewell, *Software Metrics, Establishing a Company-wide Program* (Englewood Cliffs, NJ: Prentice-Hall, 1987)] on the long-term IS development metrics program at Hewlett Packard provide an excellent source of comparative cost information for measurement efforts.

17. *International Quality Study: The Definitive Study of the Best International Quality Management* (New York: Ernst & Young, 1991).

18. See note 14.

3

Characteristics of High Performance IS Organizations

To build a sustained level of improved performance in the future state IS organization, we need to identify the characteristics and behaviors we are looking for in a highly productive IS development organization. There is much to be learned from the leading practices of existing IS organizations, even though these practices may not of themselves provide everything needed for sustained high performance. By identifying what works well today and analyzing where this falls short of our desired future state, we can begin to create the detailed vision of where we would like to be and to design the transition process required to get there.

In his book *Future Edge*,[1] Joel Barker, one of the earliest and most eloquent proponents of the concept of "paradigm shift" and its effect on organizations, lists three key capabilities needed by an organization to be consistently successful in the future.

- **Excellence**. Long considered the goal of the quality movement and yet to be achieved consistently by more than a handful of organizations, Barker cites *excellence* as the price of entry into the ranks of the successful by the end of the 1990s. Businesses that are not routinely excellent in everything they do will not be able to compete with those that are.
- **Innovation**. Beyond excellence, *constant innovation* is the cost of achieving membership in the small group of businesses that will lead and dominate each industry or market. Only by continuously innovating processes, products, and services will an enterprise be able to create the flow of investment capital that leadership requires to sustain it.
- **Anticipation**. With excellence as the price of entry, and innovation the price of success, leaders will be distinguished by an ability to *anticipate* the needs of customers, so that capital and creativity can be focused on innovation in areas where there is as yet little or no com-

petition. The true leader will create new markets as well as compete effectively in existing ones.

Although Barker is writing about the enterprise as a whole, his points apply to the requirements for a successful, high-performance IS organization. This chapter discusses some of the key characteristics needed by a high-performance IS organization in order to enable consistent levels of excellence, innovation and anticipation. The characteristics considered here are derived from a number of sources, including observations and research on the following:

- The behaviors associated with high-effectiveness teams, extrapolated to include consideration of the cultural and organizational context within which the team is formed, works, and is managed.
- Total Quality and the ability of an organization to continuously learn and to continuously improve its performance.
- The experiences and lessons of the relatively few organizations that have been able to radically redesign at least some of their business processes through the innovative use of technology.
- The experiences and practices of those (very few) organizations that have been able to achieve and sustain consistently high levels of performance over a significant period of time.

Note that the ability to deliver occasional periods of high performance is not of primary interest here, except for what can be learned about the reasons that performance falls off after a period of time. Sustained high performance must be the goal.

Although "high performance" has many dimensions, this chapter focuses on seven in particular:

Mission, which gives the information systems (IS) organization its purpose and provides a vision of what it is trying to achieve

Culture, which determines the way in which members of the IS organization behave toward each other and toward their customers

Organization, which describes how the processes of the IS organization are managed and sets out the key roles that members of the IS organization will play

Processes, which describes the work of the IS organization and the ways in which this work is carried out

Customer interface, which defines the nature of the relationship between the IS organization and its customers

Infrastructure, which describes how the IS organization uses technology, organizational design, standard practices, and desired behaviors to support its internal processes and management structures

Economics, which defines the approach to resource allocation and priority assessment used to map available IS resources to meet customer demand

Clearly, these dimensions are not really orthogonal. Indeed, any high-performing organization must seek to achieve a synergy between these and other aspects of its situation. Chapter 8 introduces and discusses the use of a model framework—the Diamond Model—that can be used as a tool to map out these aspects of high performance in an organization and show how they interact. Part III of this book explores some of the most important issues that need to be confronted to achieve the required synergy between these dimensions.

Mission

Research[2] and observation have established that all highly effective organizations and teams have a clear and commonly understood sense of mission. Any formal mission statement for the IS organization must link its work with the goals of the enterprise and must provide strategic direction over an extended period, even though the details of the mission will change as business direction changes. As a straw man mission statement, consider:

> *The IS organization is the center of excellence within the enterprise for creating and sustaining business value through the cost-effective deployment of information technology in support of business processes.*

Mission statements are notoriously easy to generate and equally hard to make meaningful. It is essential, therefore, to go behind the statement itself and look at what the highly effective IS organization really seeks to do. Successful IS organizations need to remember these axioms:

- **The IS organization does not exist in isolation.** It must recognize that its purpose is to provide active support for a continuing program aimed at improving the enterprise's ability to operate and compete effectively. The IS organization must therefore develop strategies, priorities, and plans to ensure that this goal is understood, communicated, and promoted. There must also be an active program to promote effective use of all current information assets, including installed technology, enterprise data, process knowledge, and IS services to create and sustain recognizable business value within the enterprise.
- **The IS organization cannot rest on past successes.** It must seek, in collaboration with a broad range of enterprise managers and customers, opportunities to use information technology as an enabler to improve or innovate business processes through a program of continuous process redesign.
- **The IS organization cannot assume that it cannot or need not do better.** It must recognize a need to continuously improve and innovate its own internal

processes, infrastructure, and capabilities, even when these are perceived as being among the leaders.

This is a complex mission, but it recognizes that the IS organization must exist and be successful in a complex and constantly changing world that it cannot completely control.

Culture

Culture in this context is the set of shared beliefs, traditions, and values that determines the instinctive and habitual behaviors of members of a group or society. The IS organization must build and sustain a culture that allows its mission to be implemented successfully. Although there will be a variety of possible successful IS cultures, the following description provides a good starting point for the "culture design" effort.

The culture must value excellence and reward all those whose efforts contribute to achieving it. Nothing can be achieved unless it is valued. Many cultures espouse a belief in excellence, but readily accept much less. A high-performance organization needs a culture in which everyone wants to do his or her best and take every opportunity to improve.

The culture and its values must be resilient to high levels of change. Most cultures grow up and mature by investing in some form of stability in societal practices and environment. Even cultures that are initially innovative and challenging often begin to seek stability as members achieve their initial goals and want to enjoy the results of their success.

Over time, therefore, the culture tends to become averse to change, and even to "fossilize." The successful IS culture must seek to balance the need for continuity of experience and the development of effective practices and behaviors with the equally strong need to evolve the context within which experience, practice, and behavior are applied.

Eventually, the culture and its members must be able to drop from consideration those experiences, practices, and behaviors that are no longer valid or relevant to their purpose.

The culture must value and reward judicious experimentation. This is often a difficult behavior to internalize, inasmuch as acceptance of experimentation implies acceptance of failure in some cases. Clearly, a pattern of constant failure, for whatever reason, must be avoided. But it is axiomatic that cultures that do not allow some proportion of attempts to fail soon stagnate as experimentation is penalized and innovation is stifled. As a direct corollary of this axiom, the culture must be able to accept bad news without unduly penalizing the bearer.

The culture must understand that individuals play different roles according to circumstances and need. This is one of the bases of the *empowered work group* model and is among the most difficult behaviors to implement in organizations that have traditionally equated role with organizational position, influence, or power. Creating a culture in which, for instance, the lead is from time to time taken by the individual who is best suited to deal with the situation of the moment, is a difficult challenge when cultural and organizational aspects mitigate against such behavior.

The culture must recognize the value of both heterogeneous and homogeneous skills and encourage and reward individuals for their development. Despite the increasing sophistication and complexity of the technologies it uses, the IS organization must acquire both narrowly focused technical skills to cope with that complexity, and broadly focused general management skills to cope with the application of the technology to business problems.

Individuals need to be encouraged to choose between these skill sets, but must not be penalized for their choice. Where the rare individual is identified who can be equally at home with both technical complexity and business applicability, he or she should be encouraged to develop in both areas and not be pigeonholed into one or the other.

The culture must accept and encourage objective assessment of performance through comprehensive measurement programs for both processes and participants. In many cultures, measurement is seen as a threat, often because management uses it that way. Yet both processes and people must be measured if they are to improve. Measurement is a necessary basis for certification of competence and must be used as an aid to improvement, not just as a penalty for poor performance.

It is the nature of the real world that processes and individuals perform across a range of values, whatever the measure used. It is also part of the real world that the performance of an individual will seldom be the same relative to all other individuals on all possible measures. No one is the best or worst at everything. Therefore, rather than a "management weapon" to weed out the poor performers and reward the best, measurement needs to be viewed as a tool for improving everyone's performance by helping to ensure that capabilities are matched to the requirements of processes and that help is provided when and where it is needed.

The culture must encourage the acquisition and dissemination of new learning from both inside and outside the organization. "Not invented here" plays no part in the highly effective organization's culture or behavior. Just as the IS organization does not exist in isolation within the enterprise, neither does the enterprise exist in isolation from other enterprises in its field.

Ensuring that internal best practices are uniformly adopted is only the first step in becoming highly effective. Looking outside, at the best practices of partners and competitors, also provides a valuable source of ideas for improvements and innovations. Notice that this traffic works best if it is two-way. Effective organizations do not fear to share the "secrets" of their effectiveness with others—they have sufficient confidence in their abilities to remain competitive, and they understand that true competitive differentiation depends on an ability to adapt rapidly to changing circumstances, not on a singular process or capability of the moment.

The culture must promote values of openness and receptivity to ensure that all assets and resources are used as effectively as possible. It is a truism that no one alone is as smart as all together. Yet successful cultures can sometimes forget this and become too dependent on the knowledge and vision of their assigned leaders. Highly effective leaders find ways to keep all members of the culture engaged as active participants in the continuous improvement and innovation process.

The cultural model we are suggesting here may be termed "loose adhocracy," with a high value placed on team participation and synergistic relationships as the primary vehicles for delivering individual contributions.

Organization

Just as there are many possible cultures for a high-performing IS organization, so there are many possible organizational approaches as well. Chapter 5 explores the factors affecting organizational design in more detail. In general, however, the IS organization needs to adopt a model that provides an effective balance between five organizational elements:

1. **A customer-focused group,** dealing with strategic alignment and customer requirements specification issues. This is the group that has an in-depth understanding of the key issues facing business managers in making effective use of technology. To keep its requirements feasible, the group also needs to blend in relevant technical skills, using a combination of individuals with hybrid skills, if available, and multifunctional group processes analogous to those used for concurrent engineering. This approach helps ensure that requirements are determined primarily on the basis of real business needs and that appropriate solutions are selected primarily on the basis of technical feasibility.

2. **A development, assembly, and delivery capability** organized on a variant of the "Software Factory" model,[3] with flexible manufacturing and concurrent engineering analogies. As the actual delivery of information systems moves away from the creation of new software and toward the assembly of previously developed and tested components, a factory production process becomes feasible. However, that does not imply a mindless production-line model, with the poor levels of motivation, skills, and quality that this approach has come to imply. Because conventional manufacturing processes have already evolved beyond this to encompass flexible work cells and self-directed team-based assembly, the software factory may be able to jump straight to these approaches without the intermediary evolution and its undesirable side effects. Note, however, that, as with the International Quality Study (IQS) findings, appropriate levels of process and infrastructure maturity are needed to lay down the necessary building blocks for the software factory concept to work.

3. **An infrastructure management and provisioning group,** which has the objective of ensuring that the right processes, standard practices, appropriate support technology, and effective performance support capabilities are available and that these are effectively integrated into the IS working environment. This implies a primarily—but not exclusively—inward focus, with continuous improvement of the infrastructure capabilities as an objective. The group will have members who rotate between infrastructure work and either development- or customer-focused work to ensure that it does not lose touch with the real needs of customers.

4. **Program and project sponsoring groups,** which provide both initiating and sustaining sponsorship for the IS

organization's work and which are potential advocates for innovation and improvement within IS processes. The group contains both business sponsors, who provide a customer perspective and the determination of business value, and IS organization sponsors, who contribute commitment of resources and technology.

5. **A technology enablement group,** to research, select, and integrate new technology-based capabilities. This is a separate group because it must often look at new technologies before they are really ready for general use, and understand the role that such technologies could play in process innovation—both for the enterprise as a whole and for the IS organization in particular. This contrasts with the improvement orientation and IS organizational focus of the infrastructure management and provisioning group. Despite these different orientations, the two groups need to work together to gain the maximum value from infrastructure investment.

Within this organizational structure, work programs—sets of related projects with common objectives—and projects are staffed by multifunction teams. The fundamental organizational unit is therefore the team—not a fixed organizational hierarchy. Reporting relationships will vary over time as individuals shift roles within a team and between teams. This places emphasis on an effective management infrastructure that can deal with the shifting organizational environment. It also puts emphasis on the role of the team manager—and requires an investment in creating and sustaining project and team management skills.

Within the team-based organizational framework, there should be a continuous staff development program. It is an objective of the organization to keep skilled staff turnover as low as possible, because recruitment and training costs will remain high. The pattern of skills development will shift over time, and all staff should be encouraged to participate in a continuous re-skilling process.

Information Technology Processes

A process is the set of logically related activities that transform a defined input into a defined output. Processes have process owners and customers. As such, processes are predictable and, therefore, repeatable. **Information technology (IT) processes** describe the actual work of the IS organization, and how it chooses to carry out that work. Although the processes described here are internal to the IS organization, it is important to remember that they exist within a wider organizational context that extends beyond the boundaries of the IS organization to support all aspects of information technology in the enterprise. This wider context creates a "process landscape" that is described in more detail in Chapter 4. Here we deal only with the "deliver and evolve IT components" major process.

Process Specialization

To be effective, processes must be derived from a common set of principles, so that IS staff and their business customers are always familiar with the general nature of the work flow. Yet to be efficient, processes must also be specific enough to fit a particular problem or project, so that there is no wasted or duplicated effort. This objective can be achieved by a combination of common project design approaches, common work flow management processes, and common standards, all of which should be provided as a part of the IS infrastructure. To ensure that all projects are assessed on an equivalent basis, a common assessment framework and common initial assessment approach should be used to evaluate all proposals for application development, application evolution, and solution delivery projects.

Once assessed, projects are scoped and planned using a set of enterprise-specific *route maps*, tailored to meet the individual needs and objectives of each project. There are sets of common standards easily available and in use in all appropriate areas of activity. These standards are reviewed for relevance, effectiveness, and applicability on a continuing basis and the extent of their use is also monitored. IS staff are encouraged to devise and offer for consideration any new practices or standards that they discover to be needed during project activity.

Delivery Flexibility

In "world class" organizations, information systems are developed using *models* that can be implemented in more than one target environment without change to the business requirements or the way that requirements are supported. Target environment independence has to be achieved through an evolving combination of processes, standards, techniques, tools, and technology. As a consequence of this delivery flexibility, information systems can be scaled from platform technology to platform technology in order to meet changing usage demands at different times in their life in use. Customers do not have to learn new processes as the technology changes; thus, disruption to the business is minimized.

Technology opportunity analysis is used on a regular basis to determine the most appropriate combination of platform technologies for an information system. All information systems use a flexible design architecture, based on a cooperative processing model, even when the implementation is not intrinsically cooperative, to ensure transferability.

Business process redesign opportunities are reviewed as a routine part of all new developments and major enhancements to existing systems.

Focus on the Future

Development and delivery processes are designed to focus on building for long-term maintainability, so that the cost of ownership of information systems is low, both in comparison with their value to the enterprise and in terms of absolute resources required to support them.

Productivity and quality targets are set and monitored for all projects. Project team performance is measured, and assistance is always available if required. Levels of quality and performance are expected to increase over time.

Continuous Improvement

The IS organization promotes a process of managed evolution within which applications are initially delivered rapidly, with most of the required functionality available and with a low level of defects. Applications are then evolved to meet proven and value-justified business and customer requirements. Applications are not regarded as finished until formally replaced by completely redesigned business processes.

Process Maturity

It has become fashionable to preach continuous process improvement as a means to solve the ills of all organizational units, including the IS organization. Although continuous process improvement is indeed a powerful tool, evidence is emerging that it is not, by itself, enough to guarantee long term excellence in all processes.[4] Initial and mid-term results from improvement programs are often excellent. However, in the longer term there seems to be a plateau effect and improvements taper off. After a time, the cost of continuous improvement is not offset by the benefits of the improved process. The process is now a candidate for innovation before a new round of improvements can begin. It also seems likely that processes mature at different rates. Certainly, improvement efforts start at different times. At any given time, therefore, the processes in the IS organization will be a mixture of the mature (awaiting innovation), the maturing (undergoing continuous improvement), and the new (recently innovated and still stabilizing before improvement starts), forming in total a "footprint"[5] of variable shape across the spectrum of possible maturities. This is a much more complex situation than generally described by business redesign enthusiasts. Much more effective and sophisticated process measurements will be required to ensure that process maturity states are correctly assessed and the correct improvement actions are applied.

Customer Interface

Customer interface defines the nature of the partnership between IS and its customers within the enterprise. To form a true partnership, there must be a variety of recognized, active roles for both partners, not just a passive service role—"we'll do whatever you ask for"—or a professional delegation relationship—"just fix the problem and tell me when it's done." This requires both specific understanding about the nature of partnership relationships and specific participative behaviors by both business customers and the IS organization.[6] It is important to recognize that how partnerships are thought of and organized can and should be treated separately from how they work in action; this is a key first step in establishing an effective set of customer relationships.

Participation

Customers participate actively and effectively in all key aspects of requirements analysis, design assessment, and testing for new and enhanced information systems. Customers understand the value of this participation, as demonstrated through improving measures of satisfaction when such participation occurs. This understanding makes it easy to obtain enthusiastic and relevant participants from the customer community, even though participation may have a short term impact on the effectiveness of some business processes while key staff are involved in IS-related work. As customers become more practiced participants, more team roles are available to them, including team management and facilitation.

Responsiveness

The IS function measures its effectiveness by the following factors:

- **The ability to apply agreed upon, objective, value-based criteria** when assigning priorities to new work. IS and customer resources are thus always applied to the opportunities that create or sustain the greatest business value, as mutually defined and understood with customer participants.
- **The speed of response to user requests** for new or enhanced system facilities. Solutions are always delivered while they can resolve a problem or support an opportunity.
- **The acceptability and usability,** as measured by the customer, of the systems that are developed or enhanced. Acceptability and usability are monitored throughout the life of an information system so that objective data is available to justify or support the need for preventive maintenance or enhancement work.
- **The level of defects** of all types, reported by customers and IS staff in new or enhanced information systems. Although both IS and its customers have zero defects as an objective, both recognize that the inevitable level of ambiguity in their processes will lead to defects from time to time. Nevertheless, early defect identification and rapid removal remains a priority.
- **The effective application of an appropriate set of technologies** in support of business processes. It must not be forgotten that the IS organization deals with information *technology* as well as with customers, productivity, and quality issues. Selecting and deploying the appropriate technology is another aspect of responsiveness that can and should be measured.

In all cases, improvement trends in process effectiveness and service satisfaction measures are expected to occur and are monitored.

Consideration for the Customer

Maintaining a high degree of stability within the customer's working environment is considered to be an important aspect of success in delivering effective information systems support to business processes. Coupled with managed technology growth and continuous improvement of business processes, IT-based solutions are designed to ensure that customers can continue to work effectively with new or enhanced information systems and that implementation-related disruption is kept to a necessary minimum.

Infrastructure

As used here, the term **infrastructure** encompasses all of the ways in which the IS organization uses technology, processes, practices, organizational structures, and environmental design to support its development and maintenance processes and its management structures. The basic concepts underlying the IS infrastructure are support for work groups and the use of flexible managed work flows, dynamically designed for optimal effectiveness within a project or set of related projects. This requires a series of related factors.

Automation

Automation must be provided to support the following:

- **Project management.** Support tools must be provided to assist with the design and execution of all types of projects. The use of a standardized model of a project assists with the accumulation of project histories in a form that allows for analysis and the subsequent improvement of processes and associated heuristics.

- **Process management** and the dynamic management of project work flows. Work flow management capabilities must be provided to support all types of projects and to automatically capture and accumulate actual project experience in resource usage related to outcomes.
- **Process support** tools. Comprehensive automation assistance with project work must be provided via tools for the support of application development, enhancement, and delivery processes.
- **Communications** tools. A large part of the effectiveness of a collection of individuals or teams depends on how well interteam and intrateam communication works. The IS infrastructure should assist with this communication requirement as a part of its support for work groups.

Because tools also develop and evolve new capabilities, the automation aspects of infrastructure will change over time. Thus, the strategic nature of the overall infrastructure should not be confused with the tactical selection of individual infrastructure components.

Reuse

A comprehensive automated *knowledge base* or repository of reusable information systems components and IS development practices, knowledge, and experience should be created and be made available as an enabler for high levels of reuse within development and maintenance processes. A common, IS organization-wide knowledge base should therefore be in use for all new development and for the support of continuing evolution work. All business and IS plans, architectures, information systems requirements, and delivered information systems should be modeled as views of this common enterprise knowledge base. Knowledge-base management should be a recognized infrastructure capability and project role.

Templates and generic models, stored in the knowledge base, should be available for all major and most minor custom developed information systems, application packages, and specialized technology-enabled facilities. Models should also be available for all business processes, as well as for the information systems that support them. It is a measured objective of IS development and maintenance processes to minimize the amount of newly created components required and to maximize reuse of existing material.

In this environment, development and evolution work should be primarily a component assembly process, using previously developed and tested information system requirements models, design fragments, and code. The proportion of reuse should be measured and should be expected to increase steadily over time.

Performance Support

There is widespread recognition that development and maintenance staff cannot continuously remain current with all the necessary aspects of their work, no matter how well they are initially trained. Some access to reinforcement materials during or just prior to the employment of a particular skill or specific area of knowledge can act as an effective trigger for material or competencies that would otherwise not be available in an effective fashion. Behavioral research has shown that practitioners will resort to various forms of in-the-workplace reinforcement only if they are available immediately at the moment of need and without undue effort. Extensive performance support facilities, reinforcing these basic competencies, should therefore be provided for all development and maintenance staff as a by-product of their working environment.

In addition, teams should have access to appropriate levels of coaching and mentoring at the start of and during projects.

Economics

Economics describes the approach to resource allocation and priority assessment used to map available IS resources to meet customer demand.

Focus on Business Value

Because the mission statement of the effective IS organization focuses on creating and sustaining business value, the concept of value must be central to the economic justification models used to assign priorities to the use of IS resources. These models should be developed and agreed upon with business customers, and monitored and updated as business conditions change. As a direct consequence of this approach, the value created or sustained through the use of information systems should be measured so that expected levels can be demonstrated to have been achieved.

Demonstrating Tactical Cost Effectiveness

The IS organization should be able to demonstrate cost-effective development processes on a project-by-project basis. It should be able to do this through a combination of effective project design, using the processes and infrastructure described earlier in this chapter, and a relatively small number of protected development environments and target implementation platform technologies. Within these constraints, an extensive repository of standardized components and infrastructure capabilities can be combined to deliver high-quality applications with low levels of risk. Application development and maintenance processes are therefore known to provide high added value at an acceptably low cost through the leverage of existing capabilities, skills, and experience.

Recognizing Strategic Investment Needs

As well as demonstrating tactical cost effectiveness, the IS organization is able to make and justify strategic infrastructure investments in support of continuous improvement or innovation in its internal processes. Because justifying infrastructure investment is notoriously difficult on a tactical basis, this ability implies that there are agreed-upon strategic measures of effectiveness that allow the IS organization to show where the value from its infrastructure investment is actually realized.

Conclusion

Excellence, innovation, anticipation: in our experience even the best IS organizations are often a long way from achieving these criteria for success. Yet just bemoaning the shortcomings of the IS organization is unhelpful if there is no counterbalancing strategy for addressing the issues.

In the rest of this book, therefore, we set out to demonstrate an approach to improvement that can achieve the objective of sustained high performance. There are no "silver bullets" here and very few easy answers. Creating and sustaining a high-performance organization of any kind is a complex task, requiring attention to detail in many areas and consistent effort on many fronts. After all, if it were that easy, everyone would already be doing it.

Notes

1. Joel A. Barker, *Future Edge: Discovering the New Rules of Success* (New York: William Morrow & Co., 1992). This work examines many of the key aspects of paradigm shifts and their consequences for individuals and organizations.

2. Based on research reported in Jon R. Katzenbach and Douglas K. Smith, *The Wisdom of Teams: Creating the High-Performance Organization* (Boston: Harvard Business School Press, 1993).

3. Michael A. Cusumano, *Japan's Software Factories* (New York: Oxford University Press, 1991). The "Software Factory" model was originally developed from research on high productivity software development processes introduced by Toshiba in Japan. The research looked at the productivity gains resulting from treating system (not application) software as a set of standardized "components" that were "assembled" using a "production line" model to create finished software products. Very high levels of productivity and quality were reported. Software Factory concepts were also used as analogies in the early work of Brad Cox that led to the concept of the "Software IC" and Object Oriented languages.

4. Based on internal Ernst & Young research and observation of processes where continuous improvement has been at work for an extended

period. The sample is small, the findings are preliminary, but the conclusions are nonetheless interesting.

5. The Process Maturity Footprint concept is based on research from the Ernst & Young IS Leadership Multi-Client Research Program. The authors are indebted to Mary Silva Doctor of the Center for Information Technology and Strategy[SM] for the original idea and its subsequent elaboration.

6. For an excellent treatment of the role of the IS organization in forming partnerships with business customers see John C. Henderson, "Plugging into Strategic Partnerships: The Critical IS Connection," *Sloan Management Review*, Vol. 31, No. 3 (Spring 1990: pp. 7–18).

PART II

Key Issues in Organizational Transition

In Part I, we described the current state of information systems (IS) development and created a vision for the future state of a high-performance IS organization. In Part II we provide the theoretical background for the Development Effectiveness approach in making the transition from the current to the future state.

Chapter 4 sets the context for the transition in Total Quality terms and thereby establishes a perspective for IS improvement that is customer driven, process oriented, and measured. We describe an overall process landscape for information technology (IT) and for the systems development subprocesses.

Chapter 5 discusses the organizational design issues, with particular reference to work groups and group processes. We examine the operating principles that underlie effective systems delivery and describe a process for designing a high-performance IS development organization, based on these principles.

Chapter 6 considers the nature of change and how people respond to it. It describes the key roles in managing change and discusses how to orchestrate these so that change initiatives are sustained.

Chapter 7 examines the costs and benefits that can be anticipated in using traditional cost displacement methods, and in using three nontraditional approaches. Finally, we show how to increase the value of Development Effectiveness by accelerating the realization of benefits.

4

Total Quality and Process Orientation in Information Systems Development

Total Quality Management (TQM) has proven to be an excellent organizing approach for Development Effectiveness. This chapter considers the major elements of TQM. It contrasts continuous improvement with innovation and compares product-focused and process-focused improvement strategies. Here we discuss process definition, describe a high-level conceptual framework for information technology (IT) processes, and provide an expanded definition for the systems development process.

Efforts to dramatically improve information systems (IS) capabilities can quickly be overwhelmed by complexity. Identifying customers, products, and services is a constant challenge. Multiple forms of relationship must be maintained with end users, business managers, and senior executives. Although some IS products and services are tangible, many, such as designing IT infrastructures and evaluating emerging technologies, are all but invisible.

The IS organization has to ensure continuous availability of diverse infrastructure components while managing and staffing small, large, and, sometimes, mammoth projects, all the while keeping legacy systems operational. IS must contend with rapidly shifting and often ill-defined business needs in a climate where IS costs are an increasingly significant budget item and where the value of IT is under constant scrutiny. IS is often an agent of change for the business, and increasingly will be looked to as a source of expertise in managing organizational change.

This complexity makes it difficult to know where to start an IS improvement effort and how to bring focus to it. How should the various improvement programs and projects be structured and sequenced? How can they be integrated and coordinated for maximum synergy? Can a harmonizing theme be found that helps people make the right daily decisions in the midst of the ambiguity that inevitably accompanies change?

An area of interest at Ernst & Young's Center for Information Technology and Strategy℠ is the study of management practices that lead to superior IS performance. Our IS Leadership Multi-

Client Research Program[1] has shown that TQM[2] can provide an excellent context for IS improvement. It can become a unifying theme that serves as an umbrella for the multiple change initiatives needed to transform an IS organization.

Just as TQM can help a company to align itself more broadly with the needs of customers, the capabilities of suppliers, and the motivations of employees, TQM can help to align IS and business strategies and provide an excellent framework for Development Effectiveness.

What Is TQM?

TQM (Total Quality Management) is defined as "the integration of quality management methods, concepts, and beliefs into the culture of the organization to bring about continuous improvement."

It is a blend of both scientific and humanistic principles. Prominent at the center of many significant corporate turnaround stories, and reinforced by initiatives such as the Malcolm Baldrige Award, "TQM awareness" is currently at an all-time high.

TQM has been gaining momentum since the mid-1980s and has proven itself to be a useful means for transforming all types of organizations. A management philosophy long an integral part of Japanese business, TQM has its roots in statistical quality control (SQC). SQC was developed during the 1930s and exported to Japan along with the postwar reconstruction effort. The Japanese, and others, have added much to SQC, and in its richer forms, TQM today incorporates continuous quality improvement, total customer satisfaction, employee involvement, process management, and policy deployment—a sophisticated form of business planning that aligns strategic quality goals through all levels of an organization.

Some of the talk about quality is, admittedly, little more than hype. One consequence has been a backlash in the press in the

1990s, with reports of abandoned quality initiatives and results falling far short of expectations. There is, however, overwhelming evidence that quality management can pay handsome dividends, and there is now a growing body of research into the business and social impact of TQM.

For example, a study by the U.S. General Accounting Office (GAO)[3] tracked the impact of quality programs on U.S. business. The GAO looked at the 20 highest scorers in the Baldridge competition and compared them with their peers in four categories: employee relations, operating procedures, customer satisfaction, and financial performance. The results showed a strong correlation between TQM and business performance. Not all the high scorers performed better—some actually performed worse. However, the vast majority performed significantly better than those that did not score high, or did not participate in the Baldridge competition.

The Conference Board, in New York, surveyed senior executives at large U.S. corporations in regard to their quality management practices.[4] Of the sixty-two companies that measured the impact of quality on profitability, forty-seven reported "noticeably increased" profits as a result of quality management, whereas only one company reported decreased profits because of "the increased costs of providing higher-quality products and services."

The Ernst & Young/American Quality Foundation International Quality Study (IQS),[5] the largest international study ever conducted on the nature of quality programs, tracked the performance of 500 companies in Germany, Japan, Canada, and the United States. This 1992 study focused on four major industries—automotive, banking, health care, and the computer industry—and assessed 102 types of management practices related to quality. Since 1991 researchers have collected 1.5 million data points about quality management practices and their impact on performance.

Among other things, the study examined organization, service, customer satisfaction, and corporate culture. Again, the value of TQM in its many forms was evident. By examining performance dimensions such as return-on-assets, value-added-per-employee, and an index of overall quality as perceived by end users, the IQS established correlations between quality management practices and performance outcomes. Significantly, however, this study refuted the conventional wisdom that held that any organization, regardless of its current performance, can benefit from the widespread adoption of all quality improvement practices. It found that practices that are beneficial at one level of organizational performance show no association—or even a negative association—with performance at other levels.

For example, lower-performing companies will usually benefit from the establishment of departmental and cross-functional teams. However, for higher-level performers widespread participation on department-level teams can actually be detrimental to performance. Benchmarking current practices against so-called "world class" practices, on the other hand, can be highly beneficial for higher-level performers, while it can be detrimental to lower-performing companies. The IQS thus shows that quality management practices must be carefully chosen, based on a company's current performance level and culture. When it comes to quality improvement, one size does not fit all!

Although TQM first appeared in the manufacturing sector, it has now spread to the services sector, in businesses as diverse as hotels, food services, insurance, financial services, government agencies, and even in highly creative industries such as advertising and public relations. Today, TQM is proving to be a major building block on the road to business process reengineering.

What, then, does TQM mean to the IS function? How can TQM be applied within IS? How do TQM principles support an appropriate planning framework for Development Effectiveness?

TQM and Process Thinking

TQM's power derives in part from its focus on processes. Unfortunately, although IS professionals have no problem at all relating to business processes, they often have difficulty thinking in terms of IT processes, particularly those outside the operations function.

For example, although there may be well-defined processes for disaster recovery, backup, and security, there is rarely a defined process for identifying IT-enabled business opportunities or for providing IT infrastructures.

This process myopia results in part from the *project* focus so dominant in IS work. IS professionals have been conditioned to think and act in terms of *projects*, rather than well-defined, repeatable *processes*. This is unfortunate, for it is the process rather than project perspective that enables organizational learning.

In his book on process innovation, our colleague[6] Thomas Davenport identifies three principal benefits of process thinking:

- First, taking a process perspective is synonymous with adopting a *customer perspective*. Because by definition a process must have a customer, whether internal or external to the organization, process thinking forces an organization to focus on its customers.
- Second, the ability to *measure processes* is important for identifying causes of waste and overhead so these can be reduced. Without measurement, improvement has no real meaning.
- Finally, process definition liberates employees from thinking about *what* to do and helps them focus on *how* to do it. This point is particularly relevant for IS professionals who, by and large, tend to view their work as a "craft" and resist the notion of predictable, repeatable processes for systems delivery.

Let us explore each of these aspects of TQM as they relate to IS improvement.

Customer Perspective

Customer satisfaction is so important that the phrase has become nearly synonymous with Total Quality. For the IS executive, this means coming to an understanding of whom the customers are, and of their needs and expectations.

An analysis of IS customers quickly reveals a large and diverse base, from internal members of the IS organization to clerical, administrative, and professional members of the business organization who use IT; to business unit managers, senior executives, and other stakeholders who fund IT investments, and regulatory agencies who require information in certain forms, or compliance with certain regulations; and, ultimately, to the end consumer of the company's product or service. With such a varied group of potential customers, a key to achieving customer satisfaction is to segment the possible customer base and concentrate on the "critical few"—that is, the *relatively few* customers who are most important to the company's success.

Clearly, no customer should experience poor service. However, when quality requires exciting and delighting customers and anticipating their needs, some selectivity must be exercised. IS must know whom its most important customers are, those who are truly going to help the company achieve its strategic goals. IS must formulate a strategy for dealing with each customer or potential customer segment and find ways to reach its customers, educate them, and involve them in designing IS products and services.

Often, IS views its key customers as those with whom it has the best relationship, or those who create the fewest problems, or who come up with the most exciting uses for technology, or who scream the loudest. Unfortunately, these might not be the customers who deserve the most attention. The "critical few" customers will likely be those associated with critical business processes, or for whom technology-enabled process change will have significant impact on the business.

Often the members of the IS organization itself are overlooked as both important customers, and as stakeholders in the success of IS. Insofar as the IS employees enjoy a high quality of work life that is challenging, stimulating, rewarding, and enjoyable, and that provides growth opportunities, they will produce quality products and services.

At the same time that the focus must be on the critical few customers, IS must concentrate on the critical few needs of those customers. Certain projects are more closely aligned with the strategy and growth goals of the business, and these must be the focal point of activity. The 80:20 rule usually applies here—20% of the candidate projects deliver 80% of the benefits.

Both kinds of focus, critical customer and critical project, help IS executives find the time to undertake IS improvement initiatives in the first place. It is typical to find managers who agree that improvement is important, but who are so overwhelmed by current maintenance and the development backlog that they lack the time and resources to bring a quality improvement process to bear. Concentrating on the critical few and anticipating business and customer needs can help to eliminate the trivial many and actually *create* the needed time. The question is not how to create the time to get a TQM initiative started; it is how to start a TQM initiative that will create the necessary time!

Empowerment

Historically, thanks to the work of Frederick Taylor, the corporate wisdom was that educated people became managers and all others became workers; the idea of "employee empowerment" was tantamount to letting the inmates run the asylum.

The TQM movement, in contrast, believes that although Taylor's approach may have been appropriate in the early stages of industrialization, it is wholly inappropriate in the middle of the information revolution. Today, proponents of TQM recognize that it is the workers who best understand the process, who are closest to the customer, and who are most likely to identify improvement opportunities, especially if they have the knowledge and information they need to participate in continuous improvement.

Employee empowerment, so integral to the quality movement, is also a major contributor to IS improvement. IS professionals are often close to the processes in which they are involved. When empowered to make change, they can bring process knowledge and perspective to their proposed improvements. Moreover, involving people in the change process has proven effective in overcoming resistance to cultural and organizational change initiatives, as explored further in Chapter 6.

Unfortunately, empowerment is no silver bullet. Workers empowered to make changes, without strong leadership or a richly detailed, shared vision of the future state they are trying to achieve, may well degrade processes and quality. Workers empowered to make change without access to the information they need to understand the implications of such change are unlikely to make the right change decisions. Moreover, there are those who do not want to be empowered—they just want to follow prescribed processes and have no interest in contributing to changes in those processes.

One important aspect of empowerment, related to providing workers with the information they need to make the right decisions, pertains to rewards and recognition. The way that people are compensated and rewarded is a very powerful source of information about what is important. If their self-interest is not served by delivering high quality, and by participating in quality improvement, people are less likely to support quality goals, particularly if the things that are rewarded are in conflict with those goals.

Another level at which empowerment works in IS improvement is the empowerment of end users to deploy IT for themselves. Traditionally, IS personnel assumed the role of "high priests" and keepers of IT. Access to technology by non-IS personnel was strictly controlled. Today, with powerful workstations and personal computers, simple and relatively inexpensive local and wide area communications networks (LANs and WANs), and increasingly "user friendly" software tools, IS must adopt a proactive approach to empowering users with IT and create an environment where appropriate standards and disciplines are willingly embraced. This will require a rich IT infrastructure that makes it easier to follow disciplines and standards than to disregard them. For example, business professionals can be provided with company-standard tools supported by templates to help them in creating their own solutions to simple computing needs. If these templates are supported by embedded electronic performance support systems to help them use the templates, and if software, training, and support are readily available, people will be more inclined to use these company-standard tools than to look outside for alternatives.

Scientific Method

The idea of the scientific method, translated by Shewhart and Deming to TQM and often referred to as "the Deming Cycle," is a process model fundamental to all scientific learning. As shown in Figure 4.1, it can be summarized as a simple cycle: Plan, Do, Study, Act.

In other words, one begins with a hypothesis about an improvement, plans how the improvement hypothesis will be tested, executes the test, studies the results, and then either institutionalizes the improvement or formulates a new hypothesis, thus leading to a new cycle. This process, so fundamental to science, also provides a model for continuous improvement. It can be viewed as an application of the basic measurement-feedback-control process, and as such provides guidance in the selection of IT-related metrics.

There is one potential problem in following the Deming Cycle. Scientific learning depends on the principles of careful experimental design and repeatability of results. Experiments can be designed to prove almost anything, and many tools and technologies have been acquired because a pilot project or trial "proved" the product was worthwhile.

There is a subtle comfort implied by the scientific method. In contrast to the popular quality tenet "get it right the first time," the scientific method implies that everything does not need to be right the first time as long as there is a mechanism for feedback and improvement.

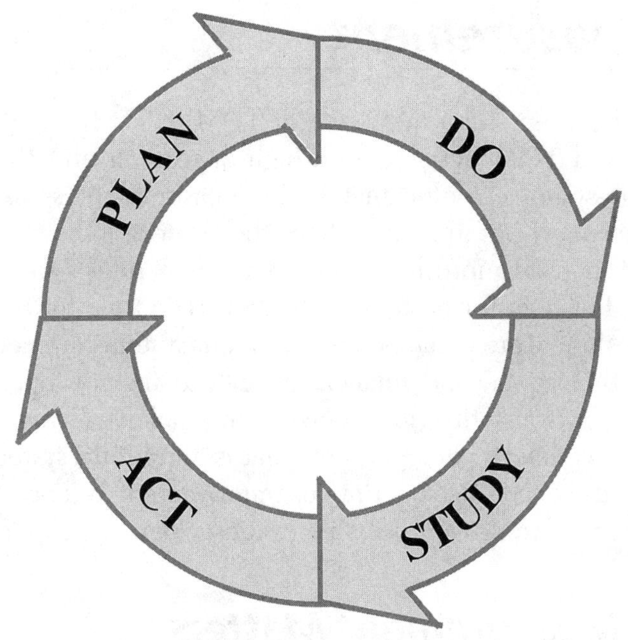

Figure 4.1 *The Deming Cycle*

The scientific method also stresses the importance of *fact-based decision making*. All too often decisions are made based on folklore and opinion, and these can be quite misleading. For example, for years conventional wisdom held that programming was the major bottleneck in systems development. This led in the mid-1970s to investments in 4GLs and code generators. Although these tools, under experimental conditions, showed coding productivity advantages over hand-coded COBOL of ten to one or more, in practice the gains over the development cycle were generally far less. It was only some years later, thanks to the rigorous work on measurement by individuals such as Barry Boehm[7] and Capers Jones[8] that people came to understand that writing program code was a relatively small part of the systems life cycle and that far greater gains were to be had by focusing on planning, analysis, and design and by looking at factors beyond automation tools.

Measurement

As stated earlier, a central theme of TQM is fact-based decision making, and TQM depends to a high degree on effective measurement systems. Unfortunately, IS measurement systems are lacking at many enterprises. Where they do exist, they are often too rigid or used more like a school ma'am's ruler—for punishment, rather than for positive motivation. The time for change is long overdue. More dynamic measurement systems are needed—systems that go beyond financial results to include operational measures; systems that look beyond internal performance and seek the customer's perception of what is important; systems that facilitate and encourage continuous improvement and provide the insight needed to drive process innovation where appropriate.

Why Measurement Matters

The British physicist Lord Kelvin once said, "When you can measure what you are speaking about, and express it in numbers, you know something about it; but when you cannot measure it, when you cannot express it in numbers, your knowledge is of a meager and unsatisfactory kind: it may be the beginning of knowledge, but you have scarcely, in your thoughts, advanced to the stage of *science*, whatever the matter may be."

Unfortunately, most IS organizations base improvement efforts on guesswork and anecdotes. Measurement is critical to any improvement initiative: it is necessary to initiate change, to focus improvement projects or teams, to evaluate progress against plans, to assess achievement of expected "bottom-line" results and to tune them. Although the "trust me" approach might be enough to begin improving systems delivery, it is rarely sufficient to sustain it.

The Roles of Measurement

Measurement can play many roles in an organization. Each role has its own requirements and purpose for being. Thus, different organizations may have very different measures because their purposes (roles) differ. And, as actors shape their roles in a play, users of measurement will further shape the measures to fit their own styles and agendas.

Measures are used to help in estimating and planning. Historical data about activities is often collected and, through extrapolation, used to estimate future needs. The nature of the data collected will vary according to use. For example, a project manager may collect data about individual projects (e.g., work effort expended, work output produced, time allocated to specified tasks, project characteristics). On the other hand, an IS department controller may collect data at a higher, overall organizational level (e.g., overall amount expended to support installed applications, level of effort devoted to new application development). The needs of the different users dictate the nature of the data in which they are interested.

Measures can be used to monitor processes and control the execution of activities. The typical pattern is to compare actual happenings with planned or expected schedules and events. Again, the users' interests will shape the specific data that is collected. The project manager might be interested in task-level data (e.g., a record of project task starts and completions versus plan). The controller, interested in higher-level issues, is likely to want to track actual expenditures versus budget at various aggregate levels, such as the department or overall IS organization. Yet a third user, interested in the performance of an installed application, may collect data about defect types and frequencies as part of an operational statistical process control scheme.

Measures can assist in the search for process understanding and improvement opportunities. The data collected is shaped by the nature of the understanding or improvement sought. For example, if the goal is shorter application-development cycle times, data about the allocation of efforts to various value-adding and non-value-adding tasks may be collected. On the other hand, if the focus of the moment is quality, the data-collection effort will be oriented toward types of defects and frequency of occurrence. A goal of delighting the customer will cause yet another, slightly different data collection direction to be established, one that includes collecting customer views about needs, expectations, and satisfaction levels. Process characteristic or attribute data is also commonly collected as part of this measurement role; it is needed in order to determine what practices and procedures were used when good results occurred versus when bad results were the outcome. Another use for measures in this role is to identify the cost of the status quo and to raise awareness of the need for improvement (this use of measures is dealt with in more detail in Chapter 7).

A variation of measurement's role in improvement occurs when the interest is in benchmarking, which has gained popularity with the TQM movement. Many of the same types of data are needed to quantify the comparisons involved in such efforts. However, the specific measures used will, by necessity, be shaped by the data commonly available from the benchmarking partners. Given this reality, if benchmarking is one of the goals of an overall measurement effort, it is well to learn about the measures that are most commonly used by companies and to use them from the start of a program. One other factor that can have a strong influence on the specific measures chosen for this role are the interests of the executives who ask for the comparative study. The questions they ask will often dictate the measures that should be used.

Measures may also be collected to strengthen the credibility of communications about IT activities. For this role, the selection of measures that the members of the intended audience can *relate* to is often of key importance. The measures need to be easily explained and, to the greatest degree possible, in terms that the recipient can relate to.

For example, at one textile company client, the IS group consciously named and described IS measures using common textile manufacturing terms. This approach made it easier for the business executives to understand what IS was trying to say. The focus on "language" is an important, though often ignored, aspect of designing measurement systems.

Finally, measures can be tools for clarifying direction and

providing leadership. For example, used to describe organizational goals in quantified terms, measures can be a powerful motivator of change. One IS group we worked with said, "Once we stated the goals we were striving to reach in measurable terms, the employees told us, 'Now we really know what you want.' It made our progress toward achieving them highly visible for everyone to watch."

Using measures for this purpose can be so powerful that caution is advised. More than one company has told us, "You must really be sure you have the right goals, and consistent goals, before you tie measures to them; if you don't, you will cause all kinds of trouble." In practice, attempting to define measures can be an important tool in clarifying goals.

A complete measurement effort will develop each measurement role that applies to the situation at hand. Because there are several roles and each is somewhat different, we have usually found it is best to work out one role, then move on to the next, completing the overall system of measurements one piece at a time. Because the measures for one role often relate to other roles, the development of later roles often goes more quickly than that of the first one or two. For example, the data collected for one purpose may prove, with just a little change in the way it is aggregated or analyzed, to meet the needs of a new role.

Measurement Goes with Good Results

With so many roles to develop, one may ask, "Is it all worth it? Can't I just do 'good things,' but skip the measurement part?" The answer is, "Yes, it is all worthwhile."

We have heard from clients, again and again, that the process of thinking through what and how to measure has a value that goes far beyond the actual numerical figures produced. Thinking about measures encourages a mental discipline that pays big dividends in a better understanding of the processes under consideration, clarifying what is important, and establishing ways to assess whether progress is really being made.

We also find that good measurement systems are often associated with organizations that perform well over the long haul. One study we know of compared IS organizations that had IS measures as part of their ongoing, regular management system with organizations that did not. Although the study was somewhat informal, it found that the organizations with consistent measurement efforts had performance levels and improvement trend rates that were higher than those of the organizations that did not. For example, it found significantly higher levels of user satisfaction with IS operations and a higher rate of improvement in application delivery productivity in the measured organizations.

A Model for Improvement

Total Quality Management and its implied process perspective can be extremely useful for planning and driving IS improvement. Defining an IT process landscape helps define IT customers, as well as their needs and expectations for products and services. Critical processes can then be selected for continuous improvement or process innovation.

A simple model linking the three dimensions of people, process, and technology is shown in Figure 4.2.

Process improvement can be effected by changing the process, the human resources associated with a process—resource allocations, skill mix, motivation, and reward structures, and so on—or by changing the technology that supports the process—eliminating human labor through automation, coordinating processes across distances—or by changing process sequences, for example.

Typically, a change to any one dimension requires a change to the other two dimensions. This has been a problem with the implementation of software development tools such as CASE. Tools are often introduced without associated process change or re-skilling of developers, with less than satisfactory results. Sophisticated modeling, prototyping, and code generation tools, for example, have been interposed into traditional waterfall life cycles, where

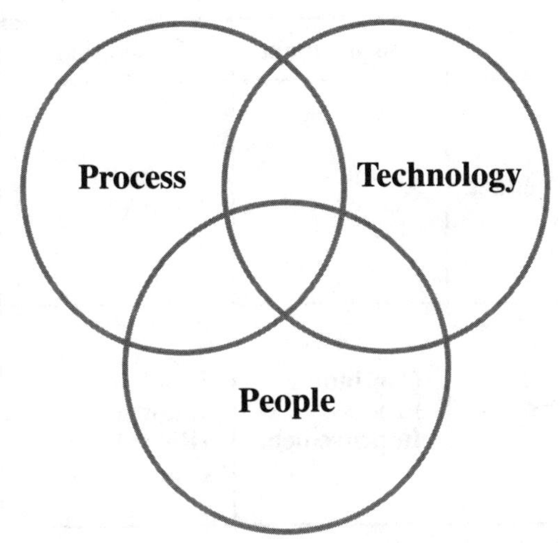

Figure 4.2 *Linking People, Process, and Technology*

the output from analysis drives design, and the output from design drives construction. The process inherent in these life cycles does not take advantage of rapid iteration made possible by the prototyping tools, or fails to bring the users together with developers in a way that enables meaningful business modeling to be done. The potential advantages of the CASE tools are neutralized (or worse) by non-CASE processes. Similar challenges exist for those introducing object-oriented approaches into CASE-based (or pre-CASE) development processes.

Which to Improve—The Product or the Process?

Improvements can be made to either the product/service, or to the process that produces it. Improvements can come from incremental, continuous change, or from innovative, discontinuous change. These modes of improvement can be represented as a 2×2 matrix, as shown in Figure 4.3.

Traditionally, IS quality efforts have focused on the end product, rather than on the process that produced it. There are several reasons for this product-dominated view, some of which

	Improvement	Innovation
Product	Product Refinement	Product Innovation
Process	Continuous Process Improvement	Process Innovation (Reengineering)

Figure 4.3 *Modes of Improvement*

are cultural. The West, for example, and the United States in particular, has been most concerned with the creative aspects of software development. It has adopted a craft approach to software, with emphasis on advanced technology with sophisticated interfaces and rich functionality. The Japanese, in contrast, have focused on developing a rigorous manufacturing process for software, most evident in the concept of the "software factory."[9] This is consistent with the Japanese obsession with continuous improvement.

There are also technical reasons. Software engineering is still a relatively immature discipline. Although E.F. Codd has provided a rigorous mathematical basis for data base management,[10] there is no current mathematical equivalent for the software procedures that manipulate data, making total automation of development difficult to achieve.

Finally, IS has traditionally been funded on a project-by-project basis. Although business customers have been prepared to fund their own projects, they have often resisted funding investment for infrastructure, and process-related initiatives require an infrastructure perspective.

How to Improve—Continuous Improvement or Innovation?

Process changes can be incremental and continuous, or radical and discontinuous. The former, often called "continuous process improvement," streamlines or rationalizes existing processes by removing non-value-added activities and by eliminating sources of defects. The latter, sometimes referred to as "process reengineering," creatively uses IT and human enablers to conceive new processes with breakthrough performance characteristics.

Continuous process improvement can be thought of as a bottom-up, current-state forward approach to effecting change. It is excellent for "tuning" processes and for providing data to support more radical change. Process innovation, on the other hand, is a top-down, future-state-driven approach. It is far more taxing on an organization's change capacity.

J.M. Juran, in *Managerial Breakthrough,*[11] wrote about "control" and "breakthrough." In today's jargon, control equates to continuous, incremental improvement, and breakthrough to process innovation, or reengineering. He described these as diverse aspects of a cycle. Both are needed and are complementary. Control (continuous improvement) tunes processes and can lead to the insights for breakthrough (innovation), and breakthroughs must be tuned and stabilized through control mechanisms.

Defining Processes

Whether through TQM, business process reengineering, or other motivations, leading companies are defining business processes in order to achieve performance—an approach we refer to as *process management.* Judging from our conversations with clients and others, we think it is fair to say that business is in the midst of a process revolution. Process management offers a way for organizations to reduce cost, improve quality, and cut cycle time. These same benefits are available to IS organizations that institute process management for themselves.

The first step in process management is to create a process landscape, or high-level conceptual model of the overall processes and their interrelationships. Further process understanding involves determining current process flows and collecting baseline performance data. This process definition information can then serve as the foundation for improvement or innovation activities.

A business process essentially defines how work is structured at a relatively high level of abstraction. A company should not view a business process as bounded by departmental, or even corporate, bounds. Indeed, some well-known examples of process innovation involve process activities that span more than one company.

We have encountered a common barrier when working with companies to define processes. Process management demands a different view of an organization and, if implemented, can lead to dramatic organizational change. Therefore, executives sometimes confuse process definition with organizational design.

We have seen many instances in which process definitions align with the existing organization structure. To the extent that these can be viewed separately, the less challenging it will be to define meaningful processes for the purposes of improvement and innovation. Any organizational redesign is best if it follows from the understanding that is developed through process management, free of organizational politics and turf issues.

Moreover, organizations need to recognize that if process boundaries are narrowed and, thus, do not cross existing organizational and functional boundaries, improving them probably will not produce the higher levels of performance improvement possible. Often, the best improvement opportunities lie at the process boundaries and interfaces.

Determining an appropriate level of granularity for each process, and therefore the number of processes, depends on the objectives of process identification. If the objective is continuous process improvement, it is sufficient to work with a larger number of narrowly defined processes. However, when the objective is radical process change, a process should be broadly defined.

There currently is no hard-and-fast rule with respect to this question. Individual companies that have defined and articulated their IT processes have commonly enumerated between five and ten.

When determining the number of IT processes, an organization must make a trade-off between having a greater potential for process innovation benefits and having a manageable project scope. With fewer processes, an organization will have a greater possibility of innovation through process integration. However, working with fewer processes, each with a larger scope, also presents greater challenges in understanding, measuring, and changing each process. When defining IT processes, companies need to view definition and boundary setting primarily as an issue of scope. Each process must be small enough to be understandable. When process definitions are more focused, change management becomes less challenging.

Figure 4.4 shows Michael Porter's model which describes generic organizational processes as a *value chain*. IT processes are part of the support activities; they are more fully described in the next section of this chapter.

The value-chain model is very different from the traditional organizational or departmental view, but it is important to think beyond departmental boundaries. The major opportunities to leverage IT lie in cross-department, and even cross-business, systems.

IS managers must help business managers shake off their stovepipe, functional orientation in favor of a process perspective. In IT planning, IS managers must also think about their *own* processes, or rather, the processes associated with IT, and effect their own process improvement and innovation initiatives.

Information Technology Processes

IT processes are an important component of a business's support activities. One model for presenting IT processes, developed in

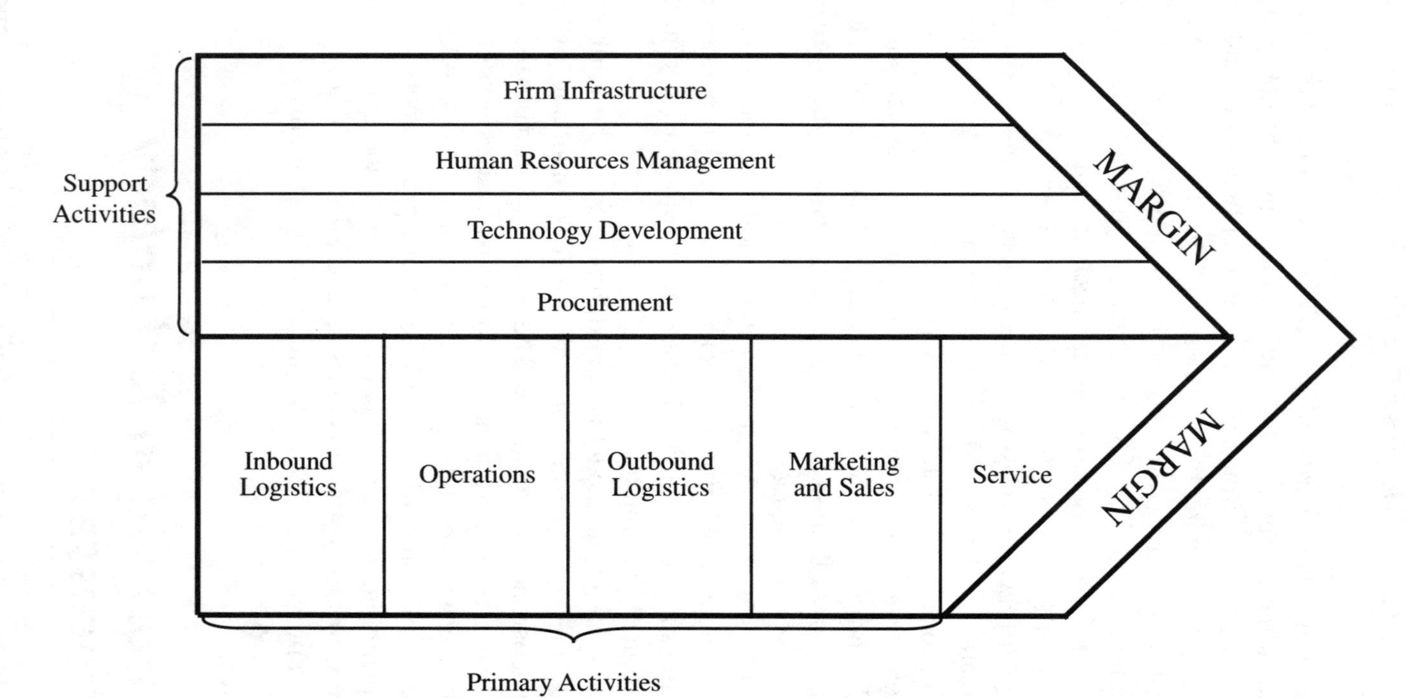

Figure 4.4 *Generic Process Value Chain*

the context of Ernst & Young's IS Leadership Multi-Client Research Program,[12] is presented in Figure 4.5.

In this model we define IT processes as those business processes that are associated with the creation and ongoing management of a company's IT resources. This definition is independent of functional boundaries, because IT creation and management activities increasingly occur throughout an organization, not just within the IS function. However, as the IS function is primarily responsible for these activities in most organizations at the present time, this set of generic IT processes also largely encompasses those processes associated with managing the IS function. In many respects, the IT process landscape described herein is defined from the perspective of the IS organization.

IT processes offer a foundation for improving the management and development of new capabilities of a company's IT resources, as well as a way to describe how IT-related services are provided to the organization. Although the IS organization is the primary locus for most of these processes in today's environment, one trend that appears to be increasing is the migration of responsibility for IT processes into other organization units. Thus, it is increasingly important to identify explicitly an organization's IT processes so that they are not overlooked as business improvement prospects are selected, and so that opportunities for shared resources are fully exploited.

The generic IT process definitions can be used to help in understanding the extent of IT processes. This knowledge is important in IT strategy and planning activities, as well as in determining the process structure with which to apply TQM improvement principles. The generic process set can also be a resource that organizations use as a template during development of their own IT process definitions and institution of process management activities.

The spectrum of IT activities can be divided into seven IT processes:

1. Identify IT-enabled business opportunities
2. Design IT infrastructure

3. Deliver and evolve IT components
4. Manage IT operations
5. Provide IT customer support
6. Plan and align IT resources
7. Manage IS resources

Figure 4.5 depicts the overall relationship of the seven IT processes. These IT process definitions were developed through analysis of the existing IT process definitions at companies participating in the IS Leadership Multi-Client Research Program. The companies represented a variety of industries and were of different sizes. Interestingly, there was a high degree of similarity in their selection of process boundaries and definitions.

Like so many activities, process definition and management are continuous learning exercises. Process definitions cannot and should not be cast in concrete. Assignment of process boundaries should be based on business requirements and capabilities and modified as these change. Therefore, this process landscape must be viewed as an iteration in a learning process, as opposed to the absolute and final truth. Illustrating this point, at least one company whose processes we studied redefined its set of IT processes during the time we were conducting our research.

Some of the landscape's generic processes will not be found in any company's set. These processes surfaced following discussions with individuals from the participating companies and others about emerging IT and business trends and strategies. Thus, the landscape of IT processes is being used to emphasize certain activities, some of which a company must focus attention on if IT is to be fully exploited, and others in which IS can and should play a more prominent role.

The test of each process is that it deliver important products and/or services to the business. Passage of this test is easily seen for five of the processes, which can be viewed as the IT "production" processes. These processes, which are depicted in the diagram as a value chain (see Figure 4.5), deliver value to the enterprise.

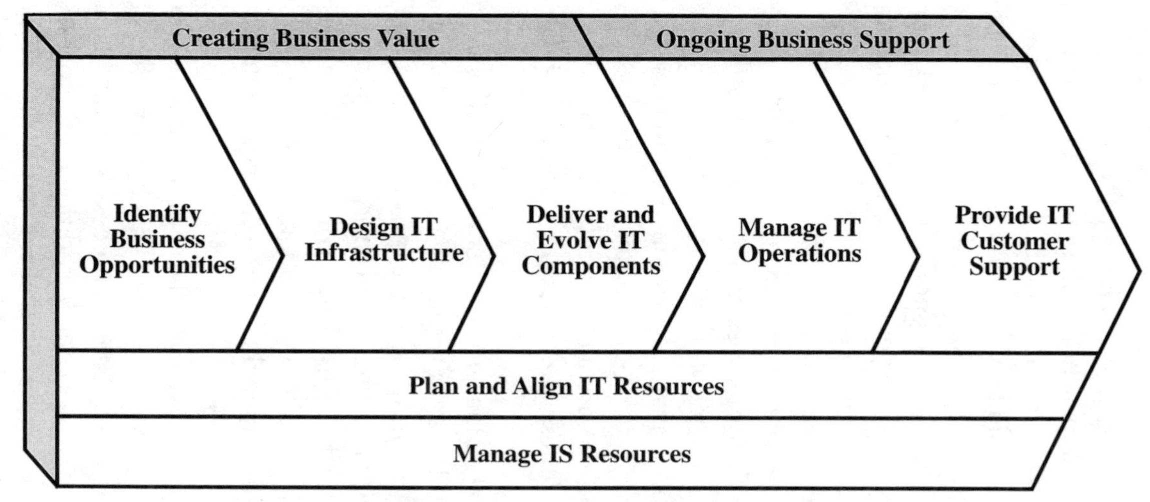

Figure 4.5 *IT Process Landscape*

The first three (Identify Business Opportunities, Design IT Infrastructure, and Deliver and Evolve IT Components) are involved with creating future value for the organization. Although developing a new application system does not provide immediate value to the enterprise, the product will someday. Therefore, these processes should be viewed as investment activities.

The last two production processes (Manage IT Operations and Provide IT Customer Support) are associated with sustaining present value by providing ongoing IT services and capabilities to the organization. These processes should be viewed within a cost management perspective.

The two remaining processes—"support" processes—are Plan and Align IT Resources and Manage IS Resources. These grew from the recognition that certain activities are required to set the stage and manage the production processes. Though the products and/or services of these support processes are less tangible than those of the production processes, they are still very real and important. These processes are essentially related to asset management.

For example, Manage IS Resources includes tactical project management and oversight planning activities that underlie and touch on each of the production processes. Plan and Align IT Resources applies to a broad, enterprise-wide view of IT. Manage IS is more inwardly focused, referring to the business management of the IS function/organization. Therefore, we have made the distinction in naming the process Manage *IS* rather than Manage *IT*.

A business process virtually always contains several lower-level processes, or subprocesses, which define the structure of work at a lower level. The subprocess structure is a hierarchy. Therefore, subprocesses contain additional subprocesses.

For example, within the Deliver and Evolve IT Components process, one typically finds subprocesses such as business requirements analysis, application development, systems testing, and system installation or deployment.

While identifying IT process customers, it became clear that a process often serves more than one customer set. Frequently, there is one type of customer that funds or sponsors an initiative but never actually uses the end product. For example, an executive might sponsor the acquisition of a new payroll system but will never actually use the system himself. We identified this type of customer as the primary customer. All other customer segments are identified as secondary customers. In the payroll system example, a secondary customer would be the accounting clerk who uses the system daily. It is important to recognize the different customer segments, because each will have different requirements and expectations from IT process activities.

Given that the topic of this book is Development Effectiveness, we focus on the three "Creating Business Value" processes—Identify Business Opportunities, Design IT Infrastructure, and Deliver and Evolve IT Components. The form of process definition and improvement strategies are applicable to the other IT processes in much the same way.

Identify Business Opportunities

The purpose of the Identify Business Opportunities process is to ensure that strategic business change activities fully exploit IT-enabled opportunities. The process is instrumental in creating future business value from IT investments. This objective is accomplished through increasing the organization's awareness of the potential benefits and opportunities offered by IT. Increased awareness is created through an assortment of seemingly unrelated activities.

One factor that caused us to delineate this process is the increasingly prominent role that IT plays in business-process change activities. A majority of participants in the IS Leadership program viewed improvement and innovation of business processes as a strategic business thrust that must involve the IS organization. Explicit acknowledgment of these activities is the first step toward ensuring that managers are focusing on them. Figure 4.6 shows the characteristics of this process.

Purpose	**To ensure that strategic business change activities fully exploit IT**
Products/Services	Proposals, assessments
Customers	Senior business executives
Subprocesses	• Participation/Leadership in Process Innovation • IT Education for Senior Executives • Participation in Business Strategy Development • Explore Emerging IT Capabilities • Participation in Business Process Benchmarking

Figure 4.6 *Identify Business Opportunities*

Based on examination of the subprocesses, it is clear that the Identify Business Opportunity process spans IS and other business functions. Thus, leadership for and involvement in its various subprocesses may come from a variety of sources. As a result of their knowledge of IT and systems approach, IS professionals should play a key, and sometimes leadership, role in their execution.

Design IT Infrastructure

An IT infrastructure is defined as hardware, software, and information elements that constitute a shareable, company-wide resource.[13] Although business units and functions may understand what technology and information are needed to run their businesses, there needs to be a global, company-wide perspective on the use of IT as well. This perspective is essential to assure integration, provide flexibility, and minimize redundancies and costs. The purpose of the process is to maintain this view while creating the flexible, rapid response environment so necessary for the success of business units in today's competitive marketplace. Figure 4.7 shows the characteristics of this process.

The establishment and maintenance of an infrastructure is a challenge facing virtually all companies. Discussions of infrastruc-

Purpose	To define and design enterprise's IT infrastructure.
Products/Services	IT architectures, enterprise models
Customers	Key stakeholders; employees who use infrastructure
Subprocesses	• Defining the IT Architecture • Developing and Maintaining Enterprise Models • Develop Architectural Standards and Policies • Develop Knowledge Base/Repository

Figure 4.7 *Design IT Infrastructure*

ture are becoming increasingly common in IT management literature. The promotion of IT infrastructure within an organization is a particularly daunting challenge, because infrastructure elements are not as visible as specific applications. In addition, infrastructure investments are virtually impossible to justify through the use of traditional methods.

IS has always had a difficult time in communicating infrastructure requirements to business management. Often, when the word *infrastructure* is used by an IS executive, it is the word *overhead* that the business executive hears. Process thinking helps both IS and the business focus on what infrastructure truly is, and how it can serve as an enabler—or in its absence, a barrier—to delivering value to the business.

One reason for explicitly defining this IT process is to promote thinking about infrastructure. Some organizations have been successful in this endeavor. One technology manufacturer, for example, has established an IT evaluation process that assesses the technology and infrastructure implications of a proposed project independently and on a par with analysis of the financial and strategic returns.

Others are also realizing that there are enormous costs associated with failure to view a project from the perspective of infrastructure. One financial services firm elected not to establish any company-wide standard for electronic mail. As a result, each business unit purchased its own electronic mail system. Over time, the company acquired 14 different systems. During a benchmarking exercise with a competitor, the company discovered that this decision had put it at a multimillion dollar cost disadvantage *annually* just in terms of electronic mail operating costs. If inconvenience, increased learning curves, and inhibited communications had been factored in, the cost disadvantage would have been even higher.

It should be noted that this process addresses infrastructure *design* exclusively. Infrastructure component development/acquisition and implementation are subsumed within the IT Component Delivery and Evolution process.

Deliver and Evolve IT Components

The Deliver and Evolve IT Components process acquires or develops, and delivers, new hardware, software, and information components for a company. Included in this process is the adaptation and/or evolution of existing components, as needed, to meet changing business requirements. Like the two preceding processes, Identify Opportunities and Design Infrastructure, this process is focused on the creation of future business value. Although all IT users will use the products of this process, the primary customers are business managers who sponsor these activities.

There are a number of subprocesses within this process, including defining component projects, analyzing business requirements, producing conceptual system designs, investigating component purchases, producing technical designs, purchasing/building elements of IT components, and delivery or deployment of components.

Selecting the appropriate subprocesses to use in a given situation will depend on the desired end product (e.g., application software, hardware). Thus, for all IT Component Delivery and Evolution process initiatives, there needs to be an initial common activity of selecting the correct subprocesses for a particular pro-

Purpose	To acquire, develop, and deliver new or improved hardware, software, and information components to the enterprise
Products/Services	New or improved hardware, software, or information components
Customers	Business sponsors; component end-users
Subprocesses	• Define Component Project • Analyze Business Requirements • Produce Conceptual System Design • Investigate Component Purchase • Produce Technical Design • Purchase/Build Elements of IT Components • Deliver/Deploy Components

Figure 4.8 *Deliver and Evolve IT Components*

ject. This is an important activity, which is one aspect of the subprocess Define Component Project. An objective of this key subprocess is to ensure that the requirements of the project are addressed by the appropriate subprocesses in light of the desired end product as well as the company's IT strategy.

Although the overall IT Component Delivery and Evolution process has a strong product orientation, the accompanying service elements (e.g., training, systems deployment, organizational change management, and project management) must not be overlooked.

Relationship to Overall Business Processes

IT processes are a subset of an organization's overall business processes. At the company level, most organizations define one or two business processes associated with the management of IT.

Although certain IT processes are in fact subprocesses of these business processes, others are subprocesses within business-change processes.

For example, the Identify Business Opportunity process might be part of the overall business planning and development processes through its contribution to the consideration of the strategic implications of IT. Even IT Component Delivery and Evolution can be viewed as a subprocess in a product development process if the new products or processes spawned by the product require new information systems.

An area of growing interest in American business that will influence this relationship is the management of information per se, regardless of the storage medium (e.g., electronic, paper) or form (e.g., document, data item). Management theorists have for some time talked of effective information management as a key to success in the current world economy.

Because modern businesses are essentially information-processing entities, there has grown a desire to better understand information management. Our colleagues McGee and Prusak[14] identify a generic information-management process model and, as shown in Figure 4.9, the major tasks associated with information management.

Although information management thinking is still in its infancy, it is clear that IT processes are a subset of information management processes. IT processes address information that is captured, stored, and distributed using information technology. As the principles of information management are further developed, the IT processes will undoubtedly evolve.

Targeting Processes for Innovation or Improvement

Once IT processes are defined, what's next? The logical step is to begin to improve them. This will initially involve determining current process flows and collecting baseline performance data.

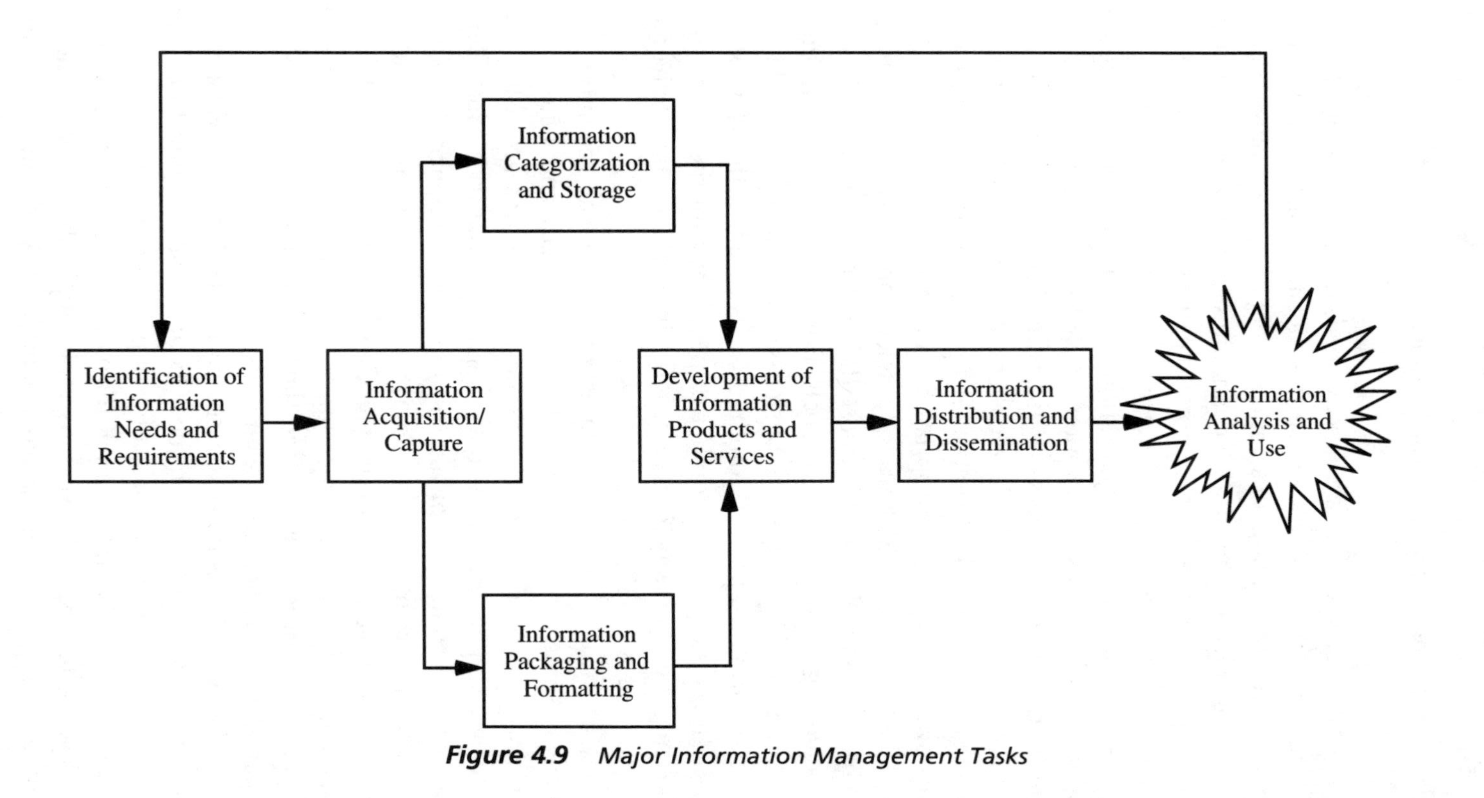

Figure 4.9 *Major Information Management Tasks*

As discussed earlier, a company needs to choose the magnitude of improvement desired, because this dictates which improvement approach to use—continuous improvement or process innovation. If a company elects to institute a continuous improvement approach, the subprocesses become the appropriate level of focus. The overall process is the appropriate scope when innovation is the goal.

However, an IS organization does not need to choose between only process innovation or continuous improvement. It can be doing both at the same time for different processes. For example, a company may decide that innovation is in order for the Deliver and Evolve IT Components process, whereas continuous improvement is more appropriate for IT Operations.

There are different ways to select processes for improvement. One way might be to choose the IT process(es) most central to achieving the organization's goals. For example, an organization could map its IT processes to business goals to see which will have the most strategic impact. Another way is to select the IT process that affects the greatest number of people within the enterprise. This might be one way to maximize the immediate value delivered by the improvement activities.

One further consideration is organizational readiness for change. An aspect in this regard is the maturity and state of the current process. For instance, some organizations are using the Software Engineering Institute's Capability Maturity Model[15] to assess the current state of the software development subprocess, which is a part of Deliver and Evolve IT Components, and to identify improvement actions. The Capability Maturity Model, for example, helps management understand where the software development process stands and the readiness of the organization to embark on the next improvement step.

The rest of this book focuses on the Deliver and Evolve IT Components process, which most IS organizations find to be the process with the greatest need for improvement. It is also the IT process that has been the target for most process innovation (new life cycles, for example, such as rapid application development) and new supporting technology (including CASE and object oriented programming).

Notes

1. IS Leadership Multi-Client Program—A multi-client research study into the implications of Total Quality Management for the Information Systems function, sponsored by Ernst & Young's Center for Information Technology and Strategy^{SM}, Boston, Massachusetts.

2. Although we refer to Total Quality Management, in practice this goes by many labels, including Customer Excellence, Leadership Through Quality, Total Quality, and so on.

3. *U.S. Companies Improve Performance Through Quality*. GAO/NSIAD-91-190, U.S. General Accounting Office, May 1991.

4. *Current Practices in Measuring Quality*. Research Bulletin No. 234 (New York: The Conference Board, Inc., 1989).

5. *The International Quality Study: Best Practices Report: An Analysis of Management Practices That Impact Performance*. American Quality Foundation and Ernst & Young, 1992.

6. Thomas H. Davenport, *Process Innovation: Reengineering Work Through Information Technology* (Boston: Harvard Business School Press, 1992: pp. 5–10).

7. B. Boehm, *Software Engineering Economics* (Englewood Cliffs, NJ: Prentice-Hall, 1981).

8. Capers Jones, *Programming Productivity* (New York: John Wiley & Sons, 1985).

9. Michael A. Cusumano, *Japan's Software Factories* (New York: Oxford University Press, 1991).

10. E. F. Codd, "Relational Database: A Practical Foundation for Productivity," *Communications of the ACM* (February 1982).

11. J. M. Juran, *Managerial Breakthrough* (New York: McGraw-Hill, 1964).

12. Mary Silva Doctor and Charles L. Gold, "The IT Process Landscape," TQM-IS Working Paper, Center for Information Technology and Strategy^{SM} (Boston: Ernst & Young, 1992).

13. Peter F. Drucker, "The Coming of the New Organization," *Harvard Business Review* Vol. 66, n. 1, (January–February 1988: pp. 45–53).

14. James McGee and Laurence Prusak, *Managing Information Strategically* (New York: John Wiley & Sons, 1993).

15. Mark C. Paulk, et al. *Capability Maturity Model for Software* (Pittsburgh, PA: Software Engineering Institute, August 1991).

5

Organizational Design for Systems Delivery Effectiveness

Many information systems (IS) organizations are struggling today with questions about how they should organize themselves as they begin to adapt to new processes for providing information systems of ever-increasing functional and technological complexity. **Organizational design** for the IS function of the future clearly needs to be different, probably very different from today's, but in what ways? This chapter looks at issues relating to the organizational structures appropriate for a constantly changing world and offers an extended and updated view of the software factory model with team-based coordination and communication mechanisms to support the effective delivery of systems.

Let us start with a simple analogy.

Three years ago, one of the contributors to this book became the coach of his then 6-year-old daughter's soccer team. He ran practices and shouted out instructions during games. He decided what drills the team needed to perform in order to develop necessary skills. He developed and employed strategies for each game.

Coordinating the tasks was simple—he did them all himself. Finding the time and energy to perform all these tasks was the problem. By the end of the season, he had lost his voice and nearly lost his patience. The next season, he solicited a friend to help him coach the children.

They split the girls into two groups during practice. Our colleague drilled the offensive players while his friend coached the defenders. During games, the friend attended to the defense while he focused on the offense. By dividing the tasks he had previously done all by himself, he found the coaching experience more rewarding, and the girls seemed to improve more rapidly.

However, new costs were introduced by taking on another coach, namely coordination and communication costs. The two coaches spent about 10 minutes before practice planning what they would work on and another 10 minutes after practice reviewing the progress the team had made. They occasionally had friendly debates over priorities, positions, or tactics, but because they were friends they quickly resolved these issues.

Once during a game they both shouted a command to the same girl at the same time. One said, "Move up!" The other said, "Drop back!" This girl was playing a midfielder's position, which means she helped to defend the middle of the field when the opposition had control of the ball, but also advanced the ball through the middle of the field when her team had possession. When she heard the conflicting commands, she just stopped and looked at the coaches with all the innocence of a 6-year-old girl. The two coaches looked at each other, and both burst out laughing.

Distributing work across an organization entails similar needs for communication and creates similar problems. The structure of an organization is designed not only to allot human energy and time to complete distinct tasks, but also to coordinate and communicate between these tasks. Addressing the questions of organizational design for effective systems delivery is infinitely more challenging than coaching a children's soccer team.

A number of issues arise:

- How should all the tasks involved in delivering information technology (IT) products and services into a business environment be allocated among workers and, equally important, how will the workers coordinate and communicate with each other, and at what cost?
- How can an organization be designed that is both effective at getting essential work done, yet flexible enough to adjust as the nature of the work changes?
- And how can this be done in such a way that the members of this organization feel comfortable with the changing organizational structures?

This chapter does not answer these questions explicitly, because there are many potentially "right" answers. Rather, it attempts to provide insights to help IS organizations rethink the purpose and value of traditional organizational structure. With this knowledge, IS organizations can design themselves to suit the prevailing business objectives, rather than just to react to current political or economic pressures.

Mechanisms for Coordination and Communication

Coordination and communication within organizations can be accomplished by three broad categories of mechanisms:[1]

Mutual Adjustment. Work is under the control of those who carry it out. The process of informal communication is used to coordinate work. Workers perform their tasks and, as needed, contact other workers, who then adjust to the new information. The coaching of the soccer team used a mutual adjustment mechanism to coordinate tasks. Self-directed work groups or teams are an example of this mechanism.

Direct Supervision. Work is under the control of a supervisor. One individual takes responsibility for the assignments of others. Communication is fed downward through instructions or orders and upward via results and status reports. The military chain of command is a classic example of direct supervision.

Standardization. Work is under the control of predetermined specifications, of which there are generally three types:

1. Standardization of work processes
2. Standardization of deliverables
3. Standardization of skills

Coordination of work is accomplished by everyone following exacting guidelines on what to do, what to produce, and/or how to produce it. The production-line manufacturing process commonly uses some form of this mechanism.

Most organizations tend to favor one coordinating mechanism

over the others, but no organization can rely long-term on only one such mechanism to communicate and coordinate all types of work effectively. Many IS organizations today tend to favor the direct supervision approach, with occasional (but regular) attempts at standardization using methodologies or specific training programs.[2] To some extent, all three coordinating mechanisms are necessary. However, each type has its values and drawbacks. Each is also suited to address a specific range of problem types.

Take a look at Figure 5.1. When problems are simple, using a *mutual adjustment* approach to coordinate and communicate makes good sense and works effectively. In our example, the two coaches were able to manage the soccer team with informal conversations at a reasonable cost.

The process used to solve simple problems is usually self-evident and requires little, if any, structure or elaboration between co-workers. However, when the problems begin to get more complex, the coordination costs for mutual adjustment rise exponentially. A minor example of this can be seen in the actions of the

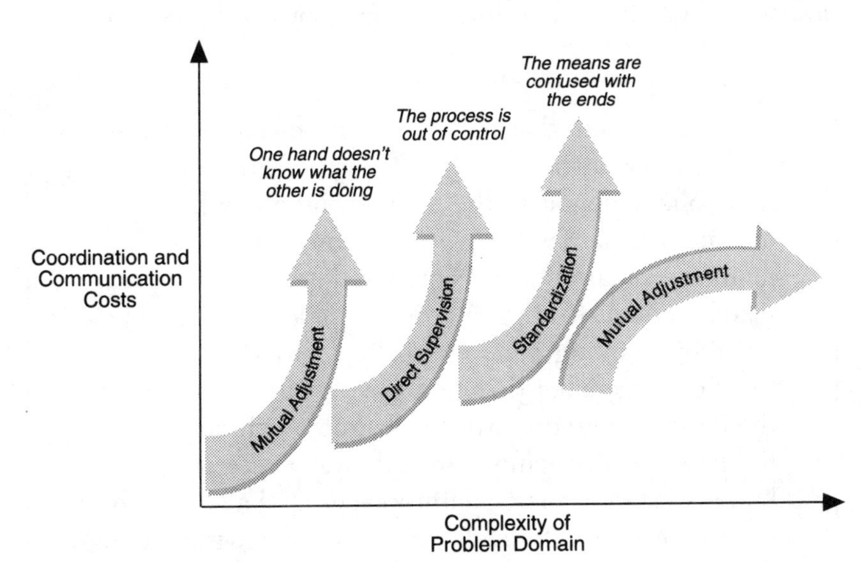

Figure 5.1 *Coordination and Communication Mechanisms Used for Increasingly Complex Problem Domains*

little girl who received conflicting commands from her two coaches. The more complex, or less standardized, the work, the less clear it is *who* is responsible for doing *what* when only a mutual adjustment coordinating mechanism is used. Eventually, a communications barrier develops that can prevent more complex problems from being solved.

At this point, most organizations cry out for order and accountability. *Direct supervision* fills the bill by having one person take responsibility for the work of others. This hierarchy provides structure around the assignment of tasks and allows a new class of more complex problems to be solved—albeit at the price of additional coordination costs, because a direct supervisor often plays no part in carrying out the work being supervised.

Direct supervision also seems to run into a barrier when it comes to handling even more complex problems. As tasks handed down from supervisors become more complex, the process needed to complete the tasks becomes harder for those doing the work to identify and perform. Eventually, the supervisors have to ask workers to perform tasks that they themselves cannot perform and for which they therefore cannot provide direct guidance.

> It has been said[3] that research anthropologists working in the 1960s attributed this "failure of group supervision" phenomenon to the early evolutionary history of human beings. Their theory proposed that the maximum size of an effective supervised group was approximately equal to the maximum practical size of a Neolithic hunting party (typically 10 to 15 people). If the group is smaller than this, the prey just as often gets the hunters. Larger parties make too much noise; thus, too much of the game is scared away and some of the hunters starve. The anthropologists believed that humans have yet to evolve beyond this environmental constraint on group behavior.

Workers are forced to invent a process each time they receive a new task. Work quickly becomes unpredictable in execution and unreliable in output. Adding either additional resources or additional supervision—or both—only makes things worse. The work process is perceived to be out of control.

To solve problems of greater complexity, many organizations have turned to *standardization,* instead of increased supervision, as a coordinating mechanism. Through standardizing work processes, outputs, or the skills believed to be necessary to do the work, the process to produce deliverables is brought under control and a new class of more complex problems can be solved, also at the cost of additional coordination effort. Mass production or assembly-line processes often use standardization effectively. The process of constructing a product from a good design can be standardized to reduce variability and to serve as a platform to improve upon.

However, like the other coordinating mechanisms, standardization encounters a limit to the complexity of the problems it can address effectively. Problems that take a very long time to solve, or have never before been solved, are difficult targets for standards. People often faithfully adhere to a known process without acknowledging the failure of the process to solve the more complex problem. In other words, the means become confused with the ends.

For very complex problems, or problems that have not been solved before, an organization must return, paradoxically, to a mutual adjustment form of coordination. Sophisticated problem solvers communicate informally.[4] Design processes require some form of mutual adjustment. When a manufacturer is designing a new product, exactly what needs to be done at the outset is not known. The knowledge develops as the work unfolds. The success of the overall effort depends on the ability of various experts to adapt knowledge, behavior, and belief to one another along their uncharted route.

This model is based on the principle that each time a problem is solved, the next time the same or similar problem arises, it is considered to some extent to be less complex than it was before.

This will be true only if an organization has an effective way to capture and codify experience and to communicate the results to workers who did not gain the experience directly.

Coordination History of Information Systems Development Organizations

The model in Figure 5.1 can shed new light on the impact organizational structures have had in developing and delivering computer systems. The following statements from the model are common to many IS organizations:

- One hand doesn't know what the other is doing
- The process is out of control
- The means are confused with the ends

Most IS organizations find that not just one of these statements, but all three, are commonplace in one form or another. This indicates several things. First, IS is incurring extremely high coordination and communication costs of various kinds. Second, IS is probably using mutual adjustment at times when direct supervision is better suited, direct supervision when standardization is needed, and standardization when mutual adjustment is required. And third, it means that the IS organization has trouble changing its ways.

Why does IS tend to overutilize any particular form of coordinating mechanism to the brink of inefficiency and fail to change? As a specific paradigm for coordination is used to solve a problem successfully, that paradigm is assumed to be capable of solving all future problems (the "silver bullet"[5] mind-set). However, this assumption of universal applicability fails because future problems are naturally new and generally more complex than those that have already been solved. The problems that could be solved have been solved. More complex problems are all that is left. The assumption also fails because once a complex problem has been solved, it is no longer as difficult to resolve a similar instance of the problem when it arises again. Most classes of problems will, therefore, change their degree of complexity over time, which implies that a different form of coordination may be more appropriate for repetitions of the same kind of problem. IS must learn to recognize that complexity is a *relative*, changing measure, and that coordination decisions must be based on present-day measures of complexity, not those of the past.

The Effect of Groups

Hardly anyone in an IS organization truly works alone—there are just not that many one-person jobs in a complex area such as developing information systems. Most people are a part of one or more permanent or transient groups of co-workers who need to collaborate to get things done. How these groups go about organizing and managing their work makes a tremendous difference in how effective the individual group members can be. The most familiar form of group is a team—either a project team or a team that is part of the IS infrastructure. Teams are special kinds of groups; they are discussed in more detail later in this chapter. For now, however, we consider some of the key behaviors of groups in general.

Most people have worked in groups that were a delight to be a part of. Nothing seemed impossible, and everyone felt that he or she was accomplishing something worthwhile. The group was regularly able to achieve results that were clearly beyond the capabilities of any of its members.

Equally, most of us have experienced the unpleasantness of being a part of a group that was just not working out. It seemed as though the group could not get anything done, even though all were working as hard as they could. No one seemed to know what was wrong, so it was hard to see what to do to put things right. All attempts at changing the way the group worked seemed to be equally disastrous. In the end, group members believed that each of them could do better on his or her own than the group could do as a whole.

Is it possible to identify what makes one group successful while another fails? Although interaction between group members is clearly important, success or failure is not just a question of whom makes up the group. Individuals who have been members of successful groups have often also been members of groups that failed to be effective. Indeed, a group that has succeeded in one circumstance can subsequently fail in another, even though the membership is unchanged.

Achieving the Group Synergy Effect

One aspect that has emerged as very important for the success of a group is its *structure of supervision.* If the group is to be overtly supervised, the form of supervision must be appropriate both to the nature of the work and to the needs of the group. Getting the level of supervision right is not easy. Both undersupervised and oversupervised groups perform badly. Perhaps a better metaphor for the supervisor's rôle is that of coach. In our opening example, the coach's job was not to play soccer, but rather to make the team as good as possible so that players could be successful through their own efforts. Similarly, the supervisor is the resource the group uses to clear obstacles from its path and to help remove barriers to success, not the sole source of direction and effort.

Another important key to success is to ensure that it is possible for the common resources of the group to be shared by all the group's members. This prevents the formation of internal ownership structures based on access to, or control of, scarce or valuable resources. Groups seem to work best when everyone feels equally valued and where group behavior supports the notion that everyone must have what he or she needs to contribute most effectively to meeting group objectives.

High-performance groups are always measured for productivity of process and quality of output. There are no exceptions to this principle. The group may well have a significant say in what form the measurement takes (indeed, most high-performing groups will insist on input to the measurement framework), but performance and quality measures are always present. Measures are seen as an essential tool for identifying and correcting process defects and for directing improvement in individual competencies. Measures and their interpretation are always shared within the group (and often between groups) both as a mechanism to encourage standardization on superior practices and as a catalyst for continuous performance improvement.

High-performing groups tend to work in close physical proximity. This encourages communication and mutual adjustment within the group and, by extension, minimizes coordination problems between groups. Physical colocation is not always easy or possible, however. Where it cannot be arranged, measures have to be taken to compensate for geographical dispersion, such as video conferences, computer-supported cooperative work environments, or a great deal of travel to allow group members to meet regularly.

> In 1990 one of the authors was involved in research into the effectiveness of video conferencing as a group-support aid for a very large distributed IS development project. Development groups were based in five different cities across Europe. Rather than continually fly to meet in one or more of the development locations, the groups used a weekly video conference to share progress and issues and to attempt issue resolution. They used the current state-of-the-art technology, with a large shared video screen, individual participant screen areas, and voice-activated point-of-view management. A real-time computerized document-exchange system supported their meetings. There were about 20 people in the weekly conference. The participants were all peers within the IS organization, but not all of them had met in person prior to the project.

At first the meetings seemed to go well. Participants kept to the meeting agenda and seldom wandered far from the topics being discussed. However, meetings were essentially devoted to exchanging information. Almost no decisions were made during the video conference sessions. The decision-making and issue-resolution processes still required face-to-face meetings, or at least telephone calls between participants who already knew each other.

As the project progressed, however, things began to change. After about 6 months, by which time the participants had all met each other face-to-face at least once, the video conferences began to be used for issue resolution. Decisions were made, and adhered to, during the weekly conferences. Face-to-face meetings and off-line telephone traffic dropped off considerably, although neither was eliminated entirely. By the time the project had been running for a year, we were prepared to publish results that indicated that the process was a success and should be used more widely, so long as participants were allowed an opportunity to meet each other face-to-face before a project actually started.

Then, within a month, five group members at three sites left and were replaced. Although the changeovers were all managed sensibly, with the new participants attending a session with the people they were replacing prior to taking over, group synergy was essentially destroyed. For the next 4 months, the conferences went back to only being information exchanges until the new members had been integrated into the group.

Dispersion does not have to occur over great distances to be an issue. Take 10 teams of 10 people and mix them up within a single working area so that no one sits next to a member of his or her immediate work group, and watch effectiveness fall off.

Colocation has always been a somewhat contentious issue. At one major enterprise where we have worked on development effectiveness, the IS development group had grown from 1 to more than 300 staff within 2 years. As new staff arrived, they were assigned places in an essentially random fashion within a single large work space. As teams were formed, no attempt was made to colocate staff. By the time the department had grown to 300 members, teams were scattered across two wings of a building and beginning to spread to a second building. As is common in such situations, there were too few phones—although everyone had a PC—limited material storage facilities, and very few meeting rooms. There was also very little individual privacy and a lot of noise.

Members of development teams routinely spent 25% of their time away from their desks looking for other team members or team leaders. Team leaders spent up to 50% of their time looking for team members. About half of all conversations took place with none of the participants at their own work places. This was almost all non-value-added activity. Totaled over the whole department, it represented a productivity loss of more than 600 hours each working day. Colocations would not have eliminated all of this nonproductive time, but we estimated that at least 520 hours per day could be saved by colocating teams.

Of course, colocation has to be a continuing process, as teams break apart at the end of projects and new teams are formed. In this example, it would have happened once or twice a year. A move would typically take 2 days—including packing, unpacking, and equipment reconfiguration—for a cost per person of 12 hours lost time.

> Therefore, for a one-time investment of about 40 hours per person—the initial move for everyone would have taken about a week and would have been truly chaotic—plus 12 or 24 hours per person per year, the IS department would have saved more than 300 hours per person per year. All the development staff wanted to do it. All the team leaders wanted to do it. But IS management claimed it would be "too disruptive" to work this way and declined to change its approach—the "cost of quality" would be too great.

Approaches to Forming Groups

Also important for successful groups are the ways in which they are formed and their membership selected. Although there is seldom a single "right" way to do this, there should always be a clear rationale behind the group-formation process, and group members should always know what it is. Group memberships will vary from time to time, and the selection criteria used should be related clearly to the purpose of the group. Grouping criteria can focus on any of the following factors:

- **The *knowledge* or *skills* of participants.** It is often important to ensure that all members of a group have more or less the same level of skills or experience in the work they will do. This allows any group member to make confident assumptions, based on his or her own experience, as to the capabilities and strengths of co-workers. Occasionally, when one objective of the group is to improve the capabilities of some of its members, a range of different skills and experience may be appropriate.

- **The *processes* to be executed by the group.** Where these processes require a blend of skills and experience, the group's capabilities should address this need. Where a narrower set of (usually technical) skills are required, there may be a less diverse membership. In all cases, there should be a group member (or members) who is conversant with most or all of the range of activities that the group will undertake. These individuals (called "hybrids" in management jargon) are rare and valuable.

- **The things that are to be produced as *deliverables* by the group.** Groups can be formed around the need to produce specific deliverables, rather than around processes. Whereas a group formed around a process may be responsible for many deliverables, groups formed around a deliverable produce only that deliverable and then disband. Where the process is significantly internally heterogeneous, this may be an excellent strategy. Some group members (user interface design or data base design specialists, for example) may transfer from group to group as the requirements for related but distinct deliverables are addressed.

- **The *duration* of a program.** In some circumstances a group may be brought together for the duration of a program of work. This is the "task force" approach, which can be a powerful and effective directional and supervisory mechanism in its own right.

- **The need to focus on a specific *customer* or group of customers.** Where the group will be dealing with a specific customer or group of customers, selection criteria focus on an ability to understand and work with the customer's circumstances, as well as technical and business skills and experience.

- **The *location* in which the group will work.** Geography, language requirements, culture, and familiarity with local customs can all be part of group selection. Where long-term assignments are involved, permanently located staff are preferred.

While by no means exhaustive, these are the majority of group-formation strategies. They can often be combined or modified but should always be understood and agreed to by the group's members.

Success Criteria for Effective Groups

Once a group has been formed, a number of factors influence its ability to operate successfully:

Clear, mutually owned objectives. This is *the* key success factor. Research[6] has shown that groups are seldom successful and never high performing without a clear, mutually owned set of objectives for work. Even in the face of considerable adverse phenomena, groups with a clear objective continue to perform well.

Well-understood process interdependencies. In creating multifunctional groups, there is also a need to ensure that all necessary processes can be carried out as required. This implies that the critical interdependencies—activity iteration and timing, discovery mechanisms, deliverable availability, and work-flow controls—are recognized and understood by everyone.

Well-understood knowledge interdependencies. Again, in a multifunctional group, it must be possible to fit together the areas of specialist knowledge that each functional discipline uses and contributes. This is generally straightforward in theory but difficult in practice because of terminology, interpretive contexts, and, in some cases, conflicting reference material and experience.

Well-understood scale interdependencies. Scale interdependencies occur when the contribution required from one or more individuals within a group appears out of scale with that required of other members. This is often inevitable when specialist contributions are required or where a particular functional discipline provides most of the required resources. Care must be taken to ensure that all team members appreciate the full value of the contribution of each member, even when it seems small in comparison to other contributions.

Well-understood social interdependencies. A group of individuals who will work together for an extended period need to build a "society" that allows them to function effectively within the changing dynamics of each individual's behavior. In particular:

- The group members need to get along with each other. Such harmony must be based on mutual respect and a willingness to work out issues and problems as they arise. It does not imply that everyone must like or admire everyone else.

- To help with the socialization process, group members need opportunities to get together outside of work. This is especially important if members have not met prior to group formation. Such meetings should occur at the beginning of the group's work, as a part of the initial familiarization and training process, and should continue at regular intervals throughout the group's existence.

Assurance that it is possible to succeed. This factor may seem obvious, but it is an important one: it must be possible for the group to be successful. Even high-performing groups often fail when faced with a seemingly impossible situation, from the perspective of time, resources, complexity, or customer expectations. Even when success cannot be guaranteed, it must at least seem possible that what is being asked for can be done.

The History of Groups in Information Systems Development Organizations

Groups, especially those that form project teams, are already common within virtually all IS organizations. Where they differ from the model described here is in how they are organized, their purpose, and how they behave. In general, groups have been:

- Permanent organizational structures, not project-based transient structures (for example, the development group or the sustaining engineering group);
- Single-function groups, not cross-functional in membership (for example, the data administration group or the quality assurance group);
- Hierarchically organized, not cooperatively organized; and
- Repositories of management status/power structures rather than working structures.

All of these characteristics mitigate against effective group behavior. It is not surprising, therefore, that sustained high performance is rare.

A Hypothetical Process for Organizational Design

How can an IS organization make good decisions about the mechanisms for coordination and communication? On what basis is mutual adjustment, supervision, or some form of standardization chosen? What groups should be formed, and what are the implications of such groupings? In order to even start to deal with these questions, an organization must understand the operating principles it wants to utilize in delivering information systems, as illustrated in Figure 5.2.

In this model, the *principles* reflect the environmental conditions and unifying guidance that make the mission of information systems delivery possible. Inherent within these principles are major implications for the *organizational design choices* that can

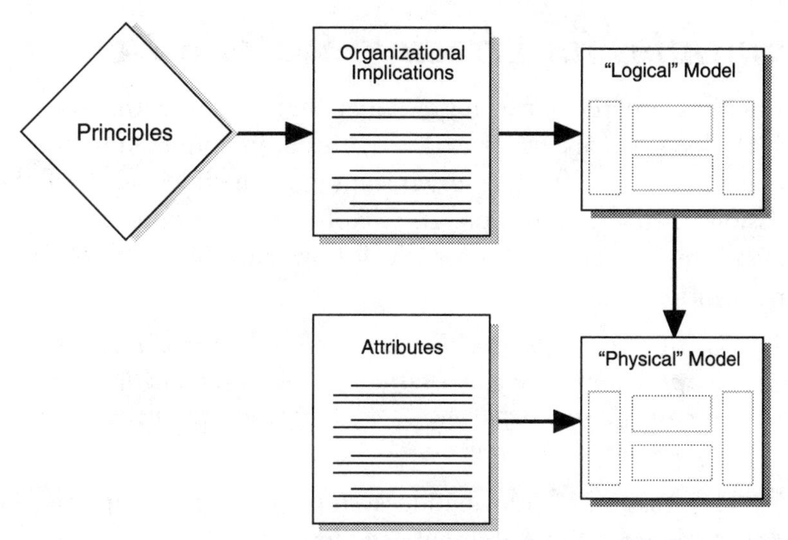

Figure 5.2 *A Hypothetical Process Model for IS Organizational Design*

be made. Together, principles and the organizational implications of those principles can yield a basic *"logical,"* or *"ideal" model* for organizational structure. But all "ideal" organizations are subject to other "real" *attributes,* such as geographical distance between units, market availability of skilled resources, and the current reputation of the organization. These attributes will affect the actual organization design decisions before a *"physical" organizational model* is completed.

The following sections of this chapter outline an organizational design process using a hypothetical systems delivery environment. The concept of a set of *best practice principles* is used as a starting point. The implications of these principles are analyzed in the context of the experiences many systems delivery organizations are facing today. Therefore, the logical and physical organizational models that are presented here should have some general applicability to any particular situation, but will require customization based on specific differences in each enterprise's actual principles and the implications of those principles.

Principles for Effective Systems Delivery

Principles are the basic ingredients that underlie the ways in which decisions are made and activities are conducted within an organization. In effective organizations, principles support the mission of the organization. In Chapter 3, we proposed the following mission statement for the future state of an effective IS organization:

> *The IS Organization is the center of excellence within the enterprise for creating and sustaining business value through the cost-effective deployment of information technology in support of business processes.*

The mission of information systems delivery groups can be interpreted from this statement as follows:

> **Continuously contribute to added value for the enterprise** through achievement of the enterprise's business goals and objectives.
>
> **Create and sustain business value** through the application of information technology to support and improve business processes.
>
> **Continuously add value to information customers** by providing the right information to the right people at the right time, in the form of superior quality information systems capabilities supporting decision making and daily operations.

This sample mission emphasizes adding value to the business, both today and in the future. The principles that follow, therefore, are based on making the most of the technology available and continuously improving so that tomorrow's requirements can be met:

- **Productivity Through Quality.** Improving quality by removing the root causes of problems in the work processes inevitably leads to improved productivity.

- **Continuous Process Improvement.** Quality is achieved not only by the occasional dramatic change, but by a steady, incremental improvement of work processes. Improvements come from the identification, reduction, and elimination of wasteful (non-value-added) activities.

- **Employee Involvement.** The people most knowledgeable about the job are the people doing the job. People will allow themselves to do their jobs better and better if they are empowered to improve the processes they use.

- **Team Learning.** The information systems delivery process involves a team of professionals. Improvements in the process help the team as a whole. If the team learns, the organization learns.

- **Collective Effort.** By group members working together to improve the process and environment, much more can be accomplished than by having individual contributors work around the faults or limitations of the process.

- **Examination Through Fact.** The quality of the development process is based on meeting and exceeding internal and external customer requirements. Measurements of the process provide the insight to either bring the process under better control, reduce variation or improve the process altogether.

- **Consistency Is the Platform for Improvement.** The reduction of process variability opens the door to successful high-speed problem identification and solution delivery. Consistency of process does not imply over-standardization. All processes can be specialized to be efficient for their required purposes.

- **Waste Reduction via Reusability.** The re-creation of system building blocks and the reinvention of existing knowledge is a wasteful, non-value-added activity. Infrastructure to support a repository of reusable knowledge and components is a prevention-based cost of quality.

- **Waste Reduction via Architecture.** "Bridge building" or interfacing multiple systems because each was built autonomously is a wasteful, non-value-added activity. Infrastructure to support enterprise-wide information architectures is another prevention-based cost of quality.
- **Waste Reduction via Strategic Alignment.** Building information systems that are not used or that are unimportant to the business is a wasteful, non-value-added activity. Infrastructure to support the alignment of information systems development with business strategy is also a prevention-based cost of quality.
- **Rapid Advancement in Information Technology Capability.** New discoveries in IT occur at shorter and shorter intervals. Many IT advancements offer levers for business process improvements or fundamental innovation.
- **Holistic Purpose.** Every member of the information systems delivery organization supports the mission of the IS organization as a whole, which, in turn supports the mission of the whole enterprise. The information systems delivery process is therefore incomplete until the enterprise is using the information system effectively.

Organizational Design Implications

- No one group can dominate the systems delivery process.

Over time, all IS delivery groups must cooperate effectively to provide excellent customer service. As a result, no single group, even the primary customer-facing group, can be seen to dominate the processes in which all groups must necessarily participate to be successful. One of the key principles of the self-directed work group—that leadership resides, from time to time, with the person currently best qualified to lead, and then passes on—should be extended to cover all the groups involved in the development process, with the lead similarly transferring from group to group as the process proceeds.

Once the concept of a shared process is accepted, the need for many types of routine direct supervision can be discounted or abandoned. Instead, a process of mutual adjustment within and between teams is encouraged, with effective arbitration mechanisms to resolve issues that cannot otherwise be adjusted.

- Innovation and improvement requires mutual adjustment for coordination.

In a real sense, innovation, and to a degree, improvement cannot be mandated to happen. All changes in working practices must be adopted and internalized by staff through a mutual adjustment process. At the beginning of this chapter, we showed how mutual adjustment is both the beginning and the end of the spectrum of organizational approaches to process management. It is very important to recognize that the maturity to handle mutual adjustment in complex problem domains seldom comes until an organization has also been through the intervening approaches at least once.

The mutual adjustment device is a team.

Here is where the specialized form of the group—the team—comes into play. Teams can be used to address complex problems only when the team members understand how to participate in mutual adjustments to the problem-solving process. And it is not just the team manager who is involved. In a mature mutual adjustment situation, *everyone* must be involved in the adjustment process, although the degree and type of involvement can and should vary. Remember that some of the best ideas come from people who are new to a process, because they see things without the preconceptions of experience. This is the only adjustment approach that supports a holistic, systems-thinking view and maintains a clear customer focus. In this approach, managers become functioning team members with special responsibility to effect coordination between the team and the external environment.

Coordinating between teams requires a degree of standardization.

Mutual adjustment between teams is possible because all teams share key aspects of the environment and work processes. There must, therefore, be a common framework that all teams have access to and use. Hence the need for the broad definition of infrastructure used in Chapter 3, and to which we return in Chapter 9. It is the totality of this infrastructure that supports and enables teams to both develop mutually comprehensible deliverables and improve the processes by which they do so.

The use of a common infrastructure also helps to reduce rework and waste:

Data models and structures become reusable resources.

Information systems components become reusable resources.

Knowledge and experience become transferable and, hence, reusable.

- Line relationships are for housekeeping.

The team focus is at odds with the conventional reporting relationships that are most familiar to IS managers and staff. These relationships are still needed, however, because team leaders should not be required to replicate "corporate housekeeping" processes for their team members. Activities related to the provision of human resources support, office services, or specialty mentoring are best collected into a line organization structure for efficiency and standardization of practices.

It is also necessary to ensure that cross-team processes that must operate fairly and identically in all teams (skills certification, performance appraisal, compensation assessment, issue management, and so on) are designed and operated externally, although here too team members can and should participate.

- Abstraction and modeling are different disciplines.

Although it runs somewhat counter to conventional thinking, we believe that the processes associated with the discovery, identification, and description of a business opportunity or problem (abstraction) are different from those associated with the development of models on which to base a solution (modeling). Different skills and experience are required, and the best approach for each varies with the situation. Thus there is a need for business process analysts in addition to solution modelers. The organizational structure should embody this distinction in the selection and formation of teams that deal with business issues and teams that develop and deliver solutions.

Opportunities are endless, resources are finite—Balance is essential.

In the ever-changing world of the future-state vision for both the enterprise and IS, only the availability of resources constrains improvement opportunities. Available resources will always be finite and less than desired. There must therefore be a balance between targeting resources to innovation and to improvement, lest opportunities in either sphere be missed.

Even this balance is insufficient in the long term. Targeting all resources to innovation and improvement in current processes with known technological and organizational enablers will miss future innovation or improvement opportunities made possible by yet to be identified enablers. Hence, there is a need for a group whose focus is on the future—undertaking the technology opportunity research that will identify or anticipate the levers for the next generation of improvement or innovation possibilities.

A Logical Systems Delivery Organization Model

Using the aforementioned principles and their consequences, it is possible to describe a "logical" structure for the future-state information systems delivery organization. Figure 5.3 shows the various components of the organization structure.

One of the most obvious aspects of this model is its movement away from a technology focus in problem identification and toward a business-process focus. Instead of seeing a supposedly seamless transition from requirements modeling to design solutions, we recognize a distinction between the business view of a problem or opportunity and the IS view of potential solutions. Instead of attempting to reconcile these views with a standardized transformation process, we borrow lessons and language from concurrent engineering principles and adopt a multifunctional multiskilled team approach.

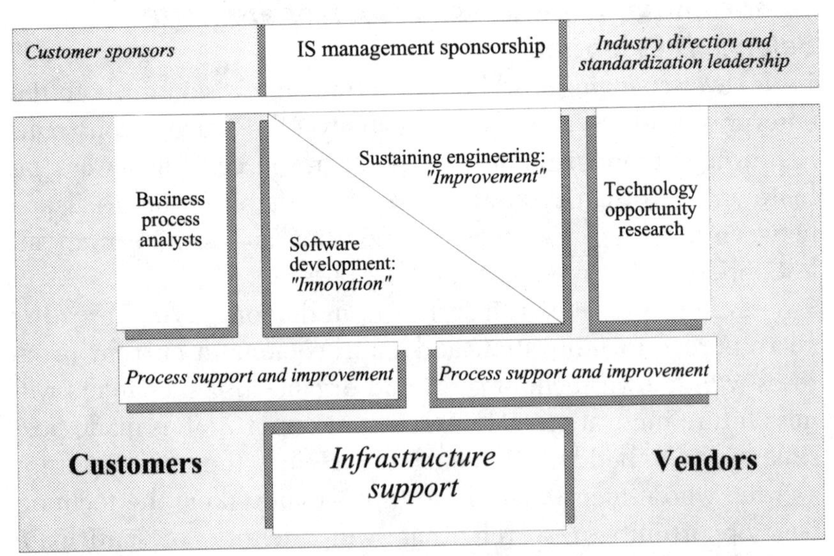

Figure 5.3 *Logical Consequences for the Future State IS Organization*

This model represents the permanent roles needed for the entire development process; the next section of this chapter presents a model that represents one possible physical implementation of the organizational structure associated with the process.

A Physical Systems Delivery Organization Model

Figure 5.4 shows an organizational structure that is consistent with the design principles described earlier. The focus is on the team as the primary organizational entity, with a line structure providing supporting services—not management controls.

It is easy to tell when you have accomplished this structure. Ask the question, "Whom do you work for?" to anyone in the organization. If the answer is, "I work for my boss," you have a long way to go. If the answer is, "At the moment, I work for the project manager of my team," you are getting close. If the answer is, "I am a member of the XYZ team—this week," you have arrived.

Cautions

There is an old joke about a man who was promoted to division head. As he was moving into the corner office, he found three sealed envelopes addressed to him with a note from his predecessor. The note said, "These envelopes represent all the wisdom I gained from my many years of experience. Open an envelope only when you are experiencing a difficulty that you cannot overcome by yourself."

After a few months, the division began to have major problems. The new boss frantically tried to solve them, but could not. He remembered the envelopes and opened the first one. Inside was a note saying, "Blame your predecessor!" He followed the advice and sure enough, the problems seemed to go away.

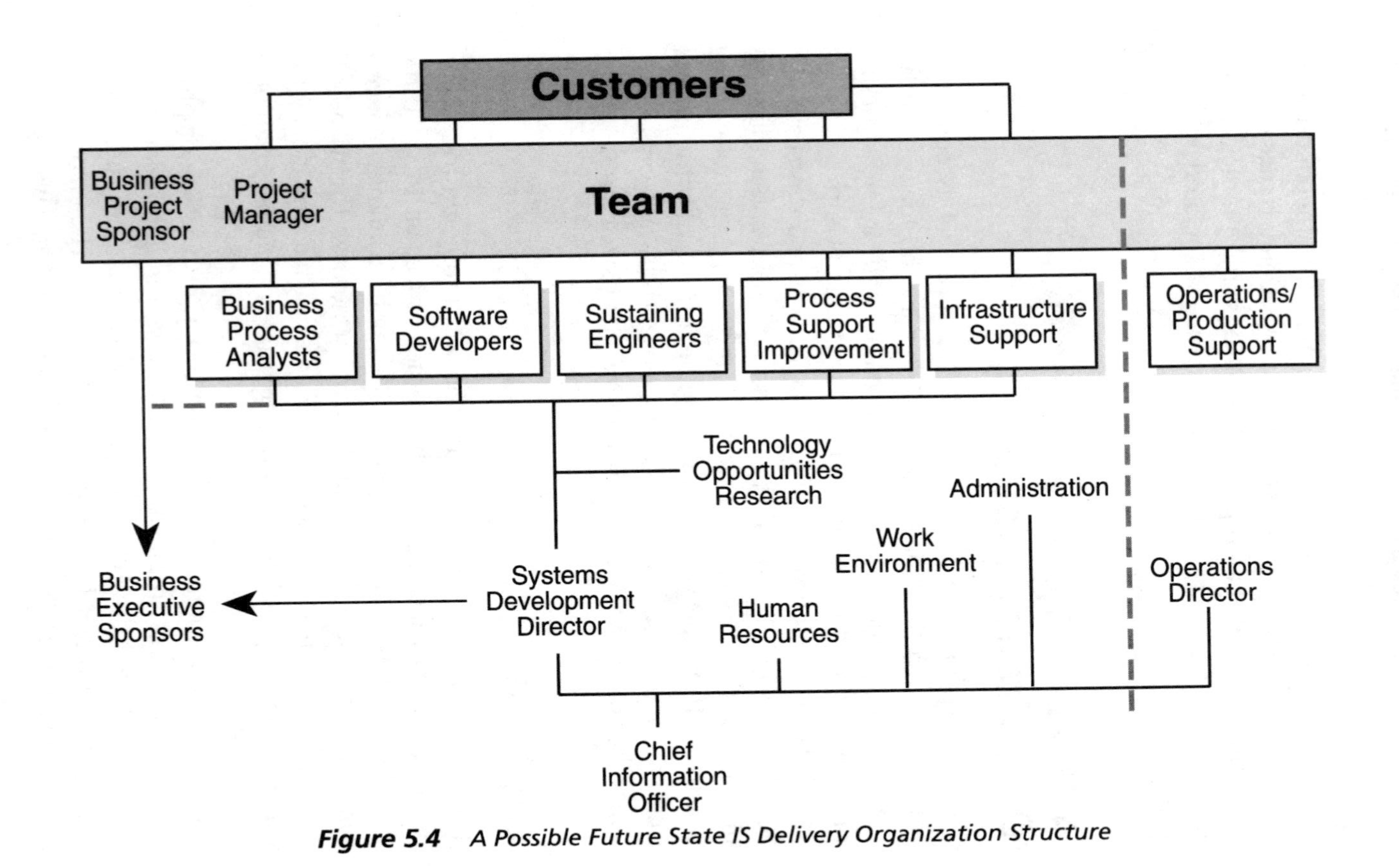

Figure 5.4 *A Possible Future State IS Delivery Organization Structure*

But not forever. Several months went by, and even more severe problems arose. The new boss tried everything, but without success. He resorted to opening the second envelope. The note inside read, "Reorganize!" He promptly plunged the entire division into a broad, sweeping reorganization. Sure enough, the advice worked. The problems subsided.

A year or so later, the problems were back, worse than ever. Everything the boss attempted was in vain. In desperation, he pulled out the third envelope and opened it. The note inside said, "Prepare three envelopes!"

This joke contains more truth about most reorganizations than we care to admit. Changing the organizational structure is a great way of diverting attention from real problems, but not necessarily a great way of *solving* real problems. When reorganizations are dictated by politics, cost cutting, or management whims, the results are not often enduring.

Even when organizational design is deliberate and rational, it is a mistake to think that change is a one-time exercise. Remember that:

- Over time, competing forces of desire for stability versus environmental change and complexity will drive the organization toward a bureaucracy as a mechanism to stifle change and defend the status quo. Do not let this happen.

- In a team-based, dynamic organizational structure, communication costs seem high. Resist the impulse to cut back on communications and communication infrastructure elements. The minimal savings will all be eaten up in the resulting loss of flexibility and effectiveness.

- Management practices are intolerant of and resistant to ambiguity. Line management may attempt to assert control over teams, re-creating old organizational paradigms that feel comfortable even though they do not work well. Keep the line organization lean and in its place.

- In the short term, this organization structure may seem as though it is not designed for achieving ordinary things, but rather for the support of extraordinary endeavors. In a sense this is true, because a highly effective development organization can achieve seemingly extraordinary performance. In fact, the organizational design we have just described aims to make the extraordinary into the routine. In the meantime, do not let a parallel structure be built up for "day-to-day" activity.
- There will always be adjustments to be made for scheduling some team members whose skills and patterns of work result in unbalanced work loads. Teams will want to retain control of these resources to ensure that they are available when needed—and have not been scheduled by another team. The more specialized the resource, the more difficult the issue becomes. Do not let such "resource hiding" take place. Encourage the teams to use mutual adjustment mechanisms to balance requirements. Remember that no one team can be successful at the expense of all others.

Good organizational design is not easy, nor is it ever finished. Just like every other aspect of the future-state vision, the organizational structure must evolve and improve as the demands on it change. What works well at the outset of transition will not be effective toward the end of the transition process. The price of effectiveness is unending vigilance and a willingness to change to improve. In the next chapter, we discuss the process of organizational change and the key issues that enable or inhibit the transition process.

Notes

1. Much of the background to this chapter stems from the organizational design research of Henry Mintzberg and his students at McGill University during the 1970s and 1980s. There is extensive resulting literature. Perhaps the best

summary of this work is Henry Mintzberg, *Structure in Fives: Designing Effective Organizations* (Englewood Cliffs, NJ: Prentice-Hall, 1983).

2. Based on an international survey of current situations and future intentions undertaken for Ernst & Young by Dialog Research in 1991.

3. We first heard this story during a social psychology class in 1972. At the time, it seemed apocryphal, but we have heard the same story from a number of other sources since. The original citation eludes us, however.

4. For an excellent treatment of approaches to complex problem solving strategies applied to technological discontinuities, see *Innovation: The Attacker's Advantage* by Richard Foster of McKinsey & Company (New York: Summit Books, 1986).

5. Frederick P. Brooks Jr., "No Silver Bullet: Essence and Accidents of Software Engineering," *Information Processing '86*, 1986. Brooks was the program manager for the development of OS/360, IBM's flagship operating system of the 1960s and 1970s. He first coined the term "silver bullet" to refer to anything seen as a single all-encompassing (but doomed to failure) solution to a complex problem. The IS profession has not been short of silver bullets in the 25 years since OS/360 was born.

6. Jon R. Katzenbach and Douglas K. Smith, *The Wisdom of Teams: Creating the High Performance Organization* (Boston: Harvard Business School Press, 1993).

6

Why the Management of Change Matters

There are many common misconceptions about the critical success factors for improving the software development process. Chief among them is that change somehow just happens. This chapter shows why this is not so and discusses the tools of organizational change management that must be applied if significant change is to be achieved successfully. It also examines the inhibitors to change, sources of resistance, and sources of support. Key roles in the change management process are introduced and described.

In previous chapters we have discussed the principles of Total Quality Management, and what this means for IS. We have described a future-state IS mission statement, and its implied principles. We have shown the organizational design implications and the need for new team-based structures. Each of these aspects of Development Effectiveness means that people must change something about their skills, beliefs, behaviors, or values.

The degree of behavior change involved in a Development Effectiveness program varies greatly, depending on the existing culture and the combination of new values, principles, tools, methods, standards, skills, and disciplines to be introduced. Some examples of the kinds of change that might be involved are shown in Figure 6.1.

This list is by no means exhaustive, but serves to illustrate that technologists have to change their beliefs and behaviors in order to make effective use of new technology. An effective and continuously improving development process is not simply a matter of new tools and technologies. It requires fundamental process changes, new skills, new roles and relationships, and a commitment to continuous personal learning and growth.

It is not only IS professionals, however, who are affected by these changes. Increasingly, an effective development process depends on significant user participation and new roles for the users of information and technology. Examples of belief shifts required by business professionals are shown in Figure 6.2.

Change From	*Change To*
A belief that programming is a craft form	A belief that systems development is an engineering discipline
A belief that every project is unique; that it is easier to "reinvent the wheel" than to reuse existing components	A belief that projects share more similarities than differences; that it is easier to reuse components than to reinvent them
A belief that defects are inevitable, and that quality should be "inspected into" systems	A belief that defects are avoidable, and that quality should be "designed into" systems
Antagonistic relationships with people in organizations who provide or use the same information	Cooperative relationships with all people who provide or use the same information
Improving the speed in which one instance of a function is completed	Continuously improving the effectiveness for all instances of a process
Project success measured by technical correctness	Project success measured by business contribution
A belief in "traditional," well-tried principles	A willingness to explore fundamentally new and innovative approaches

Figure 6.1 *Belief Shifts Required by IS Professionals for an Effective Development Environment*

This list is also not exhaustive, but illustrates that business professionals must also change their beliefs and behaviors in order to create effective information technology (IT) processes. As information technology becomes an increasingly important lever for redesigning business processes, and for creating new products and services, these necessary changes in belief and behavioral systems will become farther-reaching and increasingly important to business success.

Change From	***Change To***
A belief that systems development is someone else's problem	A recognition of the value information technology can offer and the acceptance of responsibility for its develoment
A view of participating in the systems delivery process as time spent helping the IS department	A view that time utilized during the systems delivery process is an investment in business process improvement or innovation
A prioritization approach based on increasing functional efficiency	Support for the strategic alignment of information resources to critical enterprise needs

Figure 6.2 *Belief Shifts Required by Business Professionals*

What Is Change?

Human beings are by nature control oriented. Programmed with a characteristic physiologists call *homeostasis*, people feel most competent, confident, and comfortable when their expectations of control, stability, and predictability are met. Change occurs when the balance between capabilities and the challenges faced is disrupted.

Change can be perceived as either positive or negative. The developer who believes that experience with object modeling and client-server tools will add value to his resume might view a move to an advanced development environment as a positive change. Another developer who believes that such tools and methods are inherently de-skilling, and will stifle creativity, could well view the same change as negative.

In any case, change will be resisted in some way. The reason is that, at some point, change affects people's competence, comfort, or confidence and disrupts their expectations. This refutes a popular misconception that positive change is welcomed and therefore will not be resisted. Although a change may indeed be perceived positively and may be welcomed, insofar as expectations are disrupted it will meet resistance that will consume energy during the transition process. If sufficient energy is available, the change can be sustained through completion. If insufficient energy is available, the change will stall.

The Impact of Changing Technology on People

Most attempts to improve the systems delivery process encounter objections from IS professionals, such as the following:

> These tools and methods will stifle my creativity!
>
> It's pointless measuring this, because we never do it the same way twice!
>
> We really don't need to improve. It's the users who are the problem!

Although such objections may have some basis in fact, they are often *emotional* responses to change. They arise from feelings of fear, doubt, insecurity, anger, or anxiety.

Prior to an improvement initiative, the IS organization existed in a state of *status quo*. Status quo does not imply "good" or "bad," it simply means that people knew what to expect from day to day. Even if IS processes were poor and full of confusing procedures, people knew that they were the same poor processes and confusing procedures they had used before.

Even people who complain about the status quo are not necessarily ready to change it. Psychological research shows that people tend to cling to familiar patterns of behavior even if these are not healthy for them. The colloquial expression that describes this tendency is, "The devil you know is better than the devil you don't."

When a new development process—the devil you don't know—is implemented, people often do not know what to expect or how to interpret the effects of the new process on them personally. Often, the secure and comfortable sense of control over their environment disappears. Someone who had confidence in his or her ability to get the job done now begins to experience self-doubt.

This is a natural part of being human. A new CASE tool, for example, itself represents but a small part of the total disruption people experience when systems development is automated. The implications associated with development automation are potentially far more disruptive. People will begin to have discomforting thoughts, such as:

> Will this new approach cost my friend a job?
>
> Will Joe get a promotion instead of me?
>
> Will this tool reveal my illiteracy with structured methods?

As people contemplate questions like these, their anxiety and stress levels increase. Anxiety, stress, instability, inadequacy—all are reactions to feeling a loss of control associated with change.

Assimilating Change Is Resource Consuming

In order for new development approaches to become part of the fabric of IT, people must exert energy and accept risk. They must expend intellectual energy trying to understand how to operate in the new environment: dealing with the new concepts involved in information engineering, process innovation or object modeling, for example. They must expend emotional energy dealing with the trauma caused by unexpected implications of the Development

Effectiveness program: concerns about being measured through a project management system, for example. People must expend additional emotional energy in accepting the personal and professional risks associated with the new approaches. There may be perceived personal risk, for example, that development automation could make an individual's job skills obsolete or that being part of a pilot project that fails will reflect badly on an individual's performance.

We call this energy people expend adjusting to a disruption in their expectations "assimilation." Assimilating change involves effort to deal with the cause of the change, as well as with the short- and long-term implications of the change—such as learning new communication and facilitation skills, or accommodating a workstation in addition to the mainframe computer terminal in an already overcrowded work space.

The use of intellectual and emotional energy will be expressed physically, either in the effort to understand, learn, and practice or in extra worry or concern. Change of any kind that disrupts people's expectations consumes this energy, or *assimilation resource*.

All disruptions of expectations consume some amount of this resource; the amount is determined by the degree of personal disruption one perceives. The more closely a change affects an individual, the more assimilation resource is required for the individual to adjust. A marriage requires a large amount of assimilation resource because it has a high degree of personal impact. For most people, a reorganization at work will consume less assimilation resource than a marriage, but more than environmental pollution, which has little direct personal impact despite its being a larger problem.

There are many factors that contribute to the disruption a person experiences during the change process, including the following:

- **Amount:** How many different fundamental changes are required? For a Development Effectiveness program the changes might include learning several new development tools; using a development workstation; learning new skills, including "soft" skills such as facilitation and communication; adopting new beliefs and values, such as customer focus; learning new methods; relocating into a business unit; and so on.

- **Scope:** How wide-reaching are the changes, how many people are affected, and across how many different groups and organizations? The changes could be enterprise-wide, impacting several IS units and their business customers. They could also affect suppliers and end customers of the business.
- **Time**: How much time do the people affected have to assimilate the changes? Typically, management allows insufficient time for major changes to be absorbed. For IS professionals, business demands do not wait.
- **Transferability:** How easily can the changes be communicated and understood? Some, such as new tools, are easily understood. Others—business partnership, strategic alignment, and Total Quality—are harder to comprehend.
- **Predictability:** How accurately do the people affected anticipate the ramifications of the changes? What are the full implications of relocating into a business unit? What are the ramifications of shifting from an overhead function to a "services for sale" type of structure?
- **Ability:** To what degree do the people affected by the changes feel they have or can attain the knowledge and skill to work effectively with the new technology? What skills are required for object-oriented development? What kinds of people adapt well to team-based structures?
- **Willingness:** How motivated are people to make the technology a success? What is in it for the programmer to adopt a "diagrams to generated code" development tool?

- **Values**: To what extent are people asked to change strongly held beliefs about the way they are operating? How, for example, will programmers who have thrived on technical skills for their entire career respond to a shift to automated programming and code reuse tools?
- **Emotions:** To what extent must people change their feelings about other people or processes? There is often a rift between systems development and data administration staffs, for example. How will these groups react to being integrated, or to working together in teams?
- **Behaviors:** To what extent must people modify daily routines of job-related activities? Will they have to record all their activities? Will they have to maintain multiple reporting relationships?

High measures in any or all of these characteristics indicate that existing expectation patterns will be severely disrupted, that the change is major and requires special attention for it to be successful.

The Danger of Depleting Assimilation Resources

There is a point at which assimilation resources run out. When a person faces so much disruption in his or her life, they become *assimilation bankrupt*, and may display dysfunctional behavior. Similarly, an organization that is assimilation bankrupt can no longer cope with change while continuing to perform effectively. Dysfunctional behavior manifests itself in many different ways, from mild irritation that diverts attention from work, to poor decision making, deception, chronic tardiness or absenteeism, or even sabotage.

The assimilation resources consumed by changes are cumulative. For example, a reorganization of the IS department will consume some. A Total Quality Management initiative will consume additional assimilation resources. A son's substance abuse problems in high school can consume a significant amount of the remaining assimilation resources. Even with all this turmoil, a given individual may be able to cope, until asked to participate in a CASE tool implementation. This may be more than he or she can take, and the person reaches the threshold of assimilation bankruptcy, becomes dysfunctional, and is no longer able to perform effectively.

Therefore, when considering the impact of a change initiative, it is insufficient to consider just the change at hand. The impact of all the other changes people are dealing with must also be taken into account, and this requires that the change be analyzed at a greater level of detail than is typical. It also requires some tough choices. Management usually has more change initiatives it would like to introduce than the organization has capacity to deal with. Management must decide which are the most critical changes and focus assimilation resources on those. Even then, an organization might find that it has more mandatory change to deal with than it can accommodate. In this case, the organization's resilience to change must be increased.

Increasing Resilience to Change

There are two ways to maximize an individual's or organization's resilience to change. The amount of assimilation resources required by a given change initiative can be reduced, or assimilation capacity can be increased. Assimilation resource requirements can be reduced by approaching change as a process, managing the forces that enable and inhibit change, and orchestrating the key roles involved in the change. Assimilation capacity can be increased by involving people in the change process, and by helping them understand how the change will be managed. In the rest of this chapter, we describe tactics for achieving these goals.

Some individuals or organizations are very resilient to change and constantly seek it out. Others cling desperately to the status quo. Both reactions require effort that consumes assimilation resources. Assimilation resources are used regardless of whether a change is self-initiated or imposed by other people or circumstances. Fortunately, all people and organizations can increase their available assimilation resources by learning how to become more resilient to change.

For example, attending childbirth classes has become a common practice for many first-time parents. In such classes, parents-to-be are taught the stages of labor and delivery. They may see films or take a tour of the facilities they intend to use. Months after the birth of the child, most parents have similar reactions to the classes they attended. They claim, *The class didn't relieve the pain involved, but understanding what was going on helped manage it better*. By being better prepared, their resiliency had increased.

Increasing each individual's capacity to adjust to change increases the amount of change that can be introduced without causing dysfunctional behavior. But this is only half of the strategy. The other half is to manage each change initiative more effectively in order to require less assimilation resource from the people who are affected.

Understanding Commitment Requirements

The process that people go through to adjust to a change in expectations can be studied as a change in commitment, as shown in Figure 6.3. To change, people must lower their commitment to the way things are in the status quo and increase their commitment to the way things will be in the future state.

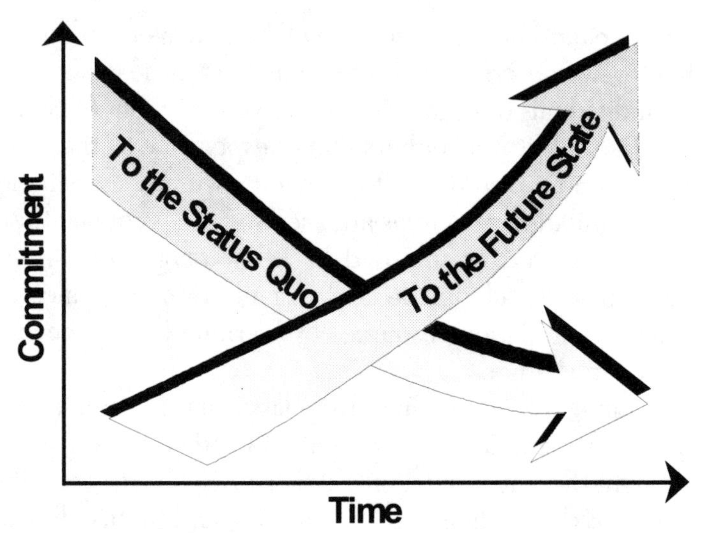

Figure 6.3 *Changes in Commitment over Time*

Commitment is an important dynamic in the change process. The degree of commitment supporting the status quo must be measured against the level of commitment required for a change to be effective. Incorrect assumptions about the level of commitment an organization has to the status quo or needs in order to reach the future state will lead to some disastrous consequences.

> **Example:** A new high-performance development workbench is designed to improve systems development cycle time and quality. Reducing cycle time is seen as a real opportunity by senior management. The workbench incorporates rapid development principles that are new to the IS organization. Part of the workbench initiative also distributes development project responsibility to business users. An implementation date is agreed to by senior management, the workbench is installed, and everyone is sent through one week's training. A large number of gripes and flaws in the workbench are noted.
>
> After a few months, development cycle time and quality are unchanged. Investigation reveals that many people are not using the new workbench, or are misusing it to support traditional development approaches. Business professionals are finding it hard to devote the time and attention required by the new environment.

Each development team offers compelling reasons for the lack of use, usually making reference to the workbench's inadequacies. Senior management is troubled but issues an edict that usage of the new workbench is mandatory. The number of complaints and noted flaws increases.

After several more months, there is still no discernible change in cycle time or quality. Senior management becomes convinced that the workbench is inadequate and considers funding a redesign project, or scrapping the whole system, and perhaps taking punitive action against the original designers.

Two assumptions about commitment were made by senior management in this example, both in error.

■ **Assumption 1:** Management assumed that because developers knew how poorly the business units perceived development cycle time and systems quality, and the significant impact this had on the business, they would have very little commitment to the existing process. Moreover, they assumed that because business units were so concerned about development cycle time and systems quality, they would be ready to participate in the new development process.

Although it was true that developers had been told that quality was poor and cycle time was too long, they had heard that story before and had come to interpret it as a senior management ploy to get them to work harder. Most saw their function primarily as providing good technical solutions to business users, and they felt they did a great job at this. Cycle time was a destiny, not a problem, and poor quality was the result of users not knowing what they wanted and constantly changing their minds about requirements. Furthermore, although business units would have liked shorter development cycle time and improved systems quality, individual business professionals were not directed by their management to shift priorities in order to make the time available to participate in the development process. These attitudes reflect a high commitment to the status quo.

■ **Assumption 2**: By issuing an edict that usage of the workbench was mandatory, senior management believed it could force *compliance*. Although some changes can be approached through compliance, the high-performance development workbench represented a fundamental change in the philosophy of systems development and therefore required a high level of personal commitment on the part of developers and users. For the environment to work, people needed to *internalize* the rapid development principles and the new "partner" relationship with the business users. People were unconsciously being asked to change what they believed in, and then to demonstrate behavior consistent with those new beliefs. A change in beliefs requires a much greater commitment than compliant behavior.

This is not to say that all aspects of a Development Effectiveness program must be approached through commitment. Many changes, such as a new electronic mail system, need only compliance—*You don't need to believe in the new electronic mail system, you just need to use it!*

Change Is a Process, Not an Event

Organizational change is a *process* of reducing commitment to the way things are and increasing commitment to the way things will be. Often, the incorporation of new technology into a business is viewed as an event by computer systems professionals—something that takes place at a specific point in time and lasts for a short duration. For example, on a specific day, the high-performance development workbench was "turned over." Workstations were plugged in, software tools were moved into production libraries, and the environment was born. One day the workbench did not exist, the next day it did. The job was considered completed when the day was over, and the systems programmers issued a sigh of relief.

But the production turnover event does not mark either the beginning or the end of the process of people adjusting to changes in their expectations. The process of change is well illustrated by

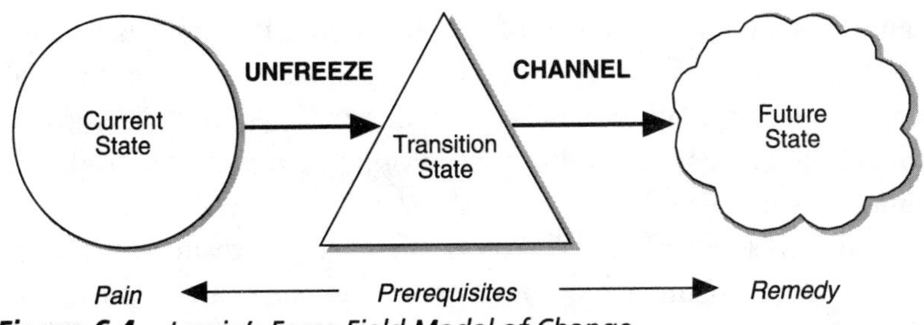

Figure 6.4 *Lewin's Force Field Model of Change*

Kurt Lewin's Force Field model, first put forward in 1958.[1] Lewin defined change as a process and described a three-state model, as shown in Figure 6.4. Each state is subject to forces, some of which act to cause motion to a different state, and others act to prevent such motion.

The Lewin model can be applied to any system—an individual, a group, or an entire organization. Although any living system is always in a state of growth, metamorphosis, or decline, all systems tend toward some sort of equilibrium. According to Lewin, equilibrium exists because of a balance between forces of change and restraining forces, which are constantly acting upon the system.

Pain: Moving Away from the Status Quo

Creating the motivation to change, or "unfreezing" the status quo, is the most important, and usually the most difficult, aspect of the change process. It requires manipulation of the forces of change and the restraining forces, such that the status quo becomes unacceptable as compared with an alternative future state.

Daryl Conner[2] refers to this manipulation of the forces of change and restraining forces as "pain management." Such pain can refer to the level of discomfort a person experiences when his or her goals are not being met (current pain) or are not expected to be met (anticipated pain) as a result of the status quo. Pain management is the process of consciously surfacing, organizing, and communicating certain information in order to generate the appropriate level of pain to discontinue the status quo. Although the term *pain* is usually equated with a problem, it can also relate to an unfulfilled opportunity, and this can often be a more powerful motivator of change. Rather than moving away from a crisis, a change can be positioned as moving toward an opportunity. Pain management is still an appropriate concept, only in this instance the pain is generated by the fear of failing to take advantage of the opportunity.

In the high-performance development workbench example, senior management was "unfrozen," but the constituency being asked to change remained committed to the status quo. To break the inertia, these people needed to develop an increased awareness of why the status quo was unacceptable. They also needed to develop a better awareness of the future state. These are the two basic prerequisites needed to move into the transition state: *pain* and *remedy.*

Remedy: Shared Vision of a Desired State

Building a shared vision of the future state establishes a context meaningful to those who must change. In the high-performance development workbench example, senior management had a vision of what needed to be accomplished (decreased cycle time, improved quality). They did not, however, have a complete vision of the conditions in which the systems delivery process would operate successfully.

Vision is frequently confused with mission. Although having a mission is a critical component of a vision, mission alone is not sufficient. A complete visioning process will visit issues such as these:

- What organizational power is needed to keep the new environment running?

- What structures are necessary to organize the new environment?
- What resources, such as time, people, equipment, or funding, are needed?
- What shared beliefs or values does the entire organization need to subscribe to?

Vision Setting Is Aimed at Effecting Change

It is best to think not only about what is written down on paper as the vision, but also what is ingrained in the organization's values. Visions vary in length and detail, and they are crafted for different levels of an organization. The vision-setting process helps people for whom the vision must be real to find the words that make the image of the vision clear. As they frame the vision, they create a picture of the future from their search for the correct words.

For example, to ensure that the various visions at the different levels fit together and add up to the total, the business plan in one division of a large telephone company is being written so that each individual plan must tie into the division's goals and action plans. Furthermore, the visions must be cosponsored. The visions that are most likely to be cosponsored are those that come from the bottom up rather than those issued from the top down.

Top-down visions often do not include key pain issues, because the executives are not close enough to the operations to know the most important pain points. Involving operational people in vision setting will help to include their feelings on pain points in the vision.

The vision must also document the new way the company will work, to help people move out of their old ways of working. A vision does not always need to be expressed in words. A graphic image may be more powerful. *Fires in the Minds of Men*[3] describes how to create a revolution. It states that songs, which carry brief messages, can capture the spirit in a way that no other mechanism can.

A change in the IS development and maintenance environment may be driven by a need to address current problems or by

The Power of a Simple Message

Consider a bottler whose vision centers on quality and service. Management has decided that the company's core competency will be the handling of acquisitions with incredible deftness, speed, and consistency. The goal is to be able to acquire another bottler, implement the company's systems within the acquisition, and instill company behaviors and vision within a couple of months. This process is down to a science, and the company is very profitable, with excellent growth as a result.

The company approaches soft drinks as a food product, which is a cultural change for many of its acquisitions. Whenever the company acquires another business, it finds a way to quickly send a visible message that demonstrates that it means what it says. For example, because quality is so important, in one large acquisition the company checked the inventory, noting the shelf date of each bottle. Then, with great visibility, the company threw away all stock that had passed its time stamp—in this case dumping $1 million worth of product. This action sent a clear message about maintaining quality.

an opportunity to position the IS organization competitively for the future. In either case, a clear vision will give the change effort meaning and direction. It should provide the context for all decision making regarding the change and for understanding the impact of the change. Setting the vision for the IS development and maintenance environment is critical for a number of reasons:

1. To clarify the business goals that will be supported by the new environment
2. To ensure that the vision of the IS development and maintenance environment supports the organization's Strategic Information Systems Plan
3. To provide the vehicle for communicating the change and associated expectations to those targeted for change
4. To provide, when combined with a clear picture of the current state, the creative tension needed to move to the new environment
5. To define concrete, realistic milestones for achieving the vision
6. To provide, when combined with a clear picture of the current state, an understanding of the gap between the two, the cost of change, and the impact of change
7. To initiate participation by sponsors, advocates, agents, and targets in the change process

The subject of vision setting is revisited in Chapter 8, "Getting Ready."

Moving Through the Transition State

F. Scott Fitzgerald wrote, "The test of a first-rate intelligence is the ability to hold two opposed ideas in mind at the same time, and still retain the ability to function." Fitzgerald was referring to ambiguity—a key characteristic of the "transition state," a learning period of transition that is often uncomfortable. People going through a transition state no longer have the set of expectations they were accustomed to, but neither have they developed a new set for the future state. It is a time when commitment to the future state is built and commitment to the status quo wanes.

The transition through a Development Effectiveness program will generate many learning experiences. People will discover the benefits of the future state, but will also discover its drawbacks. Transition will produce successes and failures. The lessons learned must be channeled into the future state for changes to take hold. The channeling process establishes the future state as the new status quo, a status quo that might include continuous change.

This entire process is described in detail in Chapters 8 and 9.

Often, new computer technology is introduced without management's clear awareness of the cost of the status quo. In the high-performance development workbench example, senior management viewed the cost of the status quo as unacceptably high, but the people who were directly affected by the new environment saw the cost of operating in the status quo as inevitable and irrelevant to their concerns.

Most people facing major change do not have a clear or accurate perception of the cost of the status quo, or do not see how it pertains to them. Just as common is an unclear or understated initial perception of the cost of change. New technology is usually justified primarily on the basis of *purchase cost*, not *assimilation cost*. In other words, costs to build or acquire hardware and software are considered; costs of people's adjusting to disruption in their expectations are not.

When the disruption to people's expectations actually does occur, the perception of the cost of change increases dramatically. Whenever people encounter the personal costs of change, unless the cost of the status quo is very clear, the equation becomes unbalanced and the change initiative will stall and possibly fail. This is how software becomes "shelfware."

Building the resolve necessary to keep the equation in balance requires an awareness of the costs of operating in the status quo, as well as the likely cost of change.

Key Roles in Managing Change

Example: The head of IS has decided that moving to a new, formal information engineering methodology, supported by the appropriate infrastructure, is critical to the organization's future success. He is committed to the change and shows this commitment by budgeting for the acquisition of workstations, tools, methodology, and training and by allocating resources for infrastructure activities. In addition, because this change is so important, he schedules a meeting of the entire IS organization to announce the change, explain how critical it is, and demonstrate his commitment to it. The meeting is convened, and this leader gives a moving speech about the future-state vision, the need for change, and how important it is for everyone to support the change. At the end of the meeting, the project managers each meet with their project teams and essentially tell them to disregard what they have just heard from the head of IS, that "this too shall pass!"

There are various rationalizations for this apparent insubordination. One manager, while acknowledging the forward-thinking vision, explains that the leader's lack of technical knowledge has blinded him to the fact that the proposed new tools and methods are applicable only to new, "green field" development projects. This team's project involves a major enhancement to an existing application and is therefore excused from the automation initiative.

Another project manager explains that her team's project involves an application package selection and implementation, to which the proposed new development environment will be totally unsuited.

Yet another project manager explains that although his team's project is a green field project, and custom software development, it is too important and visible to risk new, untried development approaches. Therefore, the team would be given special dispensation to follow the "tried and true" approaches.

And so the change directive fails. The problem here is that the IS manager has assumed that by broadcasting his message to the development community he has reached the right audience.

However, his initial target should have been members of middle management. Until they are committed to the change, they will be inclined to resist it with as much (or more) vigor as the developers. The IS manager should first have worked with the development manager, and then with the project managers. He should have gotten them involved in the change and secured their commitment before delivering the change message to the developers.

This scenario points out the importance of the various "roles" associated with the different aspects of change. Sometimes these roles are clear and explicit, other times they are blurred and overlap. The role an individual assumes can alter over time as the change progresses, and people can assume multiple roles. Even so, one of the key aspects of successfully managing change is to clarify these roles and to orchestrate them to ensure that they are being filled and that the individuals filling them understand the responsibilities of their respective roles and are prepared to fulfill those responsibilities adequately.

Change Target

Change targets, the largest group in the community of change roles, are the individuals or groups who must actually change their knowledge, skills, attitude, or behavior as a result of a change. This group is often broader than initially perceived. The establishment of a high-performance development environment, for example, has implications beyond the IS development community, and even beyond IS.

Initiating Sponsor

The initiating sponsor is the individual or group who has the power to initiate and legitimize a change for all affected targets. People often assume that the changes involved in improving IS development must be sponsored by the development manager. This is a flawed notion. To be successful, a Development Effectiveness program will likely have as an initiating sponsor a very senior executive who has the power to legitimize change throughout IS and through the business units.

Sustaining Sponsor

Although initiating sponsors start the change ball rolling, it is sustaining sponsors who make sure that the ball rolls all the way to its destination. Sustaining sponsors have the political, logistical, and economical proximity to the affected targets. Sustaining sponsorship is crucial to change initiatives, and inadequate sustaining sponsorship is one of the key factors in failed change initiatives.

For a sustained Development Effectiveness program, there will probably need to be sustaining sponsorship established both within IS and inside business units.

Change Agent

Change agents are those responsible for implementing a change. Change agents "own" the change project. Change agents require competence in interpersonal skills such as team building, problem solving, and effective communications, as well as organizational change skills. Before they can be effective, change agents must first believe in the change. Sometimes, change agents start as advocates—they believe in the change even before sponsorship has been secured. At other times, they enter the change initiative at a later point, when sponsorship has already been secured. In these cases, change agents are first change targets and must be sold on the change before they can adequately fulfill the role of change agent.

Change Advocate

Change advocates are those who want to achieve a change but do not possess legitimization power. Many individuals mistake advocacy with sponsorship or with change agency. Unless the appropriate level and degree of sponsorship for a change has been secured, the best that such interested parties can achieve is change advocacy. Acting as change agents or sponsors, without having necessary sponsorship, is a sure path to failed change. Instead, advocates should focus their energies on building sponsorship by educating sponsors on the opportunities for change, reasons to change, and their responsibilities during change through "pain management" techniques, as discussed earlier.

Cascading Sponsorship

Significant change within a target population will not occur without sufficient commitment demonstrated by the appropriate sponsors. When sponsors who lack a full understanding of the implications of a change are unwilling or unable to take the actions necessary to secure the critical resources, or are unwilling or unable to fulfill their role requirements, they must be educated or replaced.

Sponsorship can be delegated only to those who have legitimization power, not to agents. Change agents can be charged with implementation responsibilities but should never be asked to legitimize change.

Initiating and sustaining sponsors must never attempt to fulfill each other's functions. Initiating sponsors have the organizational power to start the change process, but it is sustaining sponsors who have the greatest impact on the change targets, because they have the logistical, economic, and political proximity to them.

Sponsorship must be cascaded from the initiating sponsor to the change targets, following the chains of influence and authority. In dealing with radical improvements in software-development environments, we often find that members of top management are eager for improvement. They have felt the "pain" of the status quo and are committed to change. Contrary to popular myth, we also find that most individual developers are also eager for change. They are often excited by the idea of trying new tools and techniques and enriching their resumés with the latest technologies or methodologies.

Why is it, then, that a change somehow fails to be sustained? Often, this is a failure to cascade sponsorship, as seen in the preceding example.

In dealing with change, a good initiating or sustaining sponsor must demonstrate commitment by displaying a number of relevant behaviors. It is important for them to:

- Utilize organizational power to communicate and legitimize the change with the target population.
- Surface a sufficient degree of pain regarding the status quo.
- Develop a clear definition of the future state, at both a conceptual and an operational level.
- Allocate the organizational resources (time, money, people, etc.) needed for successful implementation and demonstrate the ability and willingness to commit what is necessary to the project.
- Become educated to understand the effect the change will have on the organization.
- Demonstrate the capacity to fully appreciate and empathize with what the targets are being asked to change about the way they operate.
- Thoroughly understand the size of the group to be affected by the change, and manage the scope of the effort.
- Demonstrate the type of public support necessary to convey strong organizational commitment to the change.
- Meet privately with key individuals or groups in order to convey strong personal support for the change.

- Promptly reward those who facilitate the implementation process, and express displeasure with those who inhibit acceptance of the change.
- Ensure that monitoring procedures are established that will track progress or problems that may occur during the implementation process.
- Make tough decisions regarding the personal, political, or organizational price that may be paid for implementing the change successfully.
- Demonstrate consistent resolve/support for the change and reject any course of action with short-term benefits if it is inconsistent with change objectives.

Developing Change Agent and Advocacy Skills

In order to build sponsorship, advocates need to define precisely what they want to change and how success will be measured. They must identify the key targets who must accommodate the change and then, for each target or target group, identify the initiating and sustaining sponsor who must support the change.

Once potential sponsors have been identified, advocates need to evaluate those sponsors' level of commitment to the change.

Effective change agents are skilled in a complex combination of characteristics that can be brought to bear on a given change project. They have the ability to work within the parameters set by the sponsor. They understand the psychological dynamics regarding how individuals and organizations experience and adjust to change, and how these dynamics can be applied in developing and executing plans for major change efforts. They value the human as well as the technical aspects of a change project. They identify, relate to, and respect the diverse frames of reference of sponsors and targets.

Effective change agents generate diagnostic data regarding the organization's resistance to change and convert this information into a coherent and usable plan of action. They work to develop and sustain synergistic relationships with and between sponsors and targets. They know how to select and use alternative styles of interpersonal communication in order to effectively announce the change and respond to questions. They continually assess the level of commitment of both sponsors and targets and are prepared to take the necessary action to bolster faltering support.

Change agents must be skilled in dealing with resistance to change. They must be able to use power dynamics and influence techniques in a manner that reflects a capacity to achieve results, a concern for ethical boundaries of behavior, and a sensitivity for human dignity. They must be able to subordinate (when necessary) their personal agendas, desires, and tendencies toward the change project, so that it will succeed.

Sources of Resistance

Resistance is any opposition to a shift in the status quo. Resistance is natural and inevitable. Its occurrence does not mean that something is wrong—it simply indicates that because people are no longer able to operate as they expected, they have become uncomfortable.

It is important to recognize that disruption is the focal point for understanding resistance. It makes very little difference whether a change is perceived positively or negatively. People resist change because they resist the loss of control caused by the disruption in their expectations. As disruption increases, so does resistance; thus strong resistance will always be the companion of major change.

Resistance can be expressed either overtly or covertly. Overt resistance can be managed—its underlying sources can be ascertained and strategies developed to deal with them. Overt resistance is good. Quite often, people closest to the change can identify flaws in the change strategy that have not been recognized by its sponsors, advocates, or agents. By leaders being empathetic with the change targets and listening carefully to the messages expressed through resistance, change strategies can be adjusted and tuned.

If resistance is denied or ignored, it is often driven underground and becomes covert. Covert resistance is much harder to deal with, because it is invisible. Salespeople learn in basic sales training the need to flush objections to the surface and to discern whether these objections are real or artificial. Addressing artificial objections can create an appearance of progress toward the goal of making the sale, but it is only an illusion. As long as the real objections are hidden, no sale can be made.

> **Example**: A systems analyst reacts negatively to a proposed new project management system, complaining that it will stifle creativity. The development support consultant, in the role of change agent, tries to deal with the stated objection by explaining how creativity need not be stifled, and by reinforcing the benefits of rigorous project management. The consultant even enlists the support of a couple of other analysts who agree that good project management is not inconsistent with creative solutions.
>
> The analyst gives up the creativity argument, but then protests that the project management system will limit the team's flexibility and is inconsistent with contemporary iterative prototyping approaches. Again, the development support consultant responds to the objection, but the analyst now complains that the system is overkill for the types of project handled by the department, and so on.

In such circumstances, it is likely that the real objection is still hidden and that the stated objections are artificial—smoke screens designed to cover up the real issue, which in this case might be the fear of being measured or of being held accountable. A change agent must be sensitive to the existence of hidden objections, indicated in this instance by the continual shifting from one objection to another, and must be skillful at uncovering the real concerns. This can be done by trying to appreciate the change target's frame of reference, by being empathetic with the target, and by demonstrating a climate of open communication and trust so that change targets feel comfortable about expressing their real concerns and objections. Even then, the objection may be based on a concern that is very private, so the change agent must be skilled at reading clues and signs that may at times be quite subtle.

Resistance begins when change is initiated—when a break from the inertia of the status quo has been achieved. The amount of resistance generated is a function of the degree of disruption a person faces and his or her ability and willingness to deal with it.

To manage resistance, it is necessary first to determine its cause. Resistance can be due to either organizational or human resource issues. If the cause is organizational in nature, such as a lack of clear, compelling future-state vision, ineffective sponsorship, or weak supporting structures to reinforce the future state, it is necessary to treat that cause. People may resist a new systems development methodology, for example, because they do not understand its value or relevance to their jobs, their managers do not model the use of disciplined processes in their own activities, and it is difficult to get answers to questions about use of the methodology.

Human resource issues generally fall into the categories of ability deficiencies or willingness deficiencies. As in the earlier example of change in a systems development methodology, people might resist because they do not have the modeling skills called for by the methodology (ability deficiency) or they just do not want to be burdened with following someone else's process (willingness deficiency). Ability deficiencies should be addressed through training, whereas willingness deficiencies require consequence management—performance measures, rewards, recognition, or compensation.

The Role of Corporate Culture

In Chapter 3 culture is defined as the set of shared beliefs, traditions, and values that determines the instinctive and habitual behaviors of members of a group or society. Every organization has a unique culture made up from many subcultures. There is an identifiable General Motors culture, for example, and specific variations within the various GM business units. Cadillac Motor Division has a different culture from Chevrolet. Even within Cadillac Division, the culture in the marketing department is not the same as that in engineering or manufacturing. Cultures are not inscribed anywhere, yet their elements are soon recognized by any employee, often as "the way we do things here." Because cultures are acquired over time, they tend to be deeply ingrained and are not easily or quickly changed. Change initiatives are far more likely to succeed if they are consistent with a culture.

In understanding culture, it is important to distinguish between espoused values and beliefs and actual, deeply held values and beliefs. Chris Argyris[4] discusses why and how individuals behave as they do and how their actions affect their organizations. He identifies two distinct types of "theories" that precede and govern action: espoused theories and theories-in-use. Espoused theories are publicly held and acknowledged, reflected in statements such as "We are a people-oriented company—we put people first and invest in them as our most important resource." Theories-in-use, however, determine what people actually do. They are deeply held and internalized.

When designing change strategies, it is important to keep the change elements consistent with the theories-in-use embodied within the culture. If it is a change in the culture that is required, the difficulty of the change is greatly increased, and all the techniques in this book regarding management of organizational change must be skillfully executed.

Stages of Change Commitment

The degree to which people can commit to any change initiative can vary widely. At one extreme, they may **totally ignore** an announced change. At the other extreme, they may **fully commit** to the change and *internalize* it.

Between these extremes, people comply with change directives to varying degrees. Those in **genuine compliance** have *institutionalized* the change—they believe in the change initiative, want to follow it, and will act within the "spirit of the law" to achieve it. Unlike those fully committed to the change, however, they will not go out of their way to create the structures needed for it. Someone in **formal compliance** does not really believe in the change initiative, but will *adopt* it—follow its "letter of intent," and will go through the motions of complying, only, however, when it can be observed by someone with power or influence over them. Those in **grudging compliance** will not only "cheat" whenever possible, they will also complain as they comply with the change and may even act overtly or covertly to derail the change initiative.

One of the key decisions that change agents and sponsors must make for any change initiative concerns the degree of commitment required from the various communities of change targets. Gaining full commitment from everyone involved can be expensive, in terms of change agents' and sponsors' efforts, and can take considerable time.

When considering these minimum levels of commitment required, it is important to segment the various change target communities according to their roles in the change effort and then treat each segment according to its role. In *Managing at the Speed of Change*,[5] Daryl Conner has produced a useful model showing the stages of commitment to change, as shown in Figure 6.5.

This model identifies three stages of change and eight degrees of commitment that can build over the life of a change

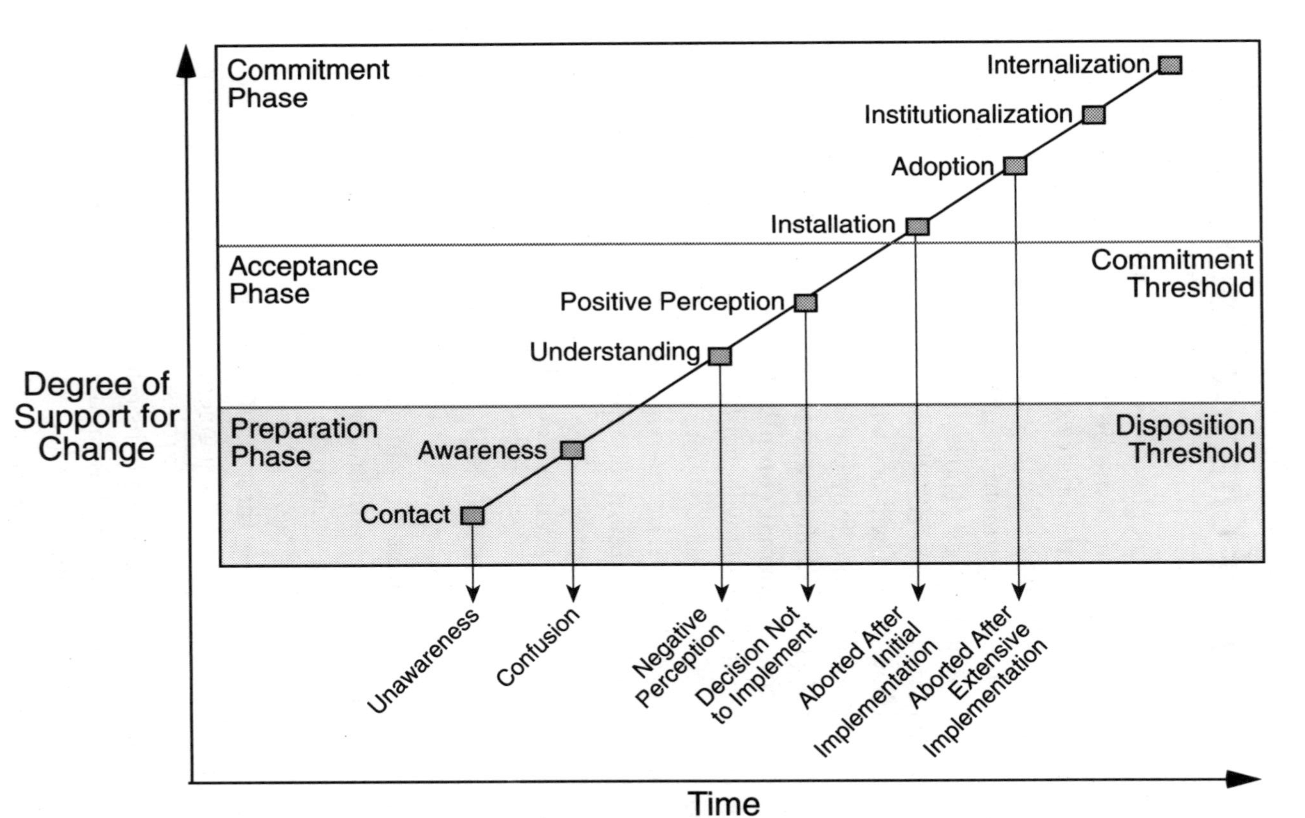

Figure 6.5 *Stages of Change Commitment (© Copyright ODR, Inc.)*

initiative. During the *Preparation Phase*, there is no predisposition toward the change, and unless the nature of the change being considered is one for which simple compliance is sufficient, then the change will not be sustained. During the *Acceptance Phase*, there is predisposition toward the change, but insufficient commitment for the change to be self-sustaining. Only during the *Commitment Phase* does the change become institutionalized or, beyond that, internalized. The following paragraphs explain the degrees of commitment to change and the implications of failing to progress from one degree to the next.

Preparation Phase

1. Contact

Before anyone can begin to support a change, that person must be aware of its nature and understand how he or she is supposed to contribute to its achievement. Many change initiatives fail at this first stage because of a lack of awareness of the reasons for the change, the nature of the change, or the change process that will be followed.

Sometimes change is announced through memos, which carries a risk that the announcement will not reach everyone concerned. There is also a high likelihood that memos will simply be ignored. A recent news report told of a New York City business that used Federal Express overnight delivery to send memos to individuals located in its own building. The argument was that Federal Express was more reliable than the company's internal mail system, and that memos delivered in a Federal Express pouch were far more likely to be read than those sent through internal mail.

Another frequent problem with announcements of change is that the change is expressed in such vague terms that people do not understand exactly what is expected of them. The announcement about the new Total Quality initiative, for example, may sound like a nice idea, but fail to tell the individual what he or she is supposed to do differently from now on.

2. Awareness

Once successful contact has been established, and people become aware that a change has been announced and understand that they are supposed to react to it, the next risk is that there will be confusion about precisely how to react. For example, mixed messages about a change are sometimes communicated. If the change has not been successfully cascaded through management levels, an individual's direct supervisor might signal that the change can be ignored.

This signaling can be direct or subtle. A supervisor may tell his or her subordinates, "You can ignore this change. This too shall pass." Or the message may be less direct—a sort of "nod and a wink" to signal that the change is not to be taken too seriously. Sometimes the signals are sent inadvertently, because of ignorance or confusion on the part of the supervisor. The supervisor tells his or her subordinates, for example, "We must now follow this Total Quality initiative, which tells us that getting it right the first time is of paramount importance." The next time the group questions tradeoffs about "getting it right" and the project deadline, the supervisor says "Well, we have to embrace the quality program, but the deadline is critical—we must be ready on the committed date." The subordinates, of course, follow their supervisor's guidance. They understand that a quality problem with this project will be more readily forgiven than a schedule slippage.

Once people are aware of the change and understand its implications for them, they have crossed the *disposition threshold.* Until this threshold is crossed, the targets are not disposed toward the change and, if they are confused about it, cannot even be forced into compliance.

Acceptance Phase

3. Understanding

If the nature of a change is such that simple compliance is required, as opposed to higher degrees of commitment, then reaching stage 3, understanding, is all that is required. If higher levels of commitment are needed, it is necessary that people affected by the change not only understand it but also perceive it positively, agree with it, and support it.

4. Positive Perception

It may not be necessary and is unlikely that all those affected by a change will perceive it positively. A critical mass of key influencers and stakeholders, however, must support a change in order to achieve higher levels of commitment. An important skill in managing organizational change is the ability to determine who those key influencers and stakeholders are and how to win their support.

Even when positive perception has been achieved by a critical mass of change targets, the change is not home free by any means. Management may shift focus or, for some reason, decide to abort the change. Even though people are aware of the change, understand it, and are supporting it, if management aborts the change at this stage there will be no lasting impact from the effort. Until the next important threshold—the *commitment threshold*—is reached, the change is not permanent.

Commitment Phase

5. Installation

Installation moves change across the commitment threshold, and from the Acceptance Phase to the Commitment Phase. Installation occurs when the technology, systems, or procedures for a given change have been physically installed. But this does not mean that sufficient commitment has been reached. Physical systems can be de-installed and the change initiative aborted after initial utilization, and, as pointed out earlier, certain types of change require deeper levels of commitment than simple installation.

6. Adoption

Adoption, the first stage of real commitment, means that not only have the physical systems been installed, but people are actually using the new procedures or displaying the new behaviors. With adoption, the change moves beyond a limited "pilot" stage to a broader impact.

Some changes can be aborted even after widespread adoption—which is what happens when a new change supplants a prior change. For some types of change, adoption is insufficient—the change must be institutionalized.

7. Institutionalization

When a change has become institutionalized, it has become part of the organizational fabric. This means that there are usually permanent structures to support the change and that it is likely to be self-sustaining, even if those who led the change effort stop pushing.

For many types of change, particularly those dealing with physical installation of new systems, institutionalization is the highest level of commitment needed.

8. Internalization

Internalization is the highest form of commitment to a change. This happens when people have an internal motivation for the change—they wholeheartedly believe that the change is right and do not even have to think consciously about it. Changes that are internalized will often transcend a particular organizational setting. Someone who has learned to use a given problem-solving tool, for example, finds real value in it, believes in it, and will likely continue using that tool even if moved to a different organization, has truly internalized the change.

Part III explores the changes associated with a Development Effectiveness program in detail. Depending on their specific culture, change agents must decide for each change initiative what level of commitment is required and then plan how they will achieve that level. Change is expensive. It is important not to buy more commitment than is needed for a given change, but to make sure to buy enough for the change to succeed.

The next chapter, discusses the costs of a Development Effectiveness program and describes ways to justify the investment.

Notes

1. K. Lewin, "Group Decision and Social Change." In G. E. Swanson, T. N. Newcomb, and E. L. Hartley (Eds.), *Readings in Social Psychology* (New York: Henry Holt & Co., 1958: pp. 197–211).

2. Daryl R. Conner, *Managing at the Speed of Change* (New York: Villard Books, 1993: pp. 92–99).

3. James H. Billington, *Fire in the Minds of Men: Origins of the Revolutionary Faith* (New York: Basic Books Inc., 1983).

4. Chris Argyris, *Strategy, Change and Defensive Routines* (Boston: Pitman Publishing, 1985).

5. Daryl R. Conner, *Managing at the Speed of Change,* p. 148.

7

Commitment and Justification

> A change of the magnitude that is called for needs long-term commitment if it is to be carried through. Creating this commitment means presenting an objective justification for the change, as well as evidence that there will be benefits to be gained once the change has occurred. This chapter discusses the typical cost of a Development Effectiveness Program and approaches for building evidence that the expenditure can be justified. It also considers areas in which benefits can be found, how they can be achieved, and strategies to accelerate benefit realization.

Justifying and securing the commitment necessary for a transition to a high-performance development environment requires answers to a number of questions.

For example: What does it really cost to effect fundamental change in the systems delivery process? What is the business benefit of halving, say, the lead time from the identification of an information technology (IT)-enabled business opportunity to the implementation of a business solution? What is the value of a rigorous methodology that improves the quality and predictability of information systems and their delivery process? How does an investment in a library of reusable models and templates contribute to the business? What is the value of a development environment that adapts to changing business situations and is always able to respond more quickly than competitors?

Finally, can all these changes lead to results that pass traditional accounting tests, such as break-even analysis, return-on-investment, and hurdle rate, proving the value of the Development Effectiveness Program?

Though difficult, these are important questions to answer in order to build the justification for a Development Effectiveness effort. In a world of scarce resources, management increasingly asks for ways to assess, compare, and choose between different business investment options; those intended to improve the performance of the IT function are not exempted from this scrutiny.

Answers to these questions are also important in setting the stage for implementation management and follow through.

Investing in Fitness

Consider the difference between an individual who says, "I will invest $300 in an exercise bicycle so that I will lose 15 pounds," and one who says, "I will invest $300 in an exercise bicycle and $20 in a set of bathroom scales. I will exercise 30 minutes every day, weigh myself every week, and thereby lose 15 pounds over the next 6 months."

The second is more likely to benefit from the investment than the first, because the costs and benefits have been linked to the change process and a more realistic scenario has been developed that includes the cost of measurement. Most important, he has defined a process change that must occur—30 minutes exercise each day—to reach the desired outcome, and has explicitly linked the investment and result via process change.

A well-designed cost-justification approach can contribute significantly to sustaining the organizational and cultural change efforts associated with Development Effectiveness.

It is worth noting that some may ask, "Why bother with justifying the business case when the benefits of improving programming development are so obvious?" Intuitively, and to some extent empirically, information systems (IS) professionals and other technology proponents know that systems investments to improve business processes have paid back and will continue to do so.

However, the danger in relying on intuition and the need for a cautious and rigorous investment approach is well illustrated by a discussion we had with a CASE-tool vendor. The CEO of this company confided that he was in the software productivity tools business because it had an infinite marketplace. He believed that companies would always buy into the promise of improved software development productivity and, because customers would never realize the gains they needed or wanted, they would keep on investing in the promise.

Cynical though this position might be, there is ample evidence to support it. When our client work involves assessing current development environments, we often find literally dozens of tools with identical or overlapping functionality that have been acquired over time. Now, with the influx of PCs and workstations into the IS organization, we are seeing boxes full of CASE tools, programming aids, project-management tools, and so on, lying unused on IS department shelves—so-called shelfware.

Software maintenance fees alone can be significant, and yet because the tools are no longer used, they deliver no value—they just add cost and sometimes complicate forward migration. If the cost of the tools were added, taking into account acquisition cost, education, training, ongoing support, and lost productivity as the result of learning curve impacts, the investment would be enormous. Given that most tools never reach a critical mass of use, one can only surmise that the value delivered was insufficient to overcome organizational inertia and sustain their adoption. Of even greater concern than the cost, however, is the fact that shelfware serves as an artifact for future software archaeologists to find—a reminder of failed promises of productivity improvement and corroborating evidence for those who would preserve the status quo.

Let us look at some principles and approaches that have proven useful to the development of disciplined business rationales for initiating and managing Development Effectiveness Programs. We start by considering how one might demonstrate that the improvement of the development process is worth looking at in the first place. We move on to consider how the costs and benefits of improving an organization's development process can be ascertained. Finally, we examine an approach for relating a justification scenario to the ongoing management of the Development Effectiveness Program.

The ideas are drawn from consulting engagement experiences and from the results of multiclient and academic research programs. Academic research is included because the justification of Development Effectiveness activities is still an emerging practice. At this time, mixing and matching actual experiences with leading-edge thinking provides the richest set of ideas to work with in constructing the necessary justifications.

Establishing the Need for Action

A hurdle often encountered in starting a Development Effectiveness Program is lack of interest. The importance of Development Effectiveness must be established before the necessary focus on justification will receive the attention needed to initiate action. There are two basic approaches.

Sizing the Development Effort

The first approach uses the argument that an activity as large as application development demands that attention be paid to how effectively it is run. It starts by highlighting the proportion of its resources an organization allocates to development activities. An interesting way to do this was explored by the IS Leadership Multi-Client Research Program sponsored by the Ernst & Young Center for Information Technology and Strategy℠.

Two Categories of IS Expenditure

This approach begins by recognizing that IS organizations contribute to the business they are part of in two major ways. First, they support ongoing business operations through such activities as data-center operations, end user and departmental computing assistance, and corrective actions when problems arise in day-to-day operations. Second, they support the continuous efforts of a business to improve by proposing IT-enabled business changes and acquiring, developing, and modifying information processing systems and applications needed by the business. This division is consistent with the two major categories of Chapter 4's IT

Process Landscape: Ongoing Business Support and Creating Business Value.

The IS expenses in the category of Ongoing Business Support are part of the operational costs of doing business. They reflect the way things are. A company is usually dependent, to a large extent, on the systems these expenses represent, the result of hundreds of decisions made over the years by current and previous management. Moreover, although the systems may now be taken for granted, they still require IS to provide operational services, ongoing user support, and necessary repair or corrective actions. Furthermore, it is clear that "de-automating" them is not a viable option—continued expenditure is inevitable.

Creating Business Value is quite different. The IS expenses in this category are part of a company's efforts to improve and change. They support the creation of new functional applications. They provide new tools to assist managers and business professionals. They enable design and implementation of elements of the IT infrastructures that are increasingly necessary to remain competitive.

Significant Resources Allocated to Development Activities

Establishing the size of the resource pie allocated to development activities within IS is a first step to securing interest in improving Development Effectiveness. Our research has found that it is not uncommon for high-tech manufacturing companies to allocate about 2% of their overall business operating budget to the IS budget for Creating Business Value activities and 4% to Ongoing Business Support activities. An expenditure at the level of 2% of overall business operating budget deserves attention. It is no wonder that these companies are interested in improving the effectiveness of their application development activities.

Further, the argument can often be strengthened by noting that the resources allocated to IT for these purpose are usually only a small part of the total. In addition to the resources consumed by IS, there are many other business resources involved—

users who provide requirement statements, managers who sponsor projects, and so on. Effective development practices usually go far beyond IT and can improve the effectiveness of business change activities throughout a company.

Two Styles of Management

The division of IT expenses into two (or more) categories has value beyond ensuring that significant resources are allocated to development activities. Once a company understands where its expenditures fall, it can focus on a number of changes that may be necessary. For example, a company that realizes it is spending minimally on new value-adding systems may determine that it is robbing its future, and that it needs to reduce costs in ongoing systems support and free up more dollars for investment in systems to support new business processes.

Generally, a different management style is needed in each of the two categories. In Ongoing Business Support, an expense-oriented style of management is usually called for. Costs must be minimized without degrading service. To achieve this, the IS manager might consider the following steps:

- Setting unit cost reduction targets,
- Exploiting falling technology prices,
- Looking for elimination candidates, and
- Reconsidering "who does" each application (e.g., does outsourcing make sense?).

On the other hand, in Creating Business Value, an investment-oriented management style is usually proper. Here the objective is not to spend as little as possible but to spend wisely on as many initiatives as possible. Of course, whatever form an investment in IT takes, the reality is that the payback will not be immediate—and, indeed, that the level of eventual payback is uncertain. It is also a reality that a company is limited in the amount that can be invested, both by cash flow and capital constraints, and possibly by skills availability and the organization's ability to absorb change. These realities mean that choosing among IT investment options is both necessary and difficult. To deal with the challenge, managers must:

- Focus on "strategically important" opportunities,
- Allocate as many resources as possible to pursue these opportunities, and
- Exploit new approaches.

The last item listed leads naturally to ongoing Development Effectiveness programs. Although a manager may receive credit for "working on the right things" by paying attention to the first two items, credit for "doing things the right way" will come only through paying attention to improving the development process.

The Importance of Development in a Changing World

Another argument for focusing on Development Effectiveness grows out of the ideas underlying the concept of the *learning organization*.[1] It starts with the notion that the ability of an organization to learn is critical. In the words of Arie De Geus, the late head of planning at Royal Dutch Shell, "The ability to learn faster than your competitors may be the only sustainable competitive advantage." Learning, however, is not enough; there must be effective conversion of the lessons learned into new products and services. In most organizations this requires an effective development organization.

An approach for making visible, and therefore important, the capabilities of the development organization to support new business processes is to display the rate at which a business's installed application inventory is turning over. The concept is simple. Business processes are reflected in the IT systems that support them; some cynics even say that the processes are all too often "cast in concrete" by the supporting applications. Thus, if a business is to change its processes, the portfolio of installed applications must change.

Given this starting point, an analysis of the rate of change in the installed application inventory, coupled with current productivity rates and size of development staff, can be revealing. Consider the following example.[2] Assume a company has an installed application inventory of 100,000 Function Points, and that 8,000 of them are new or revised within the past year. Assume further that the company has 20 people in development and delivers new systems at a rate of 40 Function Points per work-month. From these figures it follows that:

- Eight % of the company's installed application inventory turned over in the past year, and
- Working at their current rate, the development team can, at best, change 9.6% of the installed application inventory each year.

These figures indicate the rate at which the company can change its IT-supported business processes. To totally replace its systems will take nearly 10 years. This rate might have been acceptable in earlier, less turbulent days, but in today's challenging environment it may spell the end of the company. Meeting competitive gambits, responding to processing requirements imposed by governmental and other external forces, and supporting new business strategies usually call for higher rates of installed application inventory turnover. Such an increase in development capability, without simply hiring more people, is one goal of a Development Effectiveness program.

What Does Development Effectiveness Cost?

The costs for creating a high-performance development environment break down into initial investment and ongoing costs. Within these two categories it is important to consider not just the cost of technology acquisition but the cost of technology transfer, including investments in human infrastructure and organizational change.

Initial investment includes technology (hardware, software), special one-time implementation costs (installation costs, special software to integrate tool sets into the existing environment, facilities costs, and so on), and initial costs for education and skills training. The initial investment associated with organizational change management includes awareness building, readiness assessment, vision setting, and transition planning (discussed in Chapter 8). The initial investment for establishing the human infrastructure will include methods engineering, tool support, knowledge-base management, quality management, change agents, and the training organization (discussed in Chapter 9). Ongoing costs include operating and maintaining the infrastructure, including support, operations, organizational change management, software license renewal, hardware maintenance, and administration.

Figure 7.1 shows an example of the costs involved in a Development Effectiveness initiative for an organization with 150 developers. This analysis makes many assumptions about the types and number of tools that development professionals will use, workstation costs, training costs, ratio of support staff to developers, and so on. However, it provides a good starting point for plugging in actual numbers associated with a specific improvement initiative.

It should also be noted that we have assumed a ratio of 1 development support consultant per 25 developers, which is a much higher ratio of support to developers than the 30:1 to 50:1 commonly recommended.[3] In many respects, it is this emphasis on human infrastructure for guiding and supporting the transition to a high-performance development environment that distinguishes the Development Effectiveness approach from traditional software development automation initiatives. Our experience is that underestimation of the human infrastructure resource is one of the most common causes of failure in development automation efforts. We have found the higher ratio essential, especially during the first year to 18 months of the effort.

Initial Investment	
Preparation	
Visioning workshops—3 × 1–day sessions	$ 12,000
Awareness Building—10 × 1/2–day sessions	20,000
Technology/organizational readiness assesment	50,000
Transition Planning—4 × 1/2–day sessions	8,000
Workstation hardware	
150 at $5000	750,000
Workstation software (150 at $7,500)	1,125,000
Mainframe software	750,000
Staff training	
Instructors: 100 days at $2,000/day	200,000
Staff time: 15 days/150 people at $200/day	450,000
Total investment cost	$3,365,000
Ongoing Costs	
Development Center support group	
6 people at $60,000 (salary and benefits)	$ 360,000
Hardware maintenance: 15%/year	112,500
Software maintenance	
Estimated at 15%/year for PC software	168,750
Estimated at 15%/year for mainframe software	112,500
Ongoing staff training	
15 days/person at $200/day	450,000
Total annual cost	$1,203,750
Summary	
Investment	$3,365,000
Annual cost	1,203,750

Figure 7.1 *The Cost of Development Effectiveness for 150 Developers*

We have also excluded outside consultants from the cost analysis as self-serving in a book from a consulting firm. Many organizations, however, do find significant benefits in using outside consultants to help implement a high-performance development environment. Consultants can provide product and method expertise, as well as diagnostic and assessment services, and can act as mentors and assist in accelerating knowledge transfer. Such services can help to ensure that the tools and methods are used correctly and help to reduce learning-curve effects. Given the shortage of organizational change management expertise, consultants can often supplement this knowledge and help to transfer change-agent skills to the organization. Consultants can also stay above the politics inherent in any organization and bring an independent perspective to the improvement effort.

However, the work cannot simply be delegated to outside consultants if the IS organization must truly change. If the goal is to create an isolated high-performance group with contractors, that is relatively easy to achieve, but the benefits disappear with the contractors. This is tantamount to outsourcing, which might be the appropriate strategic choice for all or part of IS. However, it is beyond the scope of this book.

Where Benefits Can Be Found and How They Can Be Achieved

The benefits derived from Development Effectiveness vary widely according to the perspective of the person or group evaluating them. As McGee and Prusak point out, "To a degree, information is in the eye of the beholder. . . . Information must be discussed in the context of specific users and decision makers."[4] Different audiences are concerned with different types of costs and benefits, so in preparing cost-benefits analyses, it is important to consider the ultimate audience and purpose of the analysis.

For example, senior executives, mainly concerned with the overall business contribution, will be interested in these aspects:

- Financial return from investment in IT
- IS responsiveness to business needs
- IS contribution to identifying IT-enabled business opportunities
- Direct revenue from sales of IT products and services

- Cost and performance of IS
- Quality of information
- Alignment between business and IT strategies
- Support for executive decision making

In contrast, functional or department-level managers are primarily concerned with the impact on particular business units or departments, including:

- Cycle time to respond to business needs
- Functional quality of information systems
- Business functions enabled by IT
- Information to support business unit decision making
- Working partnership with IS
- Cost of IT products and services
- IS service levels

IS management will be concerned with satisfying executives and user/customers, but also with internal performance of the IS organization, in such areas as these:

- Productivity and quality
- Robust measures of performance and improvement
- Predictability and control of projects
- Quality of communication within IS
- Ease of enhancement to delivered systems
- Team learning
- Improved staff morale and reduced turnover

Developers' primary interest, and the interest of the ultimate end users of application systems, in addition to satisfying demands of their management, is focused on such things as job design and individual and team growth and learning, including the following areas:

- Task variety
- Task significance
- Autonomy
- Feedback
- Technical and functional quality of delivered application
- Contributions to continuous improvement
- Ability to keep up with "state-of-the-art" technologies and methods
- Attitude and morale

Chapter 9 introduces a measurement framework based on these four perspectives.

Three Major Areas of Benefits

The benefits of Development Effectiveness are seen in three broad problem areas:

1. Reducing "waste" in the traditional development organization. Our experience shows that between 40% and 50% of IS resources are consumed by activities that do not contribute to meeting the real needs of IS customers. This wasted activity includes:

- Work on systems that are never completed, never implemented, or abandoned soon after implementation.
- Work that is defective from the perception of customers, which leads to rework.
- Work delivering functionality that is not used.

- Work on inter-application interfaces that would not be required if a robust IT architecture was leveraged.
- Work that unnecessarily duplicates functionality.
- Work that is inconsistent or incompatible with previously completed work, leading to rework.
- Systems that are needed but have not been delivered, including the application backlog and work-in-progress.

2. Easing the resource requirements for day-to-day operations and problem resolution:

- Virtually everyone in many IS organizations is working on new development, maintenance, or fire-fighting activities. Very few resources are focused on improving defective processes or on helping IS reengineer its processes.
- Insofar as there are improvement efforts under way, these are often uncoordinated or even in conflict with each other. A Development Effectiveness program dedicates resources to improving defective processes and coordinating important work.

3. Assisting in the adoption of new methods and technologies, and the shifts in beliefs, behaviors, skills, and organizational structure necessary both at all levels in the IS organization and within the IS customer base:

- Learning new skills and internalizing new beliefs are extremely difficult and require resources in organizational change management, as well as educated, informed, committed sponsorship from top and middle management levels, both within IS and throughout the business community.
- This kind of culture change takes time. Our research indicates that the time needed for traditional programmers to become proficient with full life-cycle CASE

tools is about 18 months.[5] Unfortunately, we live in an age of instant gratification and short-term focus. Recursively, getting management to accept a longer-term view of change itself requires a major culture change, which is difficult to achieve when people are so focused on the immediate term. A vicious circle!

Other sources of potential Development Effectiveness benefit opportunities should be surfaced through the cost of status quo as discussed in Chapter 6.

Justifying Change in Development Activities

Once awareness of the need to improve the development process is achieved, awareness that such improvement is possible must be established and the optimum process for achieving those improvements must be determined. This is where a justification scenario fits in. It provides quantified support for the story of change and improvement that lies ahead and a basis for establishing checkpoints and indicators to monitor progress and, if necessary, redirect efforts during the implementation period.

Traditional approaches to cost justification fall short, as we shall show. We therefore look to two relatively new, but promising, approaches for justifying a Development Effectiveness program: (1) development systems as infrastructure, and (2) the changes in work patterns enabled by new development systems.

Traditional Cost Justification

The traditional IS justification approach uses a cost displacement method. In this approach, a new system is justified if it displaces or avoids more costs than it incurs, by a certain margin.

Development Effectiveness investments, however, generally

do not fit the cost displacement paradigm. Such investments are usually intended to complement the users, not substitute for them. Benefits are stated in such terms as greater productivity, rather than decreased costs. Thus, approaches to justifying Development Effectiveness have to estimate tangible benefits from improved productivity. The basic goal is to show that the gains are greater than the initial and ongoing costs associated with the improvement initiative. A group of anticipated, but often difficult to quantify, benefits, referred to as "intangibles," may also be thrown into the mix to add weight to the justification. The following paragraphs consider a typical Development Effectiveness initiative from this perspective.

Productivity and the Basic Cost-Benefit Equation

On the cost side of the equation, there are initial, one-time costs associated with technology, including hardware, software, and communications. There are initial costs for education and training and one-time implementation costs, such as special software to integrate tool sets into the existing environment, facilities costs, and so on. There are also recurring costs associated with support, new employee training, operations, software license renewal, hardware maintenance, and administration.

On the savings side, there are tangible savings realized from increased productivity, usually estimated in terms of work-effort savings and typically calculated at fully burdened average systems developer costs. This is typically such a large cost item that even a modest productivity improvement—say 10% to 15%—translates into significant savings. Instead of the cost displacement model, whereby productivity gains are translated into cost savings—fewer people needed to complete a given amount of work—the benefits are taken as cost avoidance—more work achieved without additional hiring.

Pilot projects are often used to develop productivity improvement figures for use in justification scenarios. However, caution is advised if this route is taken; almost any reasonably designed pilot project can show far greater productivity improvements than 10%

to 15%. Indeed, the influence of the "Hawthorne Effect"[6] alone often leads to productivity increases approaching 10%. The issue is whether the results will be capable of being broadly applied, and sustainable over the long haul.

Sometimes a "reverse cost justification" approach is taken. In this approach the benefits needed to justify the total costs (taking into account internal rates of return, or hurdle rates) are first calculated. From this information is derived a productivity factor that would yield the needed benefits. If this number is within the realm of reasonableness, it is simply plugged into the justification scenario. If it is not, then pilot projects or other forms of demonstration are conducted to prove that the productivity factor is reasonable. The typical IS development budget is sufficiently large that even relatively small productivity increases can lead to significant savings.

Development tools have often been justified by anticipated impact on a single specific application system. The rationale is that this application is sufficiently large or strategic that increasing development productivity or reducing implementation time on that project alone will justify a major tool acquisition.

This approach, unfortunately, usually ignores overall organizational change issues and also fails to approach systems development holistically. Systems development is usually seen as a narrow issue of *programming*, or *methodology* or *project management*, or *information engineering*, or the like. Or, even worse, *maintenance* is seen as distinct from *development*.

This lack of a holistic approach means that tools are implemented without considering their relationships to the processes in which they are used. How the tool could contribute to continuous improvement, or enable process innovation, or even eliminate processes, is largely ignored. Reuse is often expected without investment in the infrastructure necessary to achieve it, and there is rarely a formal mechanism to transfer the technical learning from the initial project to other projects and teams.

These shortcomings virtually doom the chances of a single project's realizing the high expectations for the tool investment. However, even if the project is a success, the lack of organizational learning and infrastructure confines success to the initial project. All other projects either continue to stumble along using traditional methods or become their own mini-universes, each justifying yet another new development tool. Thus the cycle of institutionalized pilots and experiments continues, and fundamental change is once again frustrated.

Cycle Time

Increasingly, benefits associated with cycle-time reduction and quicker response to IT-enabled business opportunities are being added to the cost-benefit equation. Although learning-curve effects may initially lessen these savings, once proficiency has been reached the acceleration of benefits produced by new systems can be significant—particularly if they are associated with business strategies that depend on or are enhanced by rapid time-to-market.

Quality

In addition to improvements in productivity and cycle time, a Development Effectiveness program can have a significant impact on quality. Analysis and design tools, rigorous systems methodologies, cross-functional teams and joint, facilitated design sessions can allow systems to match business requirements more closely than has been typically achievable without these approaches. Code generation, prototyping, and other systems development tools can lead to far fewer operating defects than result from traditionally programmed systems.

These improvements in both functional and technical quality provide significant benefits, although they are more difficult to quantify than productivity benefits. The savings attributable to reductions of waste and rework can also be estimated, and these can be significant. The overall business value will be a function of the nature of the application. For example, high functional quality in a marketing application designed to increase sales-order volume by 15% could have far greater impact than high functional quality in an internal financial accounting application.

Other Benefits

The inclusion of cycle time and defect-level improvements among the benefits in justification scenarios is an indication that a new wave of thinking about business measurements is taking hold.[7] Purely financial measures are inadequate to guide management decision making today; a richer set of measures (e.g., process measures, customer measures, employee measures) are necessary to understand the ins and outs of a rapidly changing business environment. Thus, many items not previously considered are receiving increased attention. Some, like cycle time and defect levels, are reasonably easy to quantify. Others are less tangible.

Intangible benefits are often the most compelling. Improved morale, ease of recruiting and retaining qualified personnel, increased organizational flexibility, improved organizational planning, and promotion of organizational learning are all benefits that can be expected from a Development Effectiveness program. Similarly, improved customer satisfaction, timelier access to information, better utilization of assets, and improved decision making are among the benefits that business units may experience from a more effective systems delivery capability.

However, quantifying these factors, and accurately determining the likelihood of achieving them can be difficult. Suggested values are easily challenged. Nevertheless, some companies have found at least a partial way around this problem—developing assessment scales for items they value. For example, one company decided that projects that improve its ability to respond to competitive thrusts should be favored. Each potential project is rated on a five-point scale ranging from "major impact" to "no impact." Though such a scheme does not result in a dollar value, it provides a way to compare competing projects and has the additional benefit of making visible the organization's values.

Nontraditional Approaches

As stated earlier, traditional approaches to cost justifying investments in increased development productivity have fallen short.

First, the cost side of the equation is often significantly understated and frequently ignores the human and infrastructure investment necessary. Second, and of greater concern, the benefits side of the equation is rarely realized. Is this because the estimated benefits are unrealistic? Or does poor implementation prevent them from being realized? Our experience indicates the latter. Clients' predicted benefits are often modest and theoretically easily achieved. Yet implementation and follow-through are so poor that even these modest gains go unrealized. The results are skepticism about many proposed systems development automation initiatives and dissatisfaction with the outcomes of those attempted.

Skepticism has been further heightened by the appearance of highly publicized studies on the failure of IT investments to pay back in productivity gains at the national level.[8] Although a thoughtful review of their findings often reveals gaps in the research (for example, many fail to account for increases in quality; others include government data which, almost by definition, introduces a "no productivity change" element), there is no question that they are having an impact on executives' perceptions.

An approach for addressing this concern is presented in the final section of this chapter, "The Value Management Framework." Before turning to the implementation issue, however, we believe there are also several new ways of looking at investments in Development Effectiveness that position the efforts in a different light or better describe potential benefits. Although these are not in wide use at this time, they open up promising avenues for the development of future approaches to justifying efforts in process improvement.

Development Effectiveness Systems as Infrastructure

The challenge of cost justifying the systems delivery function, and improvements to this function, takes on a new form when viewed from the perspective of infrastructure. Infrastructure can either enable the response to business opportunities or inhibit that response. Insofar as the right infrastructure exists, moving from the recognition of an IT-enabled business opportunity to the provision of an IT solution is simple. If there is no infrastructure, or the wrong infrastructure, moving from opportunity to solution can be a nightmare.

What Is Infrastructure?

Infrastructure is first and foremost a *shared* resource. It typically refers to aspects of the physical and human environment shared for the public good: streets, bridges, sewers, languages, monetary systems, and even schools.[9] An IT infrastructure enables IT capabilities and provides a platform for future business capabilities. Peter Weill defines IT infrastructure as "the base foundation of IT capability budgeted for and provided by the information systems function and shared across multiple business units or functional areas. The IT capability includes both the technical and managerial expertise required to provide reliable services."[10]

Weill notes that IT infrastructure is:

- Shared across most functional areas or business units,
- Budgeted for and provided by the information systems function,
- Necessary investment that business units for functional areas are unlikely to make,
- The enabling foundation for application systems that support the business processes, and
- Costly to change in both financial and political terms.

The most visible infrastructure elements include hardware, operating software, and communications technology. However, for these hard assets to be shareable there must be softer components to the infrastructure, including policies, architecture designs, operating principles, methods, data standards, and so on.

Infrastructure is relative. To a business unit executive, the corporate mainframe and shared applications are infrastructure,

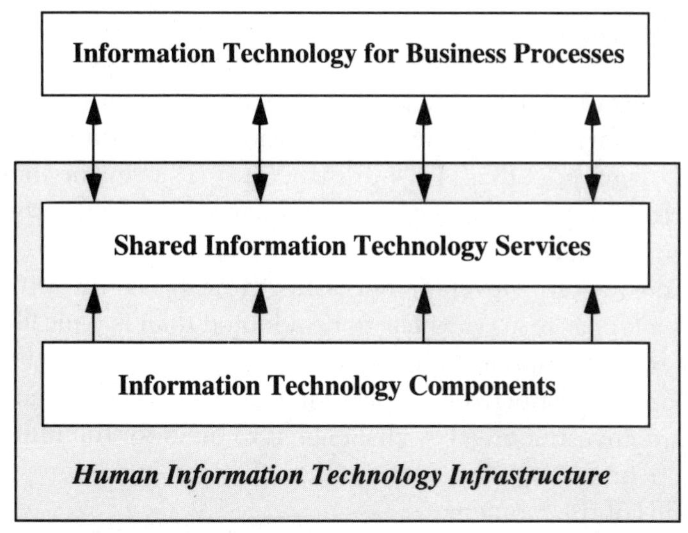

Figure 7.2 *The Structure of IT Infrastructure*

whereas the departmental computer and work-group local area networks within the business unit are dedicated resources. To the departmental head, the departmental computer is infrastructure, but the work-group local area networks are dedicated resources. To the work groups, the work-group local area networks are infrastructure, but the workstations are part of the business application.

McKay and Brockway describe infrastructure as comprising two layers—the IT components at the base and shared IT services on top of this base.[11] The human IT infrastructure of knowledge, skills, and experience molds these two levels together into the enterprise's IT infrastructure, as seen in Figure 7.2.

Applying Infrastructure Concepts to Development

Approaching the systems delivery capability as infrastructure, and viewing the costs associated with improving this capability as infrastructure investments, points to a new way to position Development Effectiveness. It also highlights both the difficulty in cost justifying such investments and some of the dangers inherent in traditional ROI (return on investment) approaches.

IT infrastructure does not in and of itself provide business benefit. Benefits are derived from the business systems enabled by the infrastructure. An IT infrastructure provides a business with the flexibility to respond to business opportunities. Peter Keen[12] contends that IT infrastructure is a major business resource and, perhaps, one of the few sources of long-term competitive advantage.

Looking at Development Effectiveness as infrastructure means a longer-term view has to be adopted than is typically used with functional applications. It must also be understood that the Development Effectiveness plan changes over time. In an infrastructure investment, a key challenge is to build for the future and to keep future options open, rather than to build for just the demands of the moment.

With regard to an appropriate management approach for treating infrastructure investments, a current trend is to speak in terms of "stealth infrastructure," hiding infrastructure investments within other projects. The rationale is understandable; given that so few top managers understand the importance of infrastructure, it is often easier to tack investments onto well-supported projects "on the sly," rather than to fight the uphill battle of education. Increasingly, however, this approach will not succeed, particularly as IT resources become more widely distributed throughout an enterprise. Instead, IS management will need to:

- Make IT capabilities and infrastructure issues more visible, and
- Relate these investments to the long-term vision of the business (particularly with regard to the need for flexibility and future technology enablement).

N. Venkatraman suggests that companies view the role of IT infrastructure from one of three perspectives: *independent*, *reactive* or *interdependent*.[13]

From an *independent* perspective, the development of infrastructure takes place outside the strategic context; infrastructure is viewed as a utility and is treated as an administrative expense.

Companies with a *reactive* perspective develop infrastructure in response to a particular strategic thrust; infrastructure plans are derived from the business plans and infrastructure is treated as a necessary business expense.

Companies with an *interdependent* perspective develop and modify infrastructure in constant coalignment with the strategic context of the business; IT infrastructure identifies and responds to business strategies and is viewed as a business investment.

Understanding which of these perspectives best describes the view of systems development in a given organization helps determine how to position the justification scenario for Development Effectiveness.

New Work Patterns

New development approaches often lead to new work patterns. For example, joint application design sessions require selected users to devote a concentrated period of time to participating in the planning meetings. Some of the new object-oriented approaches expect users to do more of their own application development. Projected benefits assume that these work-pattern changes will be made; if they are not, benefits will not be fully realized, if at all.

The expected changes in work patterns and the question of what work substitutions will take place complicate the development of justification scenarios. Simple cost displacement (i.e., the "time saved multiplied by salary" model) is no longer an adequate method for understanding the situation—especially if the time saved is not reallocated productively. Whereas the value of traditional computer systems is often to substitute computer power for routine labor, the value of many development automation efforts lies in their power to allow professionals throughout an enterprise to enhance their performance by changing work patterns and reallocating work.

One possible way to factor in work-pattern changes is the "hedonic wage model," which has been applied to office systems justification to address similar problems.[14] Underlying the application of the hedonic model is the recognition that employees involved in development activities perform a variety of tasks of different intrinsic value to their organization. It further recognizes that restructured work patterns are a major potential benefit of new IT systems. These recognitions lead to IT benefits that are based not only on increased efficiency—doing more of a given task in the same time—but also on increased effectiveness—reallocating higher-value and lower-value tasks to different employees.

A full treatment of the hedonic wage model is beyond the scope of this book. Its underlying assumptions, drawn from economics, are that:

- Management allocates resources in an efficient manner.
- Workers allocate time among available tasks efficiently.
- For each labor class (e.g., managers, developers, end users) there is a set of tasks that is appropriate for the members of the class to do. And, as work patterns shift, tasks of comparable value to current tasks remain to be done.

Given these assumptions, the following steps are required to use the approach:

- The employees involved (now or in the future) in development are grouped into employee classes.
- The activities performed by those falling in the selected employee classes are established.
- A profile of the time spent by members of each employee class performing each activity type is constructed.
- The marginal costs associated with each employee class (typically based on wages, fringe benefits, and direct overhead) and labor budget constraints are determined.
- With this data, a set of equations is solved for the marginal values associated with each employee class.

- Next, a work profile of the work distribution that will prevail after the new development system is implemented is constructed (comparing the old and new profiles highlights the changes in work patterns that are expected to occur).
- With the data now in hand, benefit figures are derived, using the calculated marginal values and the two work profiles. They are compared with the costs of the new system, which are collected as usual.

The primary difference between the hedonic model and the simpler "time saved multiplied by salary" model is the explicit recognition of the interplay of shifting tasks among employees as work patterns change. The simpler model does not recognize the changing mix of work in each employee class (i.e., the mix of work in any time saved is assumed to be the same as the mix of work before any changes are made). The model also helps surface the need to consider all the employee classes involved in the change, not just the changes that will take place in IS.

The hedonic model has been used successfully in a number of office systems studies by Fortune 50 corporations.[15]

The Value Management Framework

Once a decision has been made to invest in improving the systems-delivery process, there remains the challenge of measuring its success against the long-term goals it was designed to meet. We present here a way to measure Development Effectiveness success incrementally, to ensure steady progress toward the desired benefit, and to make timely corrections when the initiative has wandered off track.

This method, encapsulated in the Value Management Framework developed by Kathleen Foley Curley and John Henderson,[16] begins with the idea that there are linkages between investments in information technology and the outcomes from that investment. In the "Investing in Fitness" example given earlier in this chapter, the $300 investment in the exercise bicycle does not lead to the desired weight loss. The bicycle *enables* the 30 minutes of daily exercise that leads to weight loss; it is the exercise that is important. In fact, the $300 investment in the exercise bicycle can be weighed against other technologies that might enable the 30 minutes of daily exercise and lead to the 15-pound weight loss. There may be other technologies that enable exercises that burn calories more efficiently and can achieve the same result for 20 minutes of daily exercise—or a combination of diet and exercise might increase weight loss efficiency even further.

Moreover, the $20 investment in bathroom scales does not produce the weight loss, but provides a feedback mechanism to the dieter to help motivate and guide him toward the goal.

The Value Management Framework has both horizontal and vertical dimensions. The horizontal dimension, shown in Figure 7.3, connects investments in information technology to expected outcomes via anticipated process changes. Each element in the horizontal chain may have separate performance measures attached.

The implications of this linkage for measuring the contribution of Development Effectiveness are important. Ultimately, the proof of an IS investment must be assessed by its impact on economic performance. The problem, however, is that the impact cannot be measured in the short term; indeed, it may even be unmeasurable in the long term because of other variables. By contrast, the investment in a new system in terms of enabling technol-

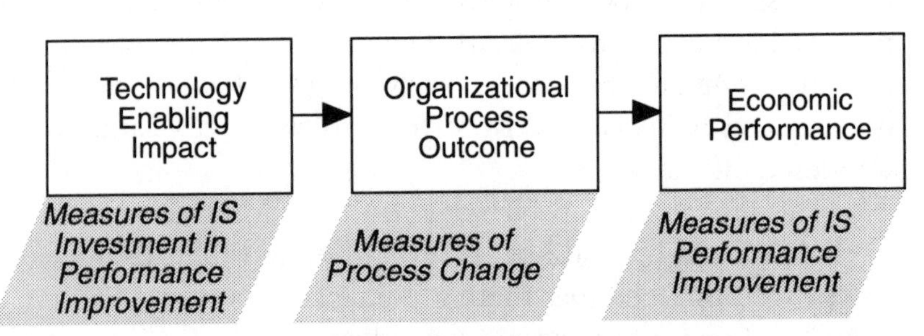

Figure 7.3 *Horizontal Linkage Between IS and the Business Outcome*

ogy can be discerned relatively quickly and easily—either it provides the intended functionality or it does not. Between these two points is the process impact, which can be discerned in the medium term. The fact that these three are linked means that it is possible to discover short- and medium-term measurements that can serve as "long-term indicators" for long-term success.

Similarly, there are vertical linkages between the actions of individual employees, the effectiveness of their work group, and the success of the business unit as a whole, as shown in Figure 7.4. Again, the performance measures applied at the individual, work group, and business unit levels are not the same. It is important, however, that they be consistent and coherent. To the extent they are, individual and work group success measures can serve as leading indicators of business unit success.

When horizontal and vertical linkages are combined, they create the matrix shown in Figure 7.5, a useful framework for displaying, understanding, and monitoring the payback of an IT investment. To use it, a manager fills in each box with the performance measures that will be employed to evaluate success at that

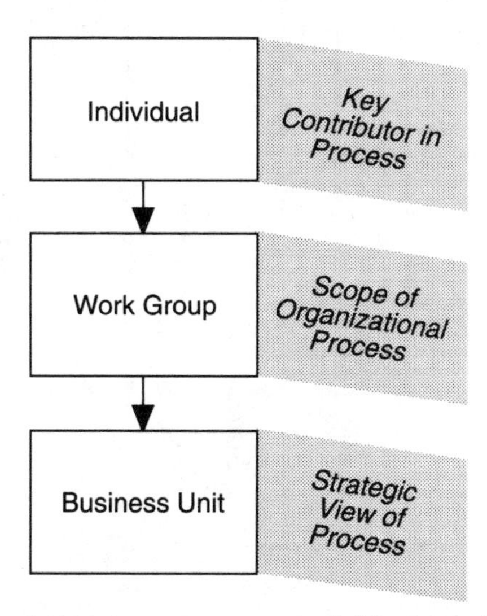

Figure 7.4 *Vertical Linkage Between Individual, Work Group, and Business Unit Actions*

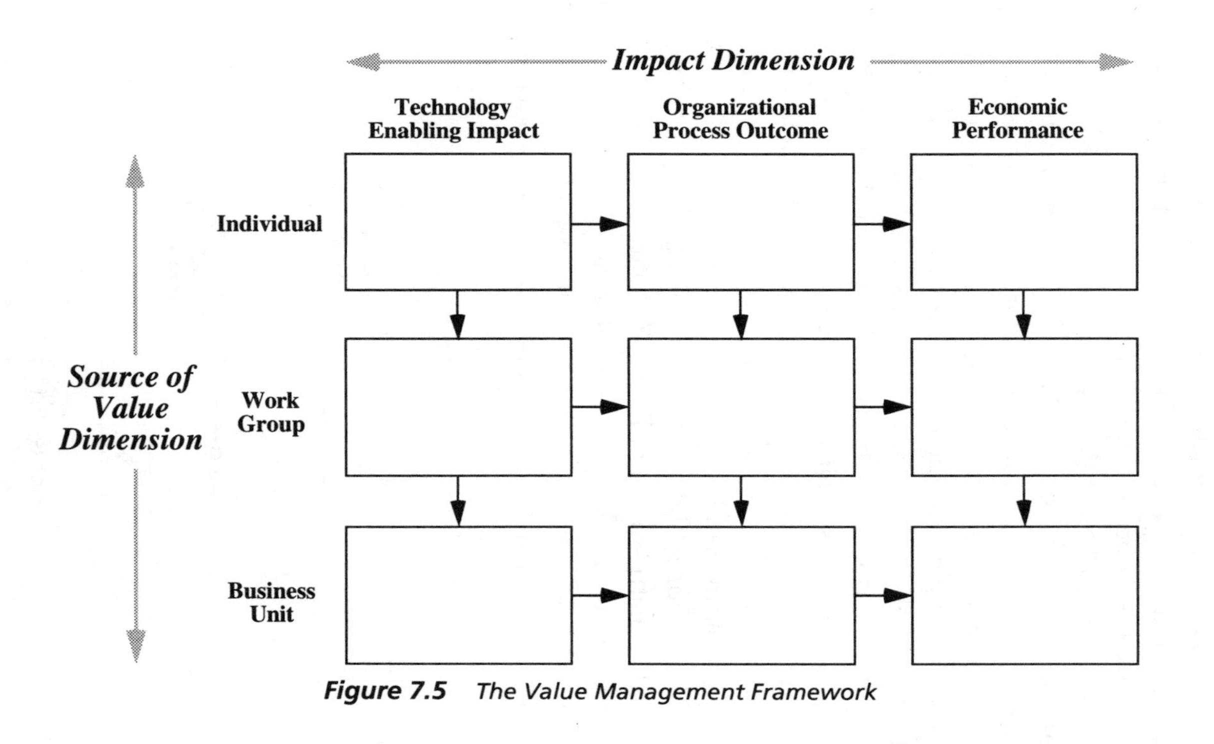

Figure 7.5 *The Value Management Framework*

level. This means beginning at the box in the lower right—which includes the performance of the business unit as a whole—and asking some very basic questions: what is it that the business is ultimately trying to achieve with this investment, and how will it know when that has been achieved? Measures at this level for a Development Effectiveness investment might be expressed in terms of reduced operational costs, faster customer response, or improved satisfaction of business requirements; whatever the measure, it should relate directly to what have been identified as the critical success factors or values of the business.

The manager then works back from those measures to fill in the remaining boxes. It is important to note that as the focus shifts toward the top left of the framework, measures become more straightforward and definitive, yet remain consistent and linked. No performance measure listed at the organizational level, for example, should motivate actions inconsistent with the business unit goals. Rather, every measure specified should be a driver of the measures in boxes below and to the right of it.

Shoshana Zuboff [17] points out that technology used to automate a function can also generate new streams of information. For example, the supermarket scanner that automated the checkout operation also yields tremendous information that can be used for inventory control, market analysis, and more. She calls this ability to generate new information as a by-product of automation "informating." Similarly, improvement systems can be "informated" by considering the investment, process impact, and outcomes for different audiences that are part of the cost-justification approach and by designing appropriate instrumentation into the systems.

To the extent that the performance measures listed are consistent and linked, the Value Management Framework provides a means of evaluating how well the improvement initiative is progressing toward its long-term goals at interim points in the short and medium term. Already tested by Henderson and Curley in several corporate environments,[18] the framework has proven useful and holds great promise for every organization that must manage IT investment spending for maximum payback.

Benefit Realization Accelerators

Chapters 9 and 10 emphasize the critical roles of Pathfinder projects as the points at which some of the earliest business benefits are achieved. In fact, the size and timing of benefits should be considered when choosing among potential Pathfinder candidates.

Although we caution about the dangers of using one major strategic application for the purposes of justifying development automation, it is reasonable to pick a set of Pathfinder projects that stage benefits realization in terms of benefit type, beneficiary, and timing.

We also discuss, in Chapter 8, the use of pilot projects to demonstrate that improvement is possible. Even though these pilots are used to secure sponsorship for transition, rather than to support the transition process itself, the benefits they yield can be positioned as benefits of the overall Development Effectiveness program and thereby accelerate benefit realization.

Sometimes the early benefits of a Development Effectiveness program manifest themselves in unforeseen ways and may even fail to be recognized as benefits. We have seen several CASE projects, for example, that were canceled during early joint design sessions. This happened because the new development process, with its redefined roles for business partners, surfaced the fact that the original perceived problem was actually a symptom of a different problem—one that would have to be solved through a different project or approach. Under the old development process, the IS development team would have tried to solve the original problem, the resulting system having to be abandoned, either prior to or at delivery. The waste of resources prevented by the new process is a real benefit and one that is achieved quickly, but it needs to be recognized as such. The danger with such a success is that it might be recognized, for example, as 1 person-month of analysis activity wasted. In reality, it is 24 person months of development activity saved! Benefits are often a matter of perception, and advocates for improvement must always take perceptions into account and continuously be "marketing" their successes. Even for pilot projects, measurement is essential to provide data for the benefit marketing campaign.

Chapter 8 discusses the need to assess the cost of status quo. Addressing this should surface particular problem areas, some of which might be candidates for early benefit realization. Given that nothing breeds success like success, every advantage should be taken of these opportunities. Pathfinder projects should be viewed as parts of a "portfolio," so that short-term opportunities are mixed in with medium- and long-term opportunities and the different potential audiences for the benefits can all share in the outcomes.

Notes

1. Peter M. Senge, *The Fifth Discipline: The Art and Practice of the Learning Organization* (New York: Doubleday, 1990).

2. The example uses Function Points, a common measure of application size and complexity, to quantify the size of the application inventory and the development organization's productivity. See *Function Point Practices Manual* by The International Function Point Users Group, Blendonview Office Park, 5008-28 Pine Creek Drive, Westerville, OH 43081-4899. Any other measure of application inventory size and development organization productivity can be used in a similar manner to make the same points.

3. Barbara Bouldin, *Agents of Change* (Englewood Cliffs, NJ: Yourdon Press, 1989).

4. James McGee and Laurence Prusak, *Managing Information Strategically* (New York: John Wiley & Sons, 1993).

5. Gregory H. Boone, Vaughan P. Merlyn, and Roger E. Dobratz, *The Second Annual Report on CASE* (Bellevue, WA: CASE Research Corporation, 1990: pp. 166–169). Now available from Ernst & Young.

6. This refers to the work of Elton Mayo, an industrial psychologist, which led to a series of experiments, called the Hawthorne Experiments, conducted at Western Electric's Hawthorne Facility. Although these experiments led to significant findings in terms of principles of individual and group involvement in quality programs, they are most famous for one finding, the so-called Hawthorne Effect. This term resulted from an experiment in which productivity was observed to increase when the lighting level was increased. When the level was then decreased, to the researchers surprise, productivity again increased. The ultimate interpretation is that people perform better when they are the focus of attention and when they try something new.

7. Robert G. Eccles, "The Performance Measurement Manifesto," *Harvard Business Review* 69: 1 (January–February 1991): 131–137; Robert S. Kaplan and David P. Norton, "The Balanced Scorecard: Measures That Drive Performance," *Harvard Business Review* 70: 1 (January–February 1992): 71–79; James V. McGee, *What Is Strategic Performance Measurement?* Center for Information Technology and Strategy[SM] Research Note (Boston: Ernst & Young, March 1992).

8. Stephen S. Roach, "Technology and the Service Sector: The Hidden Competitive Challenge," *Technological Forecasting and Social Change* 34:4 (December 1988): 387–403.

9. Thomas H. Davenport and Jane Linder, "Information Technology Infrastructure: The New Competitive Weapon?" Draft, (Boston, MA: Ernst and Young and Harvard Business School, July 1993).

10. Peter Weill, "The Role and Value of Information Technology Infrastructure: Some Empirical Observations." Center for Information Systems Research Working Paper No. 240 (Cambridge, MA: Massachusetts Institute of Technology, May 1992).

11. D. T. McKay and D. W. Brockway, "Building I/T Infrastructure for the 1990s," *Stage by Stage*, (Cambridge, MA: Nolan Norton, 1989).

12. Peter G. W. Keen, *Shaping the Future: Business Design Through Information Technology* (Boston: Harvard Business School Press, 1991).

13. N. Venkatraman, "IT-Induced Business Reconfiguration." In Michael S. Scott Morton, (Ed.), *The Corporation of the 1990s: IT and Organizational Transformation* (Oxford, England: Oxford University Press, 1991): 122–158.

14. Peter G. Sassone, "Cost-Benefit Methodology for Office Systems," *ACM Transactions on Office Information Systems* 5:3 (July 1987): 273–289.

15. Ibid.

16. Kathleen Foley Curley, and John C. Henderson, "Valuing and Managing Investments in Information Technology: A Review of Key Model." Draft, Northeastern University and Boston University, (Boston, MA: July 1990).

17. Shoshana Zuboff, *In the Age of the Smart Machine: The Future of Work and Power* (Oxford, England: Heinemann Professional Publishing, 1988).

18. For an excellent case example, see James D. Foley and John C. Henderson's article, "Assessing the Value of Corporate Wide Human Resource Information System: A Case Study," to appear in a forthcoming issue of *Journal of Systems Management*.

PART III

A Framework for Transition

Part III describes the overall Development Effectiveness transition framework. We break the framework into three pieces: *getting ready for transition, planning the transition process,* and *managing the transition projects.*

Successful transition to a high-performance development environment requires that all affected parties have a high level of awareness about the need for change, the opportunities for change, and the change process itself. They need a compelling, shared vision of the future state, one that contains sufficient detail for people to understand the behavior changes expected from them. Against this vision, an organization assesses its readiness to reach the future state from the perspective of both technical infrastructure and human resources. Chapter 8 deals with these awareness building, vision setting, and readiness assessment activities.

Chapter 9 shows how to build a comprehensive transition plan driven by the differences between the future-state vision and current reality. The plan focuses on implementing and validating the required infrastructure incrementally through "Pathfinder" projects, and addresses the ongoing management of the transition process, to ensure that change sponsorship is sustained and reward structures are aligned with the change.

Chapter 10 further describes the Pathfinder process and provides guidelines on selecting, staffing, and managing Pathfinder projects.

To sustain the high performance levels that are required from IS development organizations, the end state of a Development Effectiveness program is one in which improvement is continuous. Chapter 11 examines the implications and describes the characteristics of a continuously improving IS delivery process.

A few words are necessary to explain the Development Effectiveness Transition Framework, and its icons, illustrated below.

Although the Transition Framework is graphically represented as linear and structured, in practice the processes and

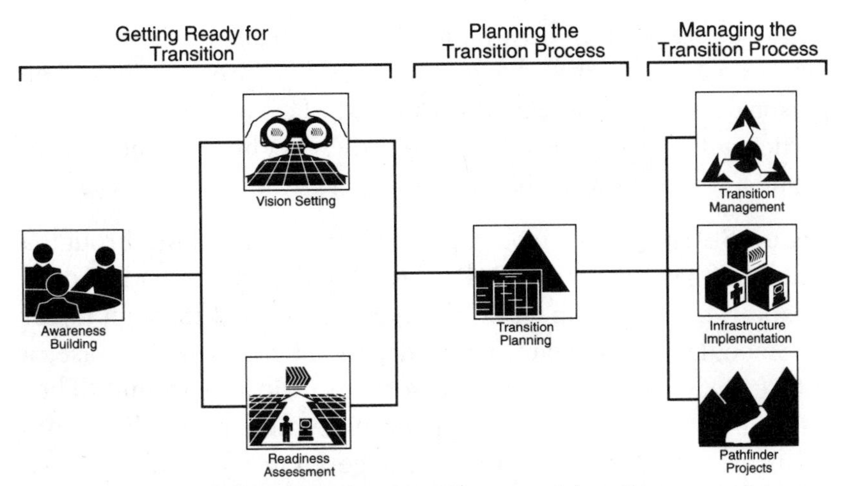

The Development Effectiveness Transition Framework

activities that comprise each component overlap, iterate, and can occur in almost any conceivable sequence. While at the highest level of abstraction it is useful to discuss the components sequentially, the reality of a given organization's situation might dictate that the process begins somewhere other than at the logical beginning—with a Pathfinder project, or Infrastructure program, for example. Certain components may be repeated over and over, at different levels of detail, or for different groups, dealing with different aspects of an overall change initiative. So many mini-projects associated with change may occur simultaneously that an overall sequence might not be discernible. However, for the purposes of communicating the intent of the Transition Framework, we will work logically from Awareness building through to Pathfinder projects.

The Transition Framework icons are intended to convey key concepts associated with each component, as follows:

Awareness Building. Although this activity typically conjures thoughts of seminars, presentations, and classroom education, we have chosen a "roundtable discussion" image to emphasize this often neglected, yet important technique for building awareness.

Group discussion can be a more effective means of communicating key issues around change, compared to presentations. The personal attention associated with face-to-face discussion, and the participants' opportunity to express their feelings about change create a sense of ownership.

Vision Setting. This icon represents the future state through a graphic image of the IT Process Landscape, introduced in Chapter 4. This is shown on the horizon, viewed through a pair of binoculars. Binoculars bring distant objects (in this case, a future-state vision of IT processes) into the foreground. They take far away objects that appear fuzzy and bring them into focus. They also add depth by exaggerating the 3-dimensional effect, just as Vision Setting adds depth and clarity to the future-state vision.

Readiness Assessment. This icon depicts the future-state IT Process Landscape on the distant horizon, with "people" and "technology" superimposed in the foreground, distanced from the horizon. This image emphasizes that there are both human and technological aspects to assessing an organization's readiness to reach its future-state vision.

Transition Planning. In addition to the prototypical Gantt chart planning icon, we have included the "delta" symbol representing change. Transition Planning is not just about planning the various programs and projects that comprise Development Effectiveness, but also about planning the cultural and organizational change implied by the transition to the future state.

Transition Management. This icon also uses the prototypical "delta" symbol to imply change, this time containing a symbolic representation of a cycle, emphasizing that continuous improvement is a never-ending cycle, and that change is an ongoing process.

Infrastructure Implementation. The icon depicts the three building blocks of infrastructure—people, process (as depicted by the IT Process Landscape graphic), and technology—reinforcing all facets of infrastructure.

Pathfinder Projects. Like a path through the mountains, Pathfinder projects help identify the way forward, through the known and unforeseen obstacles.

8

Getting Ready

This Chapter shows why *awareness building* is needed and why we cannot solve a problem we do not know or believe exists. We discuss how to find and present evidence that there is a problem and that it needs attention. "Setting a Vision" introduces an approach to deciding what the future state of information systems (IS) development should look like and examines techniques for creating and communicating such a vision. In "Assessing Readiness" we look at the need for a baseline from which to plan for transition to the future state. Organizations start from very different positions, and where an enterprise is now affects both where it wants to be and how it can get there. This chapter introduces instruments that can be used to characterize the current position and assess readiness for (and ability to) change.

Awareness Building

Most senior IS managers feel, and some will even admit[1] that all is not as well as it could be. For many of these managers, the problem is that resources are spent repeatedly to introduce and deploy new technology rather than to make better use of the technology and people they already have.

Much IS organizational energy is therefore diverted to solving problems related to symptoms, rather than to the real causes of the IS organization's ills. The idea of solving symptom-related problems is seductive. Such problems are usually limited in scope. They are real, so that solving them seems to make things better. Moreover, they often can actually be solved, which gives people a sense of achievement. Unfortunately, in most instances the IS organization remains ill and acquires another round of symptoms that requires another round of solutions, and so on.

This kind of situation, called a *type 3 error,* is very hard to eradicate. In the original theory of errors, there were two types of error. Type 1 errors related to situations in which a correct hypothesis was incorrectly rejected by a statistical test. Type 2 errors involved the incorrect acceptance of an invalid hypothesis, again using statistical testing.

Management strategists in the mid-1980s extended this error model to a third category, in which a correct hypothesis is accepted, but the hypothesis is not actually related to the nature of the problem that must really be addressed.

It is only by studying the situation as a whole that the futility of attacking symptoms instead of causes becomes visible. The key is to build awareness within the IS organization that symptoms alleviation is not necessarily true problem solving.

There is virtually no limit to the number of tactics that can be used to build greater awareness of an issue within an organization. Development Effectiveness identifies the basic categories of awareness that are most important to achieve and some of the specific methods to consider. We do not pose an exhaustive list of ways to build awareness, but rather offer a framework to help guide efforts and stimulate creative thinking. In any event, the organizational and human dynamics of any real-world organization mean that awareness building must be an ongoing process.

Commitment Requires Awareness

As demonstrated in Chapter 6, commitment is essential in successfully implementing a new development environment within the IS organization. An awareness–building process begins to establish commitment by identifying and publicizing:

1. The need to create a more effective development and maintenance environment, perhaps by contrasting the current levels of performance within the IS organization with those of competitors or with the needs of business partners
2. The opportunities available to create an effective development environment, often by focusing on where internal best practices are apparent but not yet widely used
3. The change process necessary to achieve improvements in effectiveness, productivity, and quality

If the change to a new environment is to be implemented effectively, *informed commitment*—not just consent—is necessary. Informed commitment includes an understanding of the technical methods, techniques, and tools to be integrated in the new environment. More important, however, informed commitment requires a realistic understanding of the change process, the cost of change, the cost of the status quo—the consequences of *not* changing—and the roles required to effect the change successfully.

During awareness building, education must be provided on these issues of organizational change, as well as on the technical environment in which the change will occur.

What then does an organization contemplating Development Effectiveness need to be aware of?

- The cost of the status quo
- The existence of opportunities in the new environment
- Paradigm shifts
- Change processes and issues related to managing organizational change
- The cost of change
- The need to assess the current state

Each of these subjects is examined in more detail in the following paragraphs.

Cost of the Status Quo

Few organizations will choose to undergo the effort of change if the status quo is perceived as adequate or even as comfortable. The pain of continuing to work in old, inadequate ways must be great enough to propel the organization into attempting the change process. Creating recognition of the *cost of the status quo* is therefore essential early in the awareness-building process, as it helps to form a foundation for continued justification and commitment to change. For many people in the development organization, the status quo is not a problem, it is a fate. Development just takes a long time, and is error-prone. Unless these individuals are shown evidence, in their frame of reference, that convinces them that there are burning problems within development, change will not happen.

The key to building an awareness of the cost of status quo is to surface and make visible information that will generate discomfort about a dysfunctional current state. This does not necessarily require detailed, quantifiable numbers for quality or productivity in the IS organization, although these numbers help if they are available and reliable enough to be believed. Rather, the information needs to point out the "pain" that will be experienced if a change is not made.

Such pain could be experienced because of real danger of budget cuts, reduction in staff, outsourcing, or a perceived lost opportunity to use new tools or technology. For executives, pain in the status quo is best tied to the business goals and business value that the IS department is or is not providing. For workers and mid-level managers, pain is best related to issues within their frames of reference. Exposing the cost of status quo can "thaw out" an otherwise frozen current environment so that at least a critical mass of the organization and the majority of its leadership perceive that continuing operations in their present form is risky and undesirable.

A couple of techniques useful in surfacing the cost of status quo issues are a "cost of quality assessment," and "customer satisfaction survey."

Cost of quality examines estimates of costs due to defect detection, defect prevention, rework, and cost associated with failure. Sometimes, the cost of work-in-progress is included as cost of quality. For most IS organizations, and for most IT processes, the cost of quality lies between 40% and 50% of the total cost associated with the process—more than enough to stimulate major change!

Customer satisfaction surveys examine customer perceptions along several dimensions of system and service quality, assessing customer ratings, and the importance that customers attach for each rating area. For example, a "poor" rating against an attribute that the customers considered "important" would be a major problem. Although it may be difficult to attach hard costs to customer satisfaction surveys, the results can be instrumental in creating dissatisfaction with the status quo.

Awareness of Opportunities in the New Environment

An in-depth understanding of the technology available to enhance information systems development and maintenance effectiveness is essential to building the commitment for change. Most organizations begin the venture to a new development environment without a true understanding of the implications and impact of the changes they need to make.

Education and information should provide a realistic appreciation of:

- The capabilities and use of development support technology,
- The need for and benefits of a flexible development methodology,
- The use and limitations of repository technology, and

- An understanding of Total Quality Management (TQM) principles

to help the change sponsors and targets anticipate the full effect of the change. This is particularly important where the IS organization has a history of technology-led attempts to improve productivity. Such organizations tend to see the technology of an effective development process as "the answer." The IS organization must be educated to see that this technology is only one part of the answer, which, on its own, will solve nothing.

Benchmarking, or examining other organizations' leading practices, can be an effective way to build awareness of the opportunities for change. However, benchmarking activities need to be carefully planned and managed in order to avoid the many pitfalls associated with this technique.[2]

Recognizing Paradigm Shifts[3]

The advent of some new technologies, such as object-oriented development tools or repositories, can generate or require a substantial shift in thinking patterns, roles, and behaviors. Given that emerging systems development technologies and processes represent a new paradigm for both the IS and business professional, this shift should be recognized and encouraged. Building an awareness of the required shifts in thinking before getting too far into the change process will help IS management to develop strategies for how to accomplish the new thinking patterns, roles and behaviors.

Awareness building is an essential step in helping sponsors to be aware of these changes.

Awareness of the Process and Issues Related to Managing Organizational Change

A change in paradigms requires people to adopt and become effective with new behaviors and ways of thinking. Making this happen can require a major effort. Lack of management of organizational change is the number one cause of failure in adopting a new development environment. The awareness-building process must focus on setting realistic expectations among the IS organization's leadership, highlighting that management of change is even more critical than selecting the appropriate development process or technology. Tools are replaced more easily than cultures. An essential part of awareness building is education on the following subjects:

- The issues of managing change, including resistance, disruption, and creating new frames of reference,
- The process of managing change, much of which is provided by this Department Effectiveness approach, and
- The key roles in managing change: initiating and sustaining sponsor, advocate, agent, and target.

Education is not just a facet of this stage of Development Effectiveness. As we shall see, it must continue throughout the transition and beyond.

Cost of Change

Although an understanding of the cost of the status quo is essential to motivating change, so is an awareness of the cost of making a change. A comparison of these costs is necessary for understanding whether the pain of remaining the same is greater than the cost of changing and hence whether an organization is ready to make the change, and sustain it through to completion. This comparison is called *the change equation*[4]—see Figure 8.1. Creating an understanding of the change equation is an important part of awareness building. Typically, the size of the costs of status quo is so large that even high cost of change estimates are justified. This enables more realistic cost of change estimates to be discussed than in cases where the cost of status quo is invisible.

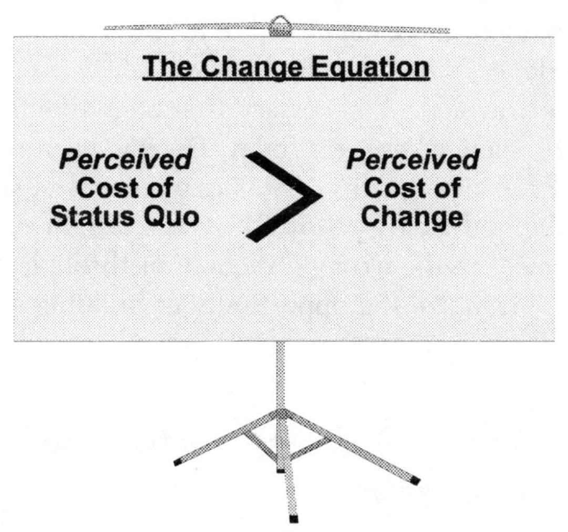

Figure 8.1 *The Change Equation*

Although the term "cost" usually connotes financial aspects, non-financial elements, such as disruption, loss of productivity through learning curve effects, and so forth should be considered as part of the cost of change. The following components contribute to the cost of change:

- Planning for the change
- Implementation and improvement of infrastructure
- Managing the transition

Less visible costs are those associated with the human and cultural changes that must take place in order for the change to be truly institutionalized.

Awareness of the Need to Assess

Many IS organizations feel that once the decision is made to change—often a prolonged and difficult process in itself—all else will fall into place automatically. However, even if the organization has a clear vision of where it wants to go, success in getting there depends on knowing both where "there" is and the distance to be traveled. A necessary first step requires the IS organization to know where it is today. During awareness building, the need for an objective assessment of the current state must be highlighted as a way to reduce the risk of moving too quickly, too slowly, in the wrong direction, or through the wrong means, and to maximize the opportunity of building on existing strengths.

Understanding Related Initiatives and Current Strengths

A key characteristic of the Development Effectiveness approach is that it can be the integrating force among all the current improvement initiatives likely to be under way, especially in large organizations. Taking stock of the current set of initiatives and understanding how they might fit with the need for managed change should be started during awareness building. This helps to leverage existing work, identifies current strengths, interests, and issues, and gives a context for fitting current work into an overall strategy for building an effective, continuously improving IS development and maintenance environment. Relating back to our comments in Chapter 6 on managing change, integrating discrete or unrelated improvement initiatives into a single program can help reduce the assimilation energy required by the change, and minimize the potential for conflict among change initiatives.

Timing Awareness Building

The length of time needed to build awareness in an IS organization to a level sufficient to begin transition planning varies. Some IS organizations may already have a substantial appreciation of the reasons to change and realistic expectations for what the change will involve. They may have already experienced some success through establishing an information technology (IT) infrastructure, or through a total quality or continuous improvement initiative. These organizations may not need to spend much time in this stage. At the other end of the spectrum are IS organizations that have a naive perception of how to use repeatable processes or development support technology, or that have underestimated the impact that change imposes on their people and culture. These IS organizations may require assistance in planning for and building awareness over a longer period of time until their perceived cost of status quo exceeds the perceived cost of changes they will need to make, and until they have built informed, committed, educated sponsorship of the change process.

Using Pilot Projects to Demonstrate That Improvement Is Possible

Chapter 10 describes the use of example development and maintenance projects to help achieve the future vision. However, there may also be a role for one or more short projects during the awareness-building stage. These "pilot" projects are *not* used as a part of the transition to the future-state IS processes, but they can provide objective evidence that:

- Current processes are inadequate, but can be improved,
- Better technology is available and can be used effectively,
- New skills can be learned by the IS organization and its staff,
- Measurement is possible and non-threatening to those being measured, and so on.

Pilot projects used in this way help to build awareness through participation, a powerful learning model.

Developing a Strategy for On-going Awareness Building

Awareness building is seldom a one-time effort. Individuals and organizations change over time and awareness must be regularly maintained as new staff are affected by the change process. There are a number of rules of thumb to follow in actively managing this constant awareness building.

Use a feedback mechanism to drive the strategy. An important piece of awareness building is creating feedback mechanisms to gauge the current state of awareness. This knowledge is then used to drive the strategy.

Gauge progress and resistance. Survey techniques are one approach to measuring awareness. These techniques can also build awareness and encourage dialogue about the change. Seeing sponsors actively engaged in the change, and "walk the talk" are better gauges, however.

Surveys of the targets about their perception of the sponsors' commitment are appropriate. A lot of time must be spent talking to people to accurately judge awareness penetration. It is essential to identify the resisters early.

Create strategies to help the resisters. When people are on the fence, one strategy is to increase their stake, and thus their involvement. Another is to scatter the vocal resisters. Still another strategy is to put a resister on the team to build the next part of the future-state process, thereby increasing their commitment by increasing their involvement.

A useful technique is to get the resisters together and let them talk about what is bothering them. Document and show sympathy for their concerns. This can be risky, however. One group that we have observed used GE's Work Out method without knowing much about it. The result was an 8-hour gripe ses-

> One organization with which we have worked used a four-quadrant matrix to gauge advocacy and resistance. By talking to first-level supervisors, the team was able to place them in one of four quadrants:
>
> 1. Those who understood the change and were advocating it,
> 2. Those whom the team thought understood the change and, with a little more prodding, would move in the right direction,
> 3. The vocal resisters, and
> 4. Silent people—the team did not know where they stood.
>
> After categorizing the supervisors, the team developed strategies for getting everyone on board.

sion, with no resolution achieved, because those with authority to respond to the problems had not attended.

Perform interviews with executive sponsors before giving them awareness training and education. In interviews, where executive sponsors are asked about their vision and the cost of the status quo, it is also often possible to assess their awareness and willingness to change.

Foster continual communications. Newsletters are great tools for continuing awareness building. In many respects, an organization can be thought of as a tree. Whereas the most visible parts are the trunk, leaves, and branches, the invisible part—the root system—often covers a much larger area. It is the invisible root system through which the tree draws its sustenance. The visible parts of an organization are the "standard procedures" it uses, equivalent to Argyris's "espoused theories," discussed in Chapter 6. Below ground is where the work really gets done—the "theories-in-use." Awareness is meant to get those real things out in the open. That is how real change occurs. Just changing the visible parts does not lead to real change. Keep the change program visible, celebrate milestones, recognize people who have participated, and create incentives for joining in.

Institutionalize organizational change. Unless training in organizational change is institutionalized as part of new employee induction, the culture will not grow, because there is constant turnover in virtually all companies, and new employees will not understand how to participate in the change process.

> One of our contributors has helped to establish a set of company-wide training programs for executives, team leaders, and team members. This training is not just for specific projects, but rather for the entire company. Thus, everyone hears the same message, receives the same training, and follows the same project process. There is no doubt or ambiguity about the company's mission or objectives, or about how the company expects to meet its goals. Everyone can feel that they are a part of the same team. As a result, awareness of the need for leadership of the change process has become part of the company culture.

Publicize a highly successful change project. One way to begin to shift a culture is to use the change process in a highly visible project and make sure that project is successful. Any success should be celebrated visibly, and larger successes should be widely publicized. Success raises awareness, making subsequent projects easier to execute.

Establish awareness forums. One of our clients has set up business and technical awareness forums. Presentations at these forums are made by those who have actually done the work. These people, rather than the consultants or change agents, spread the word.

Remember that the organizational and human dynamics of any real-world business require awareness building to be an ongoing process. Awareness builds commitment, and commitment is essential in successfully implementing a new development environment.

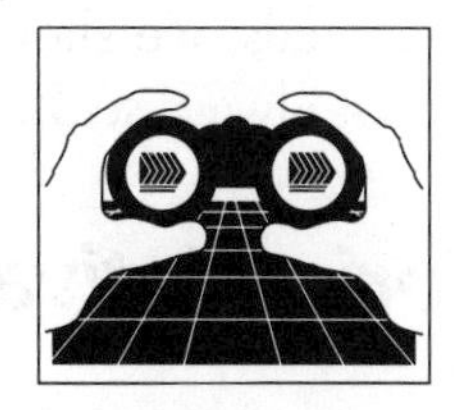

Setting a Vision

In many ways, vision setting is *the most critical* element in managing effective organizational change. Having a robust vision that people buy into and strive toward is what ultimately changes an organization. However, just having a vision is only one step. Great vision statements, framed and hanging on the wall, are not enough. Internalizing that vision throughout the organization is essential.

Vision setting is a fairly well defined element of organizational change management research, and there is a wealth of literature on the subject. Three books in particular provide significant thought leadership in vision setting. *The Fifth Discipline* by Peter Senge[5] is a rich source of ideas. *The Art of the Long View* by Peter Schwartz[6] is about using scenarios in visioning, and, most recently, *Beyond the Hype* by Robert Eccles and Nitin Nohria,[7] provides excellent insights into the role of rhetoric in articulating robust future-state visions.

A vision is not the same as a vision statement. A vision is of no value in a CIO's head; it must be shared. Nor is it just a word statement; it must be a richly detailed picture, a vivid image. Whereas purpose and direction may be similar to vision, they are more vague and abstract. A vision is concrete; it describes a very specific destination.

One of the five disciplines described in Senge's book is systems thinking. In fact, it is the fifth discipline referenced in the title. "Visioning without systems thinking adds up to painting lovely pictures of the future with no deep understanding of the forces that must be mastered to get from here to there," says Senge. As systems professionals, we should all be masters of systems thinking; yet we do not always seem to be such masters.

Powerful Rhetoric Motivates Robust Action

Eccles and Nohria link vision and rhetoric, saying that rhetoric should not have the negative connotation it now holds. Rhetoric can, in fact, be very powerful, motivating people and causing robust action through the use of metaphors and analogies, stories and myths, slogans and maxims.

Eccles and Nohria suggest that visions should include imaginative visions of the future and a realistic portrayal of the present to serve as a contrast to the future. They therefore see the necessity for balance; this thought parallels Senge's idea of creative tension as a motivator for change.

Spreading Visions

In the vision-setting stage of the transition framework, a number of goals are accomplished. Business goals are defined. A vision statement, which includes either principles or qualitative process attributes that will guide the new environment, is developed. The horizon for the full vision is identified. Boundaries, emphases, and

Contrast powerful rhetoric and mere rhetoric by comparing the words used by Jack Welch of GE and Roger Smith of GM after 1981. At that time, both took over leadership of their companies and championed change. Roger Smith was vague in his vision statements; he failed to voice the reality of GM's plights in his public statements and externalized all GM's problems. He acted as though the company's future vision was a fait accompli. In 1987 he said that GM was "the leading car manufacturer in the world by a wide margin because of [its] great organizational and financial strengths"[8]—a statement that in no way reflected GM's 1987 reality. He failed to tap his employees' frustration; and, by denying what everyone knew, he also failed to tap their energy. He followed the old school of management that espoused an approach that says "Don't tell people bad news, tell them everything is wonderful." Everyone was aware that GM was in trouble, even though its leader pretended that the company had already effected change. So people bought into neither the need for change nor the idea that GM was already reengineered into a twenty-first-century company.

Jack Welch, on the other hand, created a strong, emotion-arousing vision. In 1987, for example, he said that he wanted "people to come to work every day in a rush to try something they woke up thinking about. And that they go home from work wanting to talk about what they did that day rather than trying to forget about it. . . . factories where the whistle blows and everyone wonders where the time went, or why there was a whistle at all."[9] He was deliberately playing with people's emotions. His was not mere rhetoric, it was *powerful* rhetoric.

As we now see, GE achieved its vision, GM did not.

quantitative performance objectives are also defined. Finally, key issues and critical success factors are articulated. Vision setting is not a one-time event, or even an annual or triannual event. It should be an ongoing process. Moreover, a vision should be constantly challenged as it unfolds.

People can react to a vision in one of three ways. They can enroll in it. They can commit to it. Or they can comply with it.

When someone enrolls, he or she wants the vision and will do whatever can be done within the "spirit of the law" to achieve it. When committed to the vision, on the other hand, he or she wants it to happen, will make it happen, and will create whatever laws or structures are needed to achieve it. Commitment is thus a much stronger stance than enrollment.

Someone in compliance, however, says, "I really don't want it, so I won't go out of my way to do it. But I will do it." Compliance is not necessarily bad. For certain types of change—a new form or procedure—compliance is all right. For significant change, however, or where cultural change is needed, compliance is not good enough. At first, a crucial participant may only comply; as time goes by, that person can and must become committed.

If people do not have a personal vision and put themselves into a learning situation, they are probably not motivated to enroll. In transition management, the rewards for enrolling and the consequences for not enrolling must be clearly explained. The better the job of tapping motivations, the more likely people will become inspired.

For those with vested interests in the status quo, the future must be more attractive than the present. Many leaders believe that simply saying something will be so makes it so. As we all know, that is not true. Leaders must also understand people's pain factors and build into their vision a reduction of this pain.

The Diamond Model for Planning and Analyzing Organizational Change

Development Effectiveness provides an excellent technique for representing characteristics of an effective and continuously

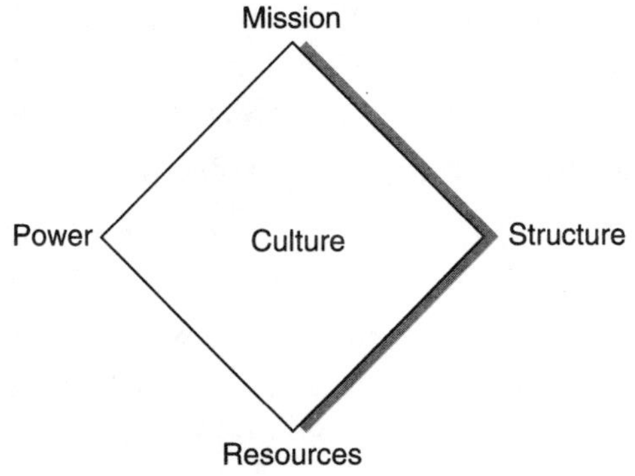

Figure 8.2 *The Diamond Model*[10]

improving development environment. This technique, the Diamond Model, is shown in Figure 8.2.

The Diamond Model is based on five interdependent dimensions that are charted in the diamond: Mission, Power, Structure, Resources, and Culture. All facets of an organization, task, project, or situation can be mapped to one or more of these five dimensions.

The Diamond Model can be used to:

- Provide a starting point and systematic framework for change analysis
- Evaluate whether all facets of a situation have been considered
- Sort large amounts of information into manageable sets of related information
- Focus attention on causes versus symptoms
- Create and test a priority list for solutions
- Introduce and explain new initiatives

The Diamond Model can be applied to any organizational unit, from an entire enterprise to a team, to an individual. The five dimensions of the model are detailed as follows:

- **Mission** refers to the purposes and directions that provide the basis for making decisions. Mission answers the questions, "What?" and "Why?" (e.g., "Why does this organization, project, or task exist?").
- **Power** is the expenditure of energy, the activity of making and adhering to decisions over time. Institutionally, power equates to authority, while personally, power is reflected in commitment—not simply compliance. Power answers the question, "Who?"
- **Structure** points to a form, plan, or regularized set of activities. Methods, procedures, and forms are examples of structure. Structure answers the question, "How?"

  Most IT organizations and people concentrate on structure because it is what they understand best and have most experience with. It should come as little surprise that structure is the most typical—although not necessarily the most appropriate—target of IT effectiveness change.

- **Resources** include anything that can be distributed or is needed to accomplish the mission. Resources answer the question, "With what?" Resources can be seen as latent power. In other words, personnel, when viewed as a cache of skills, is a resource, whereas personnel in the act of expending energy is power.
- **Culture** is the environment in which the other four factors exist. It consists of the shared values and basic beliefs of the organization.

There is a hierarchical order to the dimensions of the Diamond Model. Mission directs power; power energizes and modifies structure; and structure allocates resources. Conversely, resources limit structure; structure curtails power; and power restricts mission.

Shifts in the purposes and directions of IT (mission), for

example, must be reflected in changes to software development automation—resources, structure, and culture. These, in turn, require changes in sources of power. In the early days of computers, IS power was derived from potential business cost savings, and from the need for specialists who had mastered the technology. Today, IS derives its power from strategic alignment between the information systems activities and business needs; from joint development between technical specialists and business people; and from empowering individuals, who contribute not only to solving business problems but also to continuous improvement in processes and services delivered.

The structures through which IS power is transferred must also change with the mission. Centralized data processing organizations have dispersed into business units. Programming standards have been augmented by architectures and information resources management. Rigid-development life cycle processes have evolved into flexible and incremental rapid deployment processes.

The resources needed to accomplish the mission have changed from central hardware, data processing tools, and technical specialists to distributed hardware, end-user tools, and business professionals working together with technical facilitators.

With the shift in mission, the IS culture must change. The once-held beliefs that applications could be easily prespecified, and that users know nothing about information systems, must be replaced with the realization that applications evolve over their useful life and that users are colleagues or partners, who must be involved in information systems processes.

To be effective, the statement of vision must be formulated and *owned* by the organization. However, it is useful to start with a "template" of the characteristics of a typical vision of an effective and continuously improving development environment. This template can be organized around the dimensions of the Diamond Model.

As characteristics and critical success factors are described, specific, measurable milestones are solicited for achieving the vision. The milestones provide the starting point for measuring progress toward the vision. They are also the basis for a more detailed measurement program defined in future stages. Milestones should be defined in terms of the behavioral changes expected at each milestone. A few key measures are identified for monitoring progress against the expected changes.

In addition, each characteristic is analyzed from two perspectives:

1. How ready the organization is to achieve the characteristic, and
2. The cost to the organization if the characteristic is not achieved.

This analysis provides continued visibility to the cost of the change versus the cost of the status quo.

Assessing Readiness

To achieve a future-state vision, there must be a clear understanding of the current state of the IS environment and the IS organization's readiness for the changes that it must undergo. The assessment shows how well the current *IS infrastructure* supports the vision and evaluates how well the current *IS culture* supports the particular changes being planned.

During the readiness assessment stage, the enablers and barriers related to change can be identified and assessed. These enablers and barriers indicate the IS organization's ability to move forward and achieve its vision. The assessment, along with a clear vision and specific milestones, forms the basis for identifying shifts in thinking and working patterns, and in people's behavior, that must occur to move the IS organization successfully to the new development and maintenance environment.

The assessment of the current state of the IS organization is conducted from two perspectives: the *technical readiness* of the organization to adopt new infrastructure, and the *organizational and cultural readiness* to change to new behaviors and thinking patterns.

The technical readiness assessment addresses the existing infrastructure—development methodology and processes, tools, skills base, knowledge base, project management capability, and so on—and how well it is currently used, as well as the competencies that exist within the IS organization. The current state is compared with the infrastructure and competencies needed to achieve the future-state vision. The goal is to identify the gaps that need to be closed during the transition.

The second piece of the evaluation, the organizational and cultural readiness assessment, examines the probable impact of the changes on the organization, likely areas and levels of resistance, sponsorship commitment, history of change, capability of change agents, and compatibility of the proposed changes with the existing culture. This allows an assessment of transition readiness (see Figure 8.3).

The organization's history of change can tell much about the culture's predisposition to change. The more changes that have

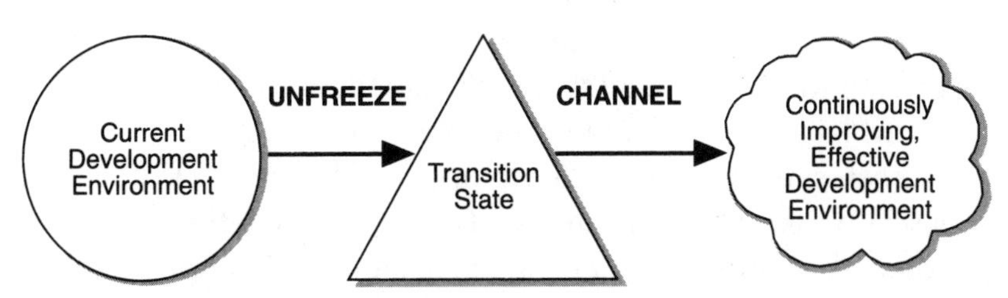

Figure 8.3 *Assessment Defines the Baseline for Transition to the Future State*

been announced, but not completed, the greater the risk that the current change project will fail.

People's perceptions about the forthcoming change, and their resistance to it, need to be assessed, as does the compatibility of the change with their basic beliefs and behaviors. Shaping a new culture is the toughest type of change. Success requires a thorough understanding of the existing culture.

The most common cause of failure in major transitions is lack of adequate sponsorship—both initiating and sustaining; therefore, one key aspect of organizational readiness is assessing sponsorship, perhaps role-mapping to identify which people fulfill the various change roles: initiating sponsor, sustaining sponsor, change agent, change target, and change advocate.

Assessment Has Multiple Objectives

The primary purpose of the readiness assessment is twofold: to understand the readiness of the organization to move to the future-state vision, and to open a dialogue between the targets of the change and their sponsors and change agents. To achieve the objective of an open dialogue, the assessment is conducted through facilitated sessions using diagnostic tools designed to encourage dialogue among the session participants.

Not only is quantitative information gathered, but also qualitative information about how the targets of change view the impact, sponsorship, and management of the change. The targets of the change are involved in examining what the changes mean to them and how they need to prepare to take on new roles and responsibilities, learn new skills, and gain new knowledge.

Involving people in the process is also an objective, because this creates energy and affects people's behavior. Just getting sponsors, targets, and change agents in a room together and focusing their discussions with change management instruments helps them understand each other's point of view.

Continuing to communicate the future-state vision is yet another objective. Readiness assessment must be performed against a desired end point. Because the vision is that end point, it forms the backdrop for discussions about readiness. These discussions should deal not only with the desired state but also with the opportunities connected with achieving it. Once the vision is explained in a focus session, group members can be asked about their perceptions of its impact, the benefits of the vision, and why they might want to achieve it.

Readiness assessment is also aimed at identifying the enablers and barriers to change. A successful history of implementing change, as well as an appreciation of those factors that led to success, will help enable the proposed change, because people will have a preconception that this change will really happen just as past changes have taken place. Conversely, a history of inability to change anything will be a barrier, often leading to a "This too shall pass" attitude. Studying the "force field"—both the driving and the inhibiting forces—helps in laying out strategies to strengthen the enablers and overcome the barriers. It is important to identify the strengths, not just the weaknesses, so they can be leveraged in the change process.

Many organizations mistakenly say, "We do not need to do readiness assessment because we already know where we stand. We know we do not have what we need, and we do not have people with the skills we need." Cutting out this stage, however, can cause other objectives to be missed—such as communicating the vision to a wider audience, and improving communication between those in various change-related roles.

As discussed in Chapter 6, there can be some confusion about who plays which roles—sponsor, change agent, advocate, and target—because a person's role often shifts as the change proceeds. For example, even change agents start out as targets. Until they are truly on board with a change, they are unlikely to be effective change agents. In addition, some people can play multiple roles—a sustaining sponsor for one group can be a change agent for a different group. Finlly, how the roles work is not always obvious; and this can cause ambiguity at first. Expect confusion; decide which roles certain people need to play and then guide them toward those roles.

There is also some blurring between the elements of the transition framework. These are not "stand alone" elements. Activities in one often overlap or combine with those in other elements. There are very few definite dividing lines. Therefore, some activities in readiness assessment are arguably better performed (or revisited) in transition planning, and vice versa.

The Readiness Assessment Process

The readiness assessment process begins with preparing and planning how data will be collected, in concert with the vision and the purpose of the change.

The second step is collecting and assessing the data. The core of the human and organizational data pertains to six areas: sponsor effectiveness, change agent readiness, likely impact of the change, resistance to the change, alignment of the culture to the proposed change, and the organization's change history—where it has had implementation problems or successes in the past.

The third step is analysis of risks of implementing the change. Good data in four of these areas—sponsorship, change agent skills, resistance, and culture—will lead to understanding the organization's existing strengths in implementing change, as well as the change inhibitors. Risk analysis on these four risk factors yields both building blocks that change agents can use to foster the change and implementation barriers that change agents must surmount.

The fourth step is feeding the data back, and the fifth step is follow-up.

Over time we have learned that readiness assessment is best performed in a cycle. As the change management team collects, assesses, and feeds data back to the participants, it typically discovers that some people were missed. Thus, a second round of data collection is generally needed. This follow-up leads to at least one more iteration of the readiness assessment process. Remember that readiness assessment can also build awareness, so this activity has a double impact. Missing key individuals in readiness assessment might mean failing to build awareness of change in those individuals.

Data collection is done in cascading cycles, moving from initiating sponsors to change agents, then to sustaining sponsors, and finally to the targets. This helps the change team lessen the gap between the perceptions of the sponsors and the targets. The goal is to bring the thinking of all constituencies together and understand why they feel the way they do about the change.

To collect and select data, specialized tools[11] are required to help change teams evaluate the organizational and individual impacts of a proposed change. They are used to assess technical knowledge, skills, and experience in such areas as methodology, infrastructure, and so forth.

Because feedback is so important to the assessment process, the feedback approach must be laid out at the outset. The sponsors need to receive feedback from the information they provide, as well as from that provided by the targets. The targets need to receive their own feedback. In these feedback loops, the change team needs to address both confidentiality and timing.

It is also possible that an assessment can show that an organization is *not yet ready* to begin transition. When this happens, Development Effectiveness offers a number of alternative strategies to begin the buildup to the point where a transition process could be started. The spectrum of possibilities is illustrated in Figure 8.4. In most of the scenarios we have seen in real-world assessments, there is insufficient initial awareness of the problems with the current state, insufficient recognition of the opportunities available in an improved future state, or unrealistic perceptions of the cost of the change process. Unless all three of these factors are appropriately understood, the transition stands a significant chance of failure. More, perhaps much more awareness building must precede the transition effort. Only when all factors are aligned correctly should a full Development Effectiveness transition be contemplated.

Feedback affects behavior, and a lack of feedback increases resistance. So the change team needs to explain how it plans to use the collected data; otherwise, people will be unwilling to provide more information in the future. It is best to feed the data back interactively, so that energy is created. That energy may be used to fight or deny the data. Denial is not necessarily bad,

Perception of Improvement Opportunities	*Perception of Dissatisfaction with Current Conditions*	*Perception of Change Implications*	*Preferred Approach*
Limited	Low	Narrow	Long-term Awareness Building
Limited	Low	Broad	Long-term Awareness Building
Limited	High	Narrow	Long-term Awareness Building
Limited	High	Broad	Short-term Awareness Building
Broad	Low	Narrow	Long-term Awareness Building
Broad	Low	Broad	Transition Plan and Review of Commitment
Broad	High	Narrow	Short-term Awareness Building
Broad	High	Broad	Full Transition Plan and Implementation

Figure 8.4 *Typical Readiness Assessments and Related Actions*

because it surfaces resistance, thus allowing the change team to see it and create strategies to deal with it.

If a sponsor denies the data, saying, "I am not like that!" it may be helpful to get the sponsor together with the people who supplied the data to produce more qualitative or quantitative data. Another strategy is to present the sponsor with anonymous quotes captured during the discussions, to support the numerical data. These quotes show the sponsor what he or she did and how the targets interpreted that action. Some of these responses could be misinterpretations, but the sponsor needs to understand the targets' perceptions. The sponsor can then change his or her behavior to correct those perceptions.

Data collection and analysis in readiness assessment raises several issues. One is confidentiality: people want to know whether the data is being associated with a person or kept anonymous. They also want to know who is using the data. They want to know what will happen to the data, and they want to understand the transition process and how their information will be used to produce the transition plan. People have to see results, because they get very tired of surveys that do not result in change.

One way to make results more visible is to post factors of concern on large charts, using colored dots—red, yellow, and green, for example—to represent high, medium, and low risk. This creates a visual map of what a particular group of people think about specific factors. In one such group that we worked with, green clusters appeared around willingness, whereas red ones appeared around scope and sponsorship. This map helped focus the discussions on the areas of greatest concern.

One of the authors travels regularly to Chicago on business. For what seems like forever, the freeway from O'Hare airport to the downtown area has been a mass of road works. There is no good alternative route and the resulting traffic congestion has been horrendous and unavoidable. Every day a local TV station broadcasts the "days to go" count as a part of its regular news sessions. While this doesn't make the traffic any better or lessen the frustration caused by the road building, it *does* provide a visible symbol of progress—feedback that really helps to keep people focused on the future state while suffering through the transition.

Gaining Participation

Sponsors sometimes do not adequately communicate why participation in the process is important. One mechanism for improving this communication is the use of an "invitation to participate" memo as one of a series of communications to get the word out, using the right words and explaining the process.

Readiness assessment does not equate to a climate survey. Climate surveys do not take account of the future-state vision; therefore, they do not assess willingness or resistance to change.

In a readiness assessment, the vision also must be detailed enough, or at least have near-term milestones, so that people understand its impact on their behavior, on whom they socialize with, on their budget, and so forth. Only then can they participate in the assessment process intelligently.

Why Assessment May Be Resisted

Many IS organizations feel that they have been assessed to death, either by external agencies forced on them by their business or by internal IS planning projects, and may resist. Assessment within Development Effectiveness is often seen as just another attempt to assign blame for poor performance or as a preliminary to another round of downsizing activity.

If the Assessment team finds this kind of situation, it has several options:

- **Return to the awareness building phase.** There may well have been a failure in communication about the change process, the improvement requirements, or the future-state vision.

- **Build on previous assessments.** It is rarely necessary to repeat fully any recent assessment work, although it should be recognized that the value of an assessment is in part determined by the reason that is was undertaken. Assessments that result from TQM initiatives or from

Strategic Information Systems planning projects are excellent sources of material and should be used.

- **Look for the root cause of the resistance.** There may be conflicting sponsorship agendas, disenfranchised stakeholders, or other sources of resentment. Surfacing these sources can ensure that a vision is created that is not too radically out of step with the capabilities and beliefs of the current IS organization.

Because assessment is important, however, it should always be carried out in some form.

Readiness Assessment Drives Transition Planning

The quantitative and qualitative information gained through the readiness assessment process feeds the development of a transition plan (the subject of the next chapter) that identifies the gap between the vision and the current state, addresses the barriers, and builds on the enablers. A critical step in readiness assessment is feeding back the information to the change sponsors and targets and illustrating how the data they provided has influenced the vision and the transition plan.

Notes

1. Annual surveys of the top 10 concerns of CIOs and equivalents are available from a variety of sources, including Index Group, the Center for Studies in Data Processing (CSDP) at George Washington University and the Center for Information Systems Research (CISR) at MIT. The actual concerns vary from year to year, but have shown a steady transition away from pure technology issues and towards the need to support strategic alignment and the demonstration of business value.

2. Camp, Robert C., Benchmarking: The Search for Industry Best Practices That Lead to Superior Performance (Milwaukee, WI: ASQC Quality Press, 1989).

3. For more discussion on the concept of a paradigm shift and its consequences, see: Joel Arthur Baker, *Paradigms: The Business of Discovering the Future* (New York: Harper Business, 1993).

4. Based on work first reported by Kurt Lewin in: Kurt Lewin, *Group Decision and Social Change* and G. E. Swanson, T. N. Newcomb, & E. L. Hartley (Eds.), *Readings in Social Psychology* Rev. Ed. (New York: Holt, 1952).

5. Peter M. Senge, *The Fifth Discipline, The Art and Practice of the Learning Organization* (New York: Doubleday/Currency, 1990).

6. Peter Schwartz, *The Art of the Long View* (New York: Doubleday, 1991).

7. Robert Eccles and Nitin Nohria, *Beyond the Hype,* (Boston: Harvard Business School Press, 1992).

8. As reported in an article in *Fortune* magazine, 1987.

9. As reported in an interview for *Business Week,* 1987.

10. Adapted, with permission from work by Robert W. Terry, Reflective Leadership Center, Humphrey Institute of Public Affairs, University of Minnesota, and Kent Boesdorfer, Ernst & Young.

11. We use the term "tools" in its broadest sense. Consultants who specialize in organizational change typically develop tools and instruments to assess organizational characteristics such as strength of sponsorship for a change project, target attitudes toward a change and resilience to change. Specialized training is almost always required to use these tools effectively because of calibration and interpretation issues. For more information on the types of tools and training available, contact the Ernst & Young Professional and Organizational Development Group, Cleveland, OH 44114 or ODR, 2900 Clamblee-Tucker Rd, Building 16, Atlanta, GA 30341-4129.

9

Planning for and Managing Transition

Knowing where you are and where you want to get to are only the first steps in achieving transition. Many things will need to be changed along the way and a plan for making all of the necessary changes in the right order is essential. This chapter considers the following questions: What should be in the plan? What time frame should it cover? How should the transition process be communicated? How will we be able to create and validate the infrastructure that the transition will require?

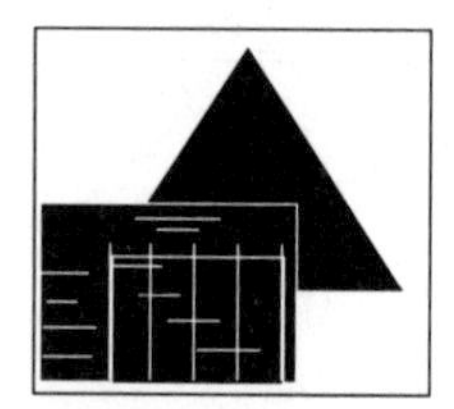

Transition Planning

A transition plan sets out the overall strategies and describes the specific plans for achieving the IS organization's future-state vision. Transition planning must be viewed not merely as an exercise, but as the development of core guidelines for a successful change process, linking the vision to a realistic set of steps that takes into account a particular organization's culture and state of readiness (see Figure 9.1).

The results derived from vision setting and readiness assessment activities must be synthesized during transition planning, and integrated programs of change must be designed to move the IS organization through specific milestones on the way to the vision. The transition plan addresses the key issues of change by organizing them into three major categories:

1. The use of *Pathfinder projects* to implement the changes

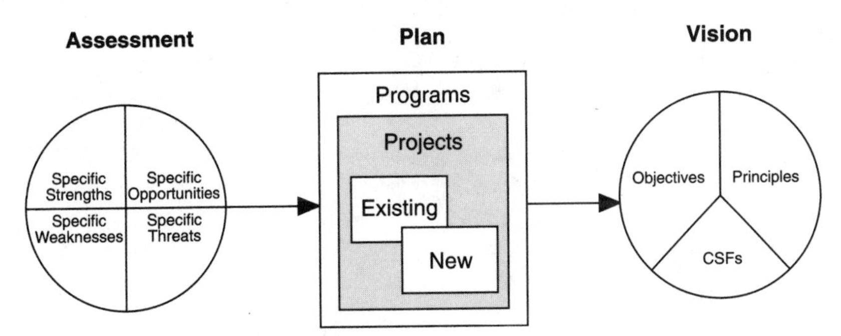

Figure 9.1 *Building a Transition Plan on the Current State Assessment*

2. The ongoing *management of the transition,* including the development and sustaining of cascading sponsorship, the identification and support of change agents, communication during the transition, and revisions to incentive and reward programs

3. The *implementation of infrastructure* components required to achieve the vision, such as roles and responsibility descriptions, training programs, metrics, new tools and methods, and changes in the organization structure

The transition plan should consist of an integrated set of programs for change, each having a specific sponsor, charter and plan for implementation (See Figure 9.2).

The very nature of any complex transition inevitably requires that the transition plan have several iterations. Some programs for change must begin immediately and can be defined in great detail, whereas others will evolve as changes are implemented. The milestones defined during future-state vision setting will drive the development of the plan, as will the variations in readiness between different target groups.

It is important to manage sponsors' expectations about the iterative nature of the plan and its ongoing evolution, in order to guide the change effort in a realistic fashion. Sponsors must understand that the transition plan is a framework that must be adjusted to incorporate past efforts and their results, as well as

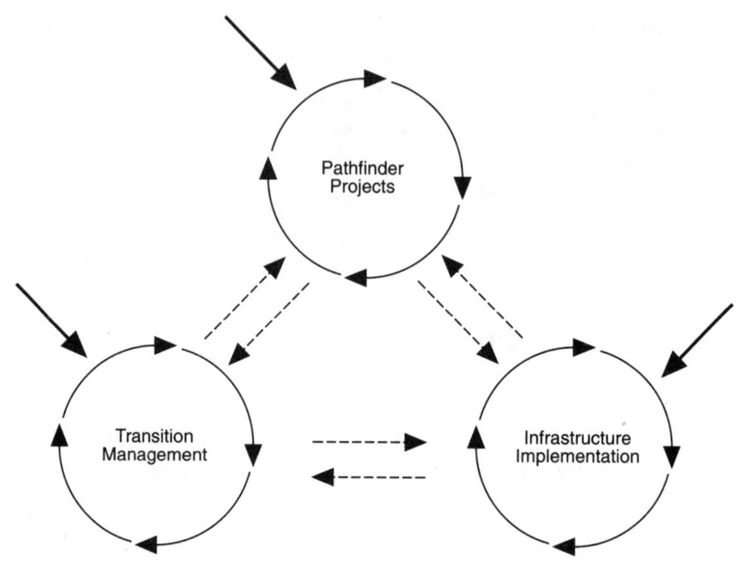

Figure 9.2 *Transition is an Integration of Themes*

changes resulting from future discovery. Because the plan provides the core guidance for the overall change effort, it acts as the integration mechanism for all the work done to this point and provides the glue that helps ensure that the individual change programs will work together during the transition. Hence it is a dynamic, evolving program—not a static map.

Managing the Transition Process

As discussed in Chapter 6, in making the transition, an organization is driven by pain, but is also drawn on by a conviction that there is a remedy to the pain and by a vision of the future state beyond the transition. The goal of transition is the attainment of that vision. In the case of organizations whose business is developing information systems, the remedy is the implementation of a set of processes and an environment in which the effective development and maintenance of information systems is routine and continually improving.

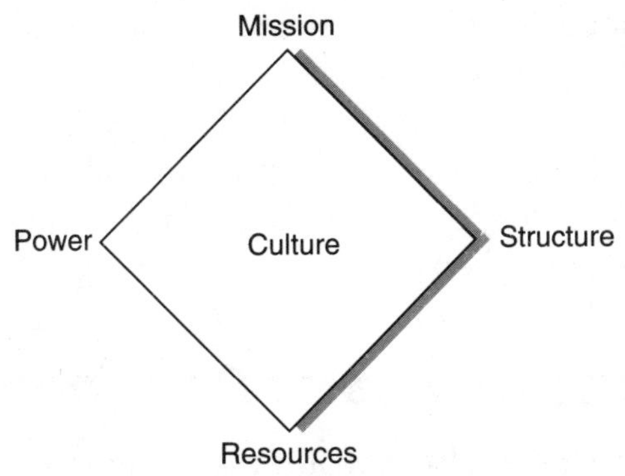

Figure 9.3 *The Diamond Model Revisited for Transition Planning*

The goal is faster development of better, cheaper, and more easily maintained systems and an environment that is continually improving on the IS organization's ability to do these things.

This environment can be described from many perspectives. A vision of the successful future state must include the resources and skills that will be used, the structure in which these resources are put to work, the empowerment of the participants, the mission that unites the participants in a shared endeavor, and the culture within which the participants work to achieve the vision. We can use the Diamond Model (See Figure 9.3) described in Chapter 8 to help organize these perspectives.

Resources and Skills

In almost all cases, the goal in changing the information systems development process and environment includes transformation of the resources that can be brought to bear in development. Shifts in capabilities, new tools, new skills, and changing attitudes to customers are all required.

Structure

A mismatch between available resources and the tasks expected to lie ahead may point to more than a need to develop and change resources, it may signal a need to address structural issues. For instance, the inability to service demands for knowledge coordination will drive demands for more trained data modeling and data administration resources. However, it is likely also to indicate the need for new elements in the IS organizational structure—adding positions for knowledge coordinators and defining the structural relationships that tie them to project team work.

Power: The Drivers of Development

The Diamond Model tells us that if the structural elements of the future state are problematic, and the implementation of those structures is likely to cause conflict, then there may be a need to focus on issues of power. Who is driving the change forward? Who will benefit from the realization of the desired future state? For which managers will the consequences of the change be deleterious? Who will lose out?

Without attention to these issues, some of the structural changes will be hard to realize. At best, there will be excessive resistance to overcome; at worst, the transition will not be completed. For instance, if the managers of the development teams are measured principally by the timely attainment of project deadlines in the short term, they will resist a change that puts a requirement for building reusable components into the development process, especially if that also entails a new line of reporting affecting people on the project. The solution lies in changing the way that consequences are managed for these managers—perhaps giving emphasis to longer-term objectives.

Power has a direction. The organizational chart may give an indication of the locus of power, but it is the examination of measures, the reward system, and the management of consequences that indicates the focus and direction of power. The vision of the future state must address these issues.

Mission

A mission should serve to make public the direction of the organization. The direction given to the exercise of power should be guided by the mission. For instance, if the organization is to be driven by the need to discover and satisfy the potential needs of the customer, then the mission statement should justify measures of performance that reflect this, rather than merely timely completion. The mission will be worked out fully as the transition progresses. Creating a mission is not simply a matter of finding the right words; commitment to the new mission will filter down through the organization as the transition progresses. However, the integrity of the vision of the future state will be greatly enhanced if it includes an indication of the main points of the mission.

Culture

If organizational culture is in conflict with the change, then the likelihood is that the change will fail. For instance, in a culture in which the technicians are customarily the arbiters of innovation, it will be difficult to introduce a systems development process in which the customers (nontechnicians) are expected to take the leading role.

It is possible to take objective soundings of the nature and strength of culture. It is vital to do this before the transition is initiated. If the transition is likely to run head-on into contrary cultural forces, then the prudent approach is to change the change. For instance, in an organization that was dedicated to the principle that Head Office does not dictate operating policy, the introduction of a common development methodology could have run straight into opposition. Instead, the vision of the future state was adjusted to be compatible with the idea that each operating unit was choosing to implement the methodology.

Continuous Improvement

There is one set of cultural expectations that will need to be built into every transition of the information systems development environment if the transition is to be a long-term success. This is the expectation that the process of development can and will always be improved. There must be a commitment in every member of the organization to the idea that he or she owns the process, shares in it, and is empowered to improve it, especially if it is found that the process is not resulting in the satisfaction of a customer's needs and ever-growing expectations.

The Transition Process

To initiate change is not enough. Each participant (the change targets) will look to his or her manager for direction on the amount of effort to be put into the transition and how much priority to assign to the change goals. Inconsistent or ambiguous signals must be avoided. Consequently, each manager has to be a consistent sustaining sponsor for the transition, a sponsor who keeps the change going and translates the overall directives and vision into concrete actions that everyone can see and understand.

The actions of each staff member will be greatly influenced by the consequences of these management actions—in areas such as praise for good work, pay raises, and promotion prospects. Sponsors who sustain the transition are those who manage the consequences for the staff who must accomplish the transition.

Managing a transition means management of a "cascade" of sponsorship from the initiating sponsor down through all levels of the organization to the lowest level of management. Initially, each prospective sustaining sponsor is a target of change; as they internalize the reasons for the transition, they should be trained in the skills required for sustaining sponsorship.

Carrying the Staff Along with the Process

The transition process is driven by a recognition that past approaches to IS development have been inadequate, at best. Usually it is either the management or the customers of the IS development process that arrive at this realization. The professionals who develop information systems are likely to be proud of their professionalism and conscious of the (self-defined) successes in their work. It can come as a shock to these people to be told that they are going to have to change much of what they have done in the past, and set off on a new tack.

The manager who takes staff through a change process that begins by rendering them "incompetent" must work hard to gain their support for the change. They have to see that it benefits them as individuals as well as the organization as a whole. Thus, transition cannot be just a top-down, management-driven process. Participants in the change must have a way of conveying their worries and a means to contribute to the direction of the change. The people who actually run the process are usually those with the clearest view of what is wrong with it and how it can be improved. If they can be recruited as active participants in the transition, this latent capacity can be a powerful motivation to participate in the change. This is as true of the information systems development process as it is of car manufacture or any other process.

Change in Bite-Sized Chunks: The Pathfinder Principle

It is possible to organize the process of change so that each effort in changing the development environment builds on past change initiatives and contributes to building the future. The principle that must be adopted is that change is made in manageable "chunks," and that each "chunk" provides a demonstration of the success of a defined part of the change within a defined context. Furthermore, each demonstrated success must be used to build momentum for the next chunk of success.

The term "Pathfinder project" is used to denominate these "chunks" of change (see Figure 9.4). A pathfinder project is a project that establishes a path for others to follow. The Pathfinder principle is described in detail in Chapter 10.

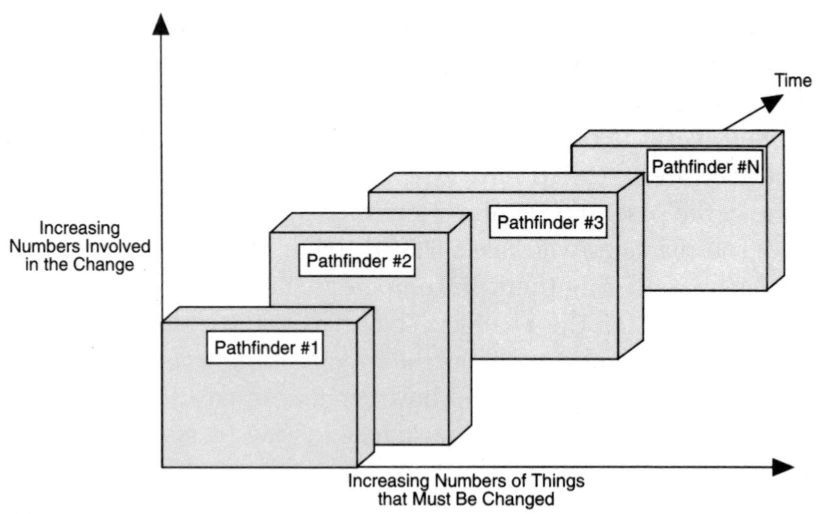

Figure 9.4 *Incremental Change and Improvement Through Pathfinder Projects*

The Bandwagon Effect

Managing the transition is partly a matter of "winning the hearts and minds" of change targets. In addition to *demonstrating* that the new development environment is effective, it is essential to *communicate* this proof to those who are working the development process and to customers of the process. Thus, it is vital that the first Pathfinder project is a success. This can usually be ensured by picking the right project, working with customers who are keen on the objectives of the transition, and providing the project with enough of the right resources. The first Pathfinder project should be followed immediately by the second; others should then follow with some overlap of start dates. Some of the members of the earlier project teams should be seeded into later teams as mentors and/or as project leaders. In this way, the bandwagon is built. When this is achieved, the turnover of the rest of the "targets" of change to the new approach comes swiftly.

Although it is important to have a good proportion of the development staff sharing a commitment to the new development process before customers are asked to join in the change, it is not possible, or desirable, to keep these two developments separate. Pathfinder projects will involve customers—this is essential if they are to be real, valuable projects, rather than toy pilots. One of the most important criteria in choosing the early Pathfinder projects is the ability to involve customers who are sympathetic to the new approach, and who will broadcast success.

> An example of a Pathfinder successful on these terms was in a U.K. building society (equivalent to a U.S. savings and loan).[1] The new development process entailed a much greater commitment from users in the analysis phase than had hitherto been the case. The first Pathfinder's target was a subsidiary business—a recently acquired insurance company.
>
> The subsidiary's CEO had been expressing concern that his business was not well understood in the parent organization. The Pathfinder project was the analysis phase of a system to support his business in the branches. The new development process involved both the customer's managerial staff and the information systems staff in extensive analysis activity. This required a substantial investment of time, but the results were greatly appreciated, precisely because the CEO and his staff were delighted to have colleagues take a serious look at the business's organization. This CEO then became a great advocate for the new information systems development process in the overall organization.

In the user organization, one wants to develop educated, committed customers as initiating and sustaining sponsors who will promote the involvement of users in the new development process. The customers for the early successful Pathfinders can be enlisted to build this sponsorship, with information systems management acting as advocates.

Putting Infrastructure in Place

Another essential component of transition is the infrastructure—the underlying framework and mechanisms that make the development process possible and effective. The infrastructure includes development tools, the repository of the results of development, the organizational structure that facilitates development, and so forth.

The desired future state will probably include a great deal of new infrastructure, including a new development process. As the new development process is introduced, one chunk at a time, so the new infrastructure must also be introduced to support it.

Experience has shown that it is essential to use the real-life laboratory of Pathfinder projects to deploy the new infrastructure. There is very often a temptation to have a preliminary project just to establish infrastructure. The source of this temptation is usually those staff who are responsible for development support—the people who acquire methodologies and infrastructure technology tools and components and are responsible for corporate information systems standards.

Their reaction to a new infrastructure is to want to establish standards, to "get it right," and then to deploy it among the developers. Beyond a certain point, this is not a good way to go about a transition. The development staff (the "customers" for the new infrastructure) will resist change if it is handed down from "on high." Their "hearts and minds" have to be won to the new infrastructure and they have to be involved in the process of discovering the right ways to use it.

This is not just a matter of psychology. It is impossible to get the infrastructure right in isolation from the real-life experience of putting it to use. On the one hand, it is essential for the development support group to act as systems integrators for the varied infrastructure components so that they are technically functional. On the other hand, if the development support people could induce the developers to make use of the development environment they had set up, they would find that the developers would immediately start modifying the environment.

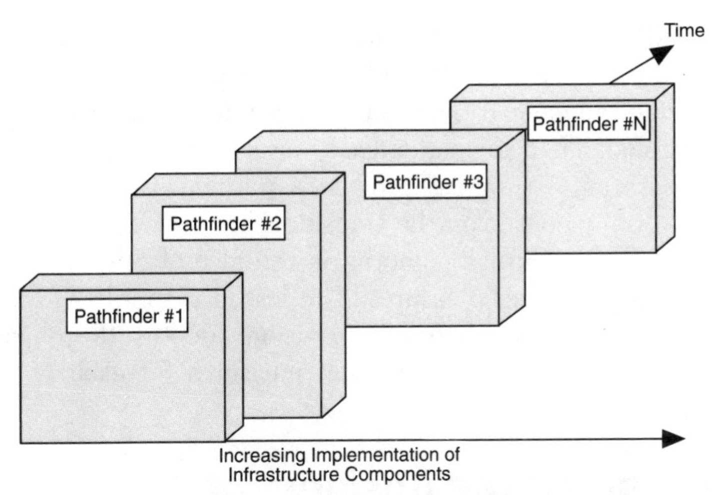

Figure 9.5 *Linking Infrastructure with Use via Pathfinders*

The right approach is to involve the customers in the development of the system and get it right at the time of implementation. The successful approach to deploying the new infrastructure is to use each Pathfinder project to put more of the infrastructure to use. Thus, the right way to use the infrastructure is established in practice through the pathfinder projects (see Figure 9.5).

One of the major challenges for transition management is to lead development support staff into the habit of working with their customers (the development teams) to establish the new infrastructure in use, rather than policing the developers' use of a preestablished infrastructure.

Achieving Measured Improvement

The new development environment—process and infrastructure—has a purpose, articulated in the future-state vision. It is essential to be able to demonstrate progress in realizing the vision through metrics in dimensions relevant to the vision.

Chapter 6 pointed out that one of the major causes of failure in managing change is the lapse of sponsorship before the change is complete. The techniques for sustaining sponsorship can be described collectively as "pain management"—managing the sponsors so they become aware, and remain aware, of the cost of not completing the change. This pain is easily forgotten. The average effective shelf life of an unattended sponsor is about 3 working days.

Measures of progress provide a positive way to keep the attention of a sponsor on the transition process. Things that are not measured are usually ignored in the face of other things for which there are clear measures. The lesson is simple—for all of the important components of the vision, identify the objective indicators of change and construct measures for each of these indicators.

Carrying on the Business of Development

For most information systems shops, the transition from traditional ways of working to a new development environment constitutes a major change in the "rules of the game." To use a phrase that has gained currency, the information systems department will be going through a *paradigm shift*. While this is happening, however, the primary business of the IS organization has to continue as near to normal as possible.

Business as Usual, Sort Of

Short of times of war, there is almost no circumstance in which there will be the universal suspension of normal expectations that makes it possible for large groups of people to make a rapid transition to new ways of working. Such a shared sense of "the burning platform"[2] is not often a feature of business life, and certainly not in large businesses. Therefore, transition must start out small, and grow as the bandwagon is built.

For the majority of the development staff it will be "business as usual," or nearly so, as the transition process begins to advance. Staff will gradually be brought into the transition either through "mass" training that will be rolled out quite late in the transition process or, much earlier, through the influence of Pathfinder projects in setting aspirations for the future.

This phased aspect of transition brings both benefits and concerns. The obvious benefit is that the amount of disturbance to the normal working of the development department can be managed, and work will continue to be delivered to the business. Schedules can be met as well as they have been in the past, and the rest of the business does not need to be shown the process of change in the development department, if that is not desired.

Of particular importance is the management of expectations among the development staff. To have some staff members accelerating through a transition to new, effective ways of working while others may see themselves as being condemned to the old rut could create tension. The management of the transition program must head off this danger, and it is relatively easy to do so through a continuing communications program.

Building The Transition Onto Regular Business

A further step can be taken toward the goal of carrying on with business during a transition. Not only can the transition be managed so that normal business is conducted around the beginning transition process, but the transition process itself can be managed so as to use essential "normal business" as a vehicle for making the change to new development processes.

Pathfinder projects are central to the explanation of this approach. A Pathfinder project is used to make the transition for a team of developers to new development processes. It is by means of a succession of overlapping Pathfinder projects that the bandwagon effect is made reality. Thus, Pathfinders fit in with the objective of managing the transition while maintaining development business.

Pathfinder projects select pieces of essential development business, such as analysis, design, or construction projects that are already scheduled, and use them as the means to put into effect new skills, new organization, and new uses of the new infrastructure. A Pathfinder project works to timetables and deadlines that meet the needs of the part of the business that commissioned the work and contributes directly to normal business.

Satisfying the Business Sponsors

As part of the IS development department's normal support for the business, most Pathfinder projects will address the needs of specific business areas. As part of the introduction of effective development processes through these Pathfinders, each project will be set up with a clear charter, naming the business sponsor(s) who is committed to the initiation and sustenance of the project and to the management of the consequences of the project.

Pathfinder projects serve two masters: the business sponsor for whom the major issues will be delivery of the business benefits through a high quality system, on time and within budget; and the change sponsor, for whom the major issues will be the transfer/acquisition of new skills, steps toward the creation of a new development environment, and the rolling out of the bandwagon. (There are some Pathfinder projects that build infrastructure for the development department itself. For these there will still be two sponsors, or at least two sponsorship concerns: for the delivery of the infrastructure component and the use of the project to contribute to the change process.)

Organizing for Transition

Although there are many possible organizational structures associated with a transition program, all contain a number of key roles that must be assigned and carried out effectively if the transition is to succeed. Many of these roles were described in Chapter 6; here we describe likely candidates for such roles.

Transition Leadership

Sponsorship is key to the management of change and, therefore, to the transition process. Effective sponsorship must exist at many levels and a number of sponsor roles must be identified and assigned.

- **Initiating Sponsors for the Transition.** There must be initiating sponsorship for the whole transition process. Such sponsorship should be external to the IS organization whenever possible, usually at the CEO level, so all those involved have a clear vision that the transition is important to the enterprise. In addition, the CIO must be at least a sustaining sponsor.
- **Sustaining Transition Sponsors.** In addition to identifying overall sponsors for the transition, a group of sponsors for the major transition programs within the transition process must be identified. These can be IS executives or a combination of IS and business customers.
- **Cascade of Sponsorship.** Along with top-level sponsorship, there must also be sponsors for each individual project or action initiative covered by the plan. This cascade of sponsorship is what makes the transition process a real and immediate imperative for everyone.
- **Transition Manager.** In addition to those in sponsorship roles, there should be an executive manager for the transition process. There may be a temptation to make transition an organizational responsibility. This supposedly dilutes the responsibility across many different people, but almost always results in no one actually being responsible for anything. Appointing a transition manager means that there is a focus for getting things done.

Some roles will be long-term and others more transitory. It is important to first educate and then remind people that they will move from role to role during the course of the transition and that their expected behaviors will also change. Because transition leaders will be seen as role models, they must be the first to recognize and adjust to this need and to "walk the talk."

It is particularly important to ensure that the transition process is not seen as the exclusive preserve of an elite few, but rather something accessible to everyone. In addition to the transition leadership, there are two key groups who should be identified and their efforts harnessed to support the change process:

- **Change Agents.** Members of this group will be part of the initial stages of the transition program and will directly influence, by their participation or behavior, progress and success. Sponsors, particularly sustaining sponsors, may also be change agents if they are directly involved in the work of transition. Because change agents have such an important impact, they should be chosen carefully and trained and supported for their role. Select those people who have a positive view of the future-state vision, and of the change process, and who will be listened to by their colleagues. Change agents need to be believable role models—those whose views are respected but who are not necessarily seen as the "stars" of the IS organization.

- **Change Advocates.** Not everyone can (or should) be involved in the first stages of the transition. The first projects will be small, and limited in scope, and typically involve less than 10% of IS staff and only a few customers. While this is going on, it is important to involve as "advocates" those who have an interest or influence in the future state and who should not feel excluded from the process. Avoid the trap of thinking of these people as change sponsors or agents. Usually, at the first stages of transition, full sponsorship has not yet been secured, so these initial supporters of change are, at best, advocates working towards gaining sponsorship.

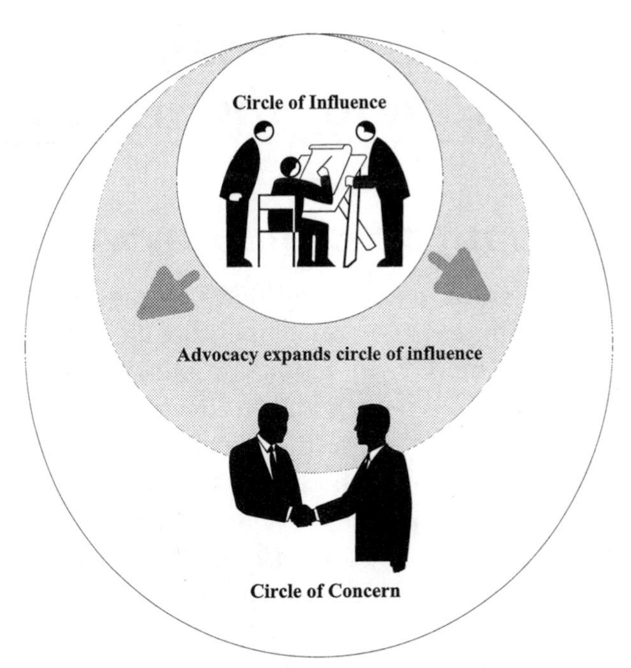

Figure 9.6 *Agency and Advocacy in the Transition Process*

One way to distinguish between agents and advocates is shown in Figure 9.6 that was adapted from Stephen R. Covey's book *The 7 Habits of Highly Effective People.*[3] People can divide the things that they believe need to be changed into two groups. The first, the *circle of influence,* contains everything an individual can directly affect through personal action. The second, the *circle of concern,* covers everything of concern, including all those things that an individual cannot influence directly, for whatever reason.

To be effective through direct action, an individual must operate within his or her circle of influence. Agency behaviors outside the circle of influence will have no effect and, if attempted, may well be a source of frustration or disillusion. To effect change outside the circle of influence requires the use of advocacy. Effective change agents recognize and operate within their circle of influence, whereas effective advocates operate outside their circles of influence but within their circle of concern.

Developing a Management Framework for the Transition

Whose Transition Is This Anyway?

Although the main focus of a transition program will be the IS organization, it is important to remember that the change affects a much wider community, both within and outside the enterprise. Because one objective is new and more effective working partnerships, the transition process must also include suppliers and customers of the IS organization, both internal and external.

A common theme in this book regarding the treatment of transition is the scope and complexity of the transition process. We have often been asked if such breadth of simultaneous action is really necessary. Certainly, it is a factor that has led a number of organizations with which we have worked to back away from a Development Effectiveness program and search for an easier way to improve. (We know of no instance where an easier way was found. These organizations either continue to flail, or return to the Development Effectiveness approach.)

In response, we are forced to contend that the whole effort is indeed necessary. In our defense, we point to the lessons of our industry's history. Whenever we tackle only some part of the effectiveness problem (be it productivity, infrastructure elements, quality, training, or any other single aspect) we fail, sooner or later, to achieve a real, sustained improvement.

Balancing Process and Structure

With so much needing to go on simultaneously, there is a great temptation to create a bureaucracy to administer the process of transition. This should be avoided, because bureaucracies tend to freeze the status quo and, hence, make it very difficult to maintain an effective change process. A better approach is to focus transition activity within a small group initially and progressively spread the change to additional groups in a managed fashion. This partitions the change effort in both time and space, achieving a balance between complexity (many things changing simultaneously) and controllability (but only for a manageable number of people). It also has the advantage that continuous improvement can begin immediately, based on the learning of the early groups.

Managing the Infrastructure-Building Programs

The partitioning approach can and should also be used in the development of infrastructure. The principle should be "Start small and prove the technology first." It is a truism worth remembering that "if you cannot do the easy things, it is unlikely that you will be able to do the difficult things." It is, therefore, prudent to start with the infrastructure requirements of a single project and expand from this experience to add more projects and more infrastructure until the work of the whole of the IS development and maintenance organization is supported.

We return to this theme in more detail in the sections of this chapter on building infrastructure.

The Pathfinder Project Managers

If the partnership theme (see Figure 9.7) is to work in the long term, all suitable roles in the IS development process must be open to appropriate staff within the business. This is a real and achievable objective as far as the project manager's role is concerned. However, early Pathfinder projects are not usually the best settings in which to introduce non-IS project managers to a process that is still being deployed. Instead, start with project managers from the IS organization, and provide them with a business "shadow" who will understudy the role and be coached

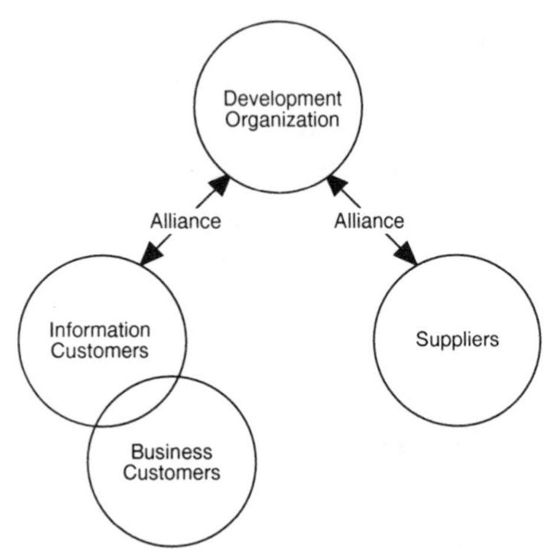

Figure 9.7 *The Future State Partnership Model*

on the process during early Pathfinder projects. It is then possible to move to customer-led projects as the Pathfinder program proceeds.

Organizing for Beyond the Transition

A transition in most large IS organizations is going to take several years. Because change tolerances must not be exceeded, the effort must pace itself to create a sustained improvement for the future-state vision. The downside of this pacing, however necessary it may be, is the creation of a sense of permanence among members of the transition process team. This must be avoided, or it will lead once more to bureaucracy and defense of the transition state as the new status quo.

From Project to Process

A good way to think of a transition is in terms of the evolution of projects within the transition into processes within the IS organization's future-state vision. As the transition is accomplished, more and more of the projects that were set up to create or change some aspect of the IS organization, process, or infrastructure will succeed, and their success will be measured by the change from a project (characterized by limited scope, specific resources, defined end, and set objectives) to a process (part of what everyone does or uses).

Of key importance is to free the process from the ownership of the project team that created it and to remember that project managers do not always make good process managers.

Projects to Improve Processes

Opportunities will still exist, however, to charter additional projects to focus on process improvement or innovation possibilities. Remember that although continuous improvement is a powerful paradigm for effectiveness, it is not of itself enough, in the long run, to maintain excellence. From time to time innovation is also required, and this is best achieved within the context of a project to improve a process.

Transition Synergy

To manage the transition process effectively and to minimize the energy and resources required for the overall change activity, every opportunity should be taken to build on interproject synergy. Evidence suggests that such synergy does not appear by itself; it must be looked for, promoted, and marketed as a continuing part of transition management.

Transition Management, Pathfinders, and Infrastructure Programs Integration

Some of the most obvious a priori areas where synergy may occur are shown in Figure 9.8. Other opportunities to cross-fertilize projects with staff, knowledge, and experience will occur throughout the program. All should be taken advantage of.

Development Environment Objectives	*Infrastructure Programs*	*Transition Management Programs*
Customer Satisfaction Through Quality	• Quality Management Program • Business Partnership Program	(Supporting every program)
Quality and Productivity Through Continuous Process Improvement	• Quality Management Program • Methodology Adoption Program • Training and Development Program	Transition Leadership Program
Team Learning and the Measurement of Improvement	• Methodology Adoption Program • High Performance Development Environments • Training and Development Program	Transition Support Program
Enterprise Ownership of Information through Architecture	• Knowledge Base Program • Planning Synchronization Program	Transition Facilitation Program
Assemble to Order Software Manufacturing	• Knowledge Base Program • Methodology Adoption Program • High Performance Development Environments	Transition Support Program
Resilience in the Face of Change and Capacity to Change	• Pathfinder Program • Organizational Design Program	Transition Support Program
Building on Existing IS Investment	• Knowledge Base Program • Pathfinder Program	Transition Support Program

Figure 9.8 *Areas of Synergy Between Infrastructure and Transition Management Programs*

Measuring Progress

The transition process needs a regular supply of performance and quality information if managers are to ensure that it is on track and that changes are being made and internalized. This provides a great opportunity to get started on measurement processes in general. However, to be successful with measurement, as with any other part of the effort, a well-thought-out approach is required.

Measurement as Part of a Management System

It is well to approach the development of measurements from a *systems* perspective;[4] that is, as part of a coherent, coordinated management system whereby all facets of measurement are considered and explicit mechanisms exist for the feedback of results to effect changes that help move the organization toward desired performance levels. Regarded in this way, a measurement system is much more than collecting numbers and producing charts. Implemented in a thoughtful way, it can help bring focus to the values an organization holds to be important. A measurement system can also play a significant role in shaping the behavior of managers and employees. To achieve these ends, however, it is necessary to fit the measures into the proper context, a context that is largely situation dependent and often changing over time. The design of measures is different for each process that is to be measured. In designing IS measures, for instance, it is important to know the characteristics of the set of processes to which the measures will be applied.

The IS Measurement Framework

Experience in establishing IS measurement systems has shown that using a guiding framework can help to ensure that all aspects of a set of IS metrics are considered. The IS Measurement Framework[5] described here is derived from work sponsored by the participants of the IS Leadership Multi-Client Research Program directed by the Ernst & Young Center for Information Technology and Strategy℠. It provides a generic outline that is useful in developing a balanced set of IS measures for a given area of information technology (IT) activity. It addresses IS measurement from four perspectives: the IS contribution to business results; the user/customer view of IS products and services; current internal operational IS performance levels; and IS preparedness for the future.

At the highest level, the four elements of the IS Measurement Framework may be summarized in terms of the following questions, each stated from an IS viewpoint:

- How do we look to senior management? (business contribution view)
- How do our users/customers see us? (user/customer view)
- How does our execution compare to industry standards? (internal performance view)
- Are we positioned to meet tomorrow's challenges? (growth and learning view)

The first question calls for measures that help management understand the costs, values, and dynamics of applying IT to meet business needs and opportunities. The second and third questions cover the operational performance of IS from both a user/customer-driven perspective and from an internal, excellence-of-execution perspective. The last question calls for developing leading indicators of the preparedness of the IS organization for future challenges.

When these generic questions are considered within the context of particular IT activity—for example, Development Effectiveness—they help stimulate a broad consideration of the measures that might be applicable to the situation. The following list describes each of the four elements of the framework in more detail. A general example of the framework in use is then presented. Finally we discuss specific examples from a Development Effectiveness viewpoint.

- **Business Contribution View.** Measures in this area help managers to understand the contributions being made by current IS activities and to weigh the benefits of implementing proposals for new uses of information technology.

Underlying the selection of business contribution measures is the need to reach agreement about how IS activities will be viewed. Business and IS management must agree on the mental models to be employed in assessing contribution. For example, it often proves useful to adopt a model that divides the IS organization's activities between those that support ongoing, day-to-day business activities and those that create new IS capabilities that underlie changes in the way the business will operate in the future. This simple split allows the first set of IS activities to be managed from the perspective of ongoing, "cost-of-doing-business-today" expenses, while the second set of IS activities is managed from the perspective of investment and future returns. The IT Process Landscape introduced in Chapter 4 achieves this.

- **User/Customer View.** Being "customer oriented" is often key to being competitive. Adoption of such a perspective is basic to implementing the principles of Total Quality Management (TQM). Thus, how IS performs in the eyes of its users/customers is becoming a concern of top priority for IS management.

  The measures chosen to address the user/customer view must not only indicate the "satisfaction" level of the customer but also reveal why the products and services of IS miss, it they do, customer "expectations." Customer satisfaction metrics should be "actionable." Experience has shown that involving customers in selecting the metrics to be used is almost always a critical success factor in this area.

- **Internal Performance View.** High-quality, responsive, low-cost service does not just happen. It depends on the processes and decisions that occur throughout an IS organization. Thus, customer-oriented performance metrics must be complemented with measures of IS's internal processes, with IS measured against applicable industry performance standards.

A key factor in selecting internal performance measures is an awareness of the possible requests for cross-industry comparisons. Benchmarking can be accomplished more easily if metrics are adopted that conform to industry practices and standards. For example, the Function Point is widely used as a standard measure of output for the application development process, and should be a candidate for collection if application delivery activities are to be covered. Another reason to choose metrics in common use is to take advantage of the learning of those who have gone before. There are few rewards for rejecting existing approaches solely because "they weren't invented here."

- **Growth and Learning View.** In addition to managing today's performance, managers must prepare for the future. Just as one would generally value more highly a company that has a strong R&D effort and plans to meet future needs, one should value an IS organization that looks to the future and focuses on more than just today's work. The challenge in selecting growth and learning measures is to identify the right leading indicators. Today, in general, this means choosing metrics related to the development of organizational capabilities.

The Right Measure

Dealing with the "What should we measure" issue means recognizing that the "right" metrics are different for every organization, vary by measurement purpose, and will change as performance changes. What is measured to guide an improvement initiative, for example, is very different from what should be measured to bill customers or to highlight the value of the IS organization.

Illustrating how measurement must change as performance improves is the experience of one company we worked with which had implemented TQM in its IS organization several years ago. As part of that effort, the company conducted a customer satisfaction survey, asking customers what IS functions were important to them and how IS was performing with regard to each function. The responses gave them the strong message that on-time, within-budget performance on new systems projects was very important and was a function that needed significant improvement.

The IS group began to measure system-delivery performance and implemented process improvements in conjunction with those measures. Performance improved dramatically. Several years later, the TQM effort was refocused with one of the typical "midlife boosters" most quality programs need, and IS again surveyed its customers. This time the message was that although systems were always delivered on time and with budget, the time taken to *fully institutionalize* new systems was a concern. On-time, within-budget delivery was now the minimum expected performance.

Focusing on meeting projected delivery led to some IS behaviors that exacerbated the new concern. Shortcuts were taken that made institutionalization of new systems more difficult. Things that were normally done prior to system delivery were now left until after delivery. In fact, the time taken to institutionalize new systems was not a *new* problem, it had been the *real* problem all along. The situation had been obscured by project cost and time overruns—another example of a Type 3 error.

There are several morals to this story. First, it is important to make sure that improvement efforts deal with the *whole* problem. For example, if this IS organization now addresses the time taken to institutionalize new systems, it is likely that the time taken to recognize a business opportunity and start a project to produce the solution will become the next problem. This is a basic systems engineering issue. Second, as one set of customer needs are met, a new set of needs will surface. What "excites and delights" the customer this year becomes minimum expected performance next year. This means that it is necessary to continuously improve the measurement system as improvement efforts

One of the participant companies in our multi-client research program is a pioneer of TQM in the IS organization and a strong proponent of measurement in support of improvement. Over the last 10 years, however, they have discovered that the usefulness of their measurements varies. Measures need to be evaluated according to their usefulness and may need to be "retired" as the benefits decline. This was a surprise to them and is somewhat counter to general thinking on process measurement. As their CIO said to us, however, "What use is all this data if no one ever looks at it or uses it to change anything?" As in most areas of Development Effectiveness, pragmatism needs to modify theory for effective practices.

are continuously realigned with shifting customer needs and perceptions.

Dealing with the second issue, measurement in a vacuum, requires careful and explicit definition of the underlying purpose for the measurement system. A common purpose of measurement is to provide *information.* McGee and Prusak point out that "Information is not just data collected; rather it is data collected, organized, ordered, and imbued with meaning and context. Information must inform."[6] This observation highlights the subjective nature of information. Information is data in use, which implies a user with a purpose for the data. To design measurement systems that *inform,* it is necessary to determine the measurement information needs of customers and stakeholders, select some starting measures, and then design and implement feedback mechanisms so that the measures drive the desired behavior change.

Measure Processes, Not People

People are inherently resistant to being measured and usually feel threatened by it. They are concerned that they will be measured according to the wrong criteria, or that they will not be measured consistently or accurately. Furthermore, individual measurement is often of little value in implementing improvement plans. Individual performance varies, both between different people and for a given individual over time. Measure enough people and plot performance levels against numbers of people, and a classic bell-shaped curve will be established—the so-called normal distribution function.[7]

This measurement approach is of no value in establishing improvement agendas. The whole performance curve must be moved higher, but that cannot be done by measuring individuals. What is needed is to improve the processes that people follow, improve the environment in which they work, and improve their skills for working in that environment. None of this requires, or is achieved by, measuring individual performance.

Instead, it is necessary to measure process capability, process characteristics, and how groups of people perform when using the process. Even though each of these measures may require that individual performance data be collected, this data should be aggregated as soon as possible. Only aggregate performance data should ever be reported, and the people being measured need to understand that this is how the data will be reported.

Picking The Wrong Measures: You Get What You Measure

There is an old adage that says "you get what you measure." This can work for you or against you. For example, if people feel that measurement systems focus on meeting project schedules and deadline commitments, they will tend to optimize their schedule and deadline performance. This is good insofar as it achieves the performance objective. However, they may do so at the expense of other factors, such as quality, customer satisfaction, and so on.

In a famous experiment[8] described in 1974, Gerald Weinberg and Edward Schulman asked five different programming teams to write the same piece of software. Each team was given a different objective to optimize, such as minimum memory size, maximum clarity, minimum number of programming statements and minimum programming time. Each team succeeded in achieving its major objective—at the expense of the other objectives and with considerable variation in productivity.

Feeding Back Progress

It cannot be emphasized too often that transition is a synergistic process: all three stages (transition management, infrastructure implementation, and Pathfinder projects) constantly refer and feed back to each other, as do most of the programs within the infrastructure implementation stage. The transition plan, as well, is actively managed, responding to the progress of the transition and modified in light of the response of development staff and the rest of the organization to change.

When Is Transition Complete?

Probably the third hardest question related to Development Effectiveness (after "Why do I need it?" and "Where do I start?") is "When is transition complete?" In a sense, transition is never complete—it is merely the first series of managed steps in an endless cycle of improvement and innovation. In practice, however, an organization that successfully manages the transition process will be able to tell when it is over. It will have the measurements to indicate that its objectives have been met and that the changes it set out to make have been internalized.

Creating and Managing an Effective Infrastructure

A successful and effective development infrastructure contains many key components (see Figure 9.9). The list that follows is a minimum and by no means exhaustive. If an IS organization misses any of the items listed, however, the chances of success are much diminished.

- **Methodology,** in the sense of a defined and deployed set of processes for the work of the IS development and maintenance organization. Without a visible, repeatable process, the change cannot get started, measurement is essentially meaningless, and improvements cannot easily be identified.
- **Project Management Support,** including both process and tools, for both designing and controlling projects. The first category ensures that project designs are efficient, and the second that project execution is effective.
- **Development Support Tools.** This category includes both "conventional" development tools and tools that address all of the things conventional tools do not. Organizing all of these tools into an environment that supports productive use of the technology is one of the major challenges of the infrastructure program.
- **Knowledge Base.** The IS organization needs to build and deploy technology and processes that assist with the consolidation, management, and reuse of knowledge, experience, models, and other IS components.
- **Communications.** Often overlooked as a facet of infrastructure, an effective intraproject and interproject communications environment should be provided, so that knowledge and experience can be easily shared.
- **Measurement.** Measurement can be greatly eased if the infrastructure supports information capture as a by-product of work flows, and if infrastructure design takes this into consideration.
- **Organization Design.** The organizational design for the future-state IS organization influences and is

influenced by the nature of the required IS infrastructure. Coordination between infrastructure and organizational design programs is therefore essential.

- **Training and Skills Development.** Creating a comprehensive performance-support environment in which all staff members can be trained and coached in effective use of the infrastructure as it becomes available, and as they need it is an integral part of the infrastructure program, not a separate responsibility.
- **Process Improvement.** It is important to remember that the aim of a Development Effectiveness program is continuous process improvement and innovation capability. Infrastructure components are needed to insure that this goal is supported.

Because the availability of an effective infrastructure underpins the ability to execute the IS development process effectively,

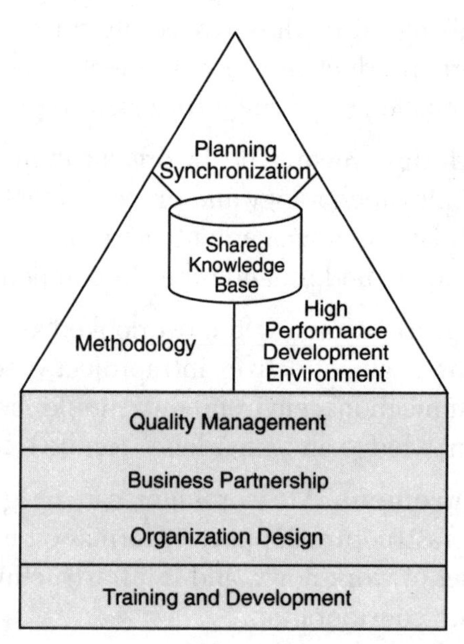

Figure 9.9 *Key Components of the Development Effectiveness Infrastructure*

infrastructure development is a key success factor within the transition. The readiness assessment will have documented the extent to which current infrastructure meets the needs of developers. The infrastructure program has to fill in the gaps in the current state, or in the worst case, create a suitable infrastructure from scratch.

A Complete Program for Infrastructure Creation

Putting an effective infrastructure together is a major challenge, perhaps especially for an IS organization that prides itself on an ability to deploy similar technology for its customers. There are many temptations to take shortcuts, go too fast, or leave out essential components. In the following paragraphs we provide a fairly detailed example of the range of activity that may be needed. Most organizations do not need to do everything that is mentioned here, but we have seen few examples where much could actually be left out safely.

A good IS development methodology can be viewed as the articulation of what the process of information systems development should be—a vision for the process. In transition, the methodology is not so much "implemented" as "realized."

One form in which successive increments in process improvement appear is in the deeper, wider, and more effective use of good methodology as the transition progresses. The process of widening and deepening the use of methodology to transform the best in the craftsmanship of systems building into excellence in engineering must continue ad infinitum. Such improvement consists of extending competency in the use of methods to more and more of the development staff, and in extending the range and depth of the methodology itself—continuously improving the process of development that the methodology describes. The methodology that is adopted must match these demanding requirements.

Organizing to Support the Methodology

Most developers do not take easily to a new methodology, whether or not they have used one before. They are especially resistant if the new methodology cannot be avoided. Like all changes, a change to a new development process must be supported, communicated, and marketed. It must also show early benefits (hence Pathfinder projects) and successes. We have found it best to start off with a specific support project for deploying the new process, chartered with the objective of making the Pathfinder teams self-confident users of the new processes. As deployment proceeds, a small group can be given responsibility for this aspect of process improvement, although membership should evolve to ensure that the "methodologists" do not lose touch with their customers among the developers.

Any good development process must be customized to match the specific needs of each group of users within the enterprise. Customizing the methodology must therefore be possible, but must also be done in a controlled fashion and preferably on the basis of demonstrated need. Customization should not be an excuse to retain outmoded working practices. Once again, use experience gained in Pathfinder projects to direct customization efforts.

Project-Support Office

Because the methodology selected must be effective in supporting the management of projects that are designed by using that methodology, consider setting up a project-support office for initial Pathfinder projects. The office can act as a training unit for project managers who are unfamiliar with the new process and its management demands.

A High-Performance Development Environment

An effective high performance development environment (HPDE) should establish a consistent tool architecture containing:

- Tools that support the whole development process so that developers can use a single environment on a project (although they may use different environments on different projects),
- A "protected environment" for groups of developers that insulates them from unnecessary technology management activity and supports reuse of existing models and components,
- A means of mapping the development support tools to the tasks of populating and using the contents of the knowledge base,
- A means of managing group work flow on a project so that appropriate tasks are assigned according to capability and appropriate tools are available at appropriate points in the development process, and
- A measurement system that automatically collects process-related information.

Establishing an HPDE for the first time can be a significant investment. However, this is repaid many times over in reduced training, process management, and technology management costs.

Organizing To Support Development Technology Long Term

It is very difficult to design and deploy a comprehensive HPDE in isolation from the situations in which it will be used and the people who will use it. HPDE development and deployment should therefore be done in collaboration with the initial projects in the Pathfinder program, providing a real-world test bed for the HPDE concepts and content. Figure 9.10 shows a common profile for the deployment of HPDE technology. Early adopters in Pathfinder projects feed improvements back to the development group, and the attractiveness of the technology grows as its use is proven and improvements are incorporated. In most instances, usage will never achieve 100%, because:

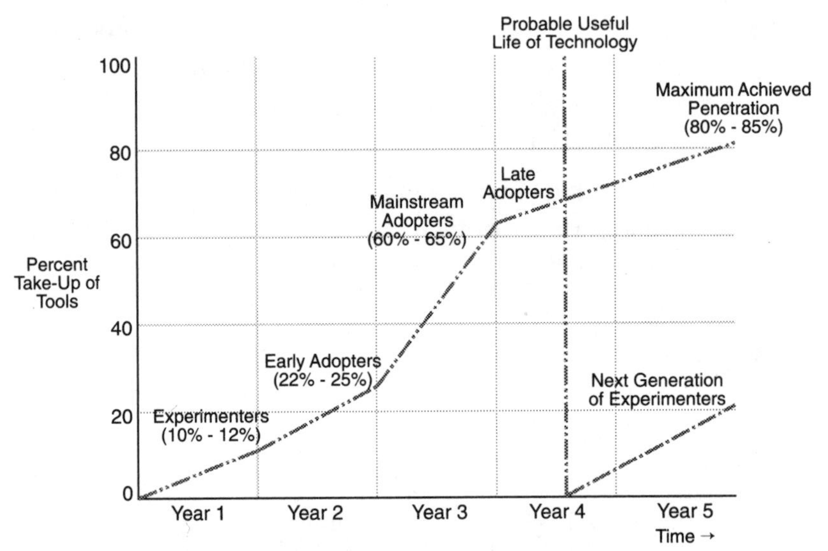

***Figure 9.10** Take-up Pattern for HPDE-like Technologies*

1. There will always be some tasks for which it will never be cost-effective to include support within the HPDE, although other forms of infrastructure support may be available.

2. A new generation of HPDE technology will probably be introduced every 4 to 5 years, faster than the deployment process would take to achieve universal usage.

This observation has some implications for the setting of deployment objectives (do not set an objective of 100% usage if it is clear that this cannot be achieved) and the justification basis for the use of these infrastructure components.

The Knowledge Base

Developing and using a common knowledge base for all IS development and maintenance work is a major cultural change for most IS organizations. Once the knowledge base is established, as much

Figure 9.11 *Data Administration Must Not Become a Bottleneck to the Use of the Knowledge Base*

as 95% of an information system can be available at the start of a development project from material already built, tested, and proven. This is an enormous potential source of productivity and quality improvement but, for IS staff, it represents a technical challenge and a completely new way of working.

In IS organizations, just as in many areas of life, knowledge is power (or at least influence), and the group that manages the knowledge is reluctant to make it too widely available, lest their power be reduced. This behavior has become quite typical of data administration and information resource management groups we have observed in many IS organizations. Rather than promote the widespread use of the models and knowledge they have collected, they hoard them, acting as the "model police" and writing procedures that ensure that other developers cannot make progress past critical milestones unless they approve (see Figure 9.11).

Implementing an effective knowledge base requires that the knowledge base managers change from being inward-looking custodians of content to outward-looking advocates of value. Instead of being a "black hole" into which all developers are required to throw the fruits of their work, never to be seen again, the knowledge base must be sold and used as the source of excellence in past work and as a resource to be used to ensure excellence in the future.

"Selling" The Knowledge Base Concept

Setting up and deploying an enterprise-wide knowledge base is a significant undertaking. The technology required is barely available, and the process is both long and resource intensive. Justification must, therefore, be significant if the project is to be sanctioned. Because an effective knowledge base is essential to much of what Development Effectiveness seeks to achieve, this justification must be clearly understood by sponsors and by developers, who may wait some time to see the promised potential realized.

Figure 9.12 shows a typical deployment model for a knowledge base and forms the basis for justifying the required resources. Note that although the buildup of content is initially slow, careful seeding of the initial content with widely used components provides a disproportionate level of improvement in the development process. Over the transition period, the knowledge base will not absorb all available material. Indeed, some of the existing information systems will never migrate to the knowledge base before they are replaced for economic or technical reasons.

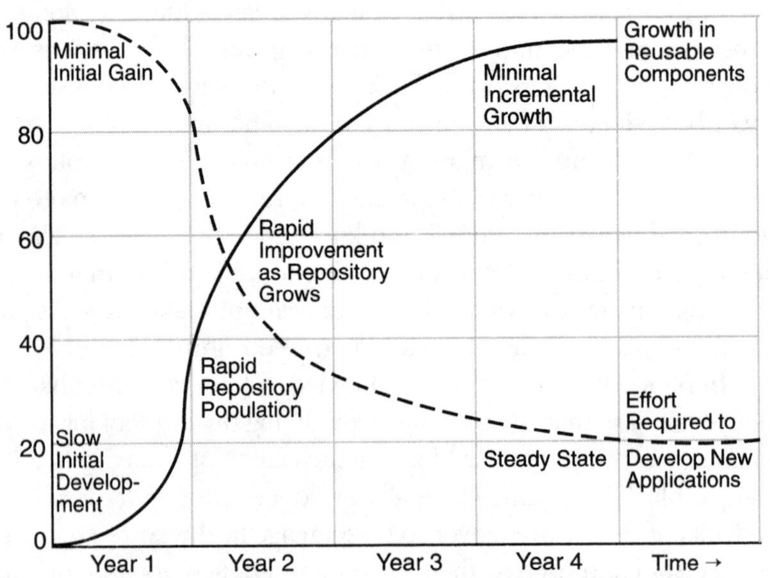

Figure 9.12 *The Economic Basis for Justification of the Knowledge Base is Performance Improvements Through Reusability*

Note also that the knowledge base will never contain everything required for new development or for the evolution of existing information systems. Once again, it is well to set expectations for content and reuse that are in accord with reality.

Populating the Knowledge Base

One way to accelerate the deployment of the knowledge base (shown in Figure 9.13) is to explicitly prepopulate the initial implementation with components and models derived from existing information systems and from enterprise-requirements models (usually for data only). This can be a powerful initial impetus to knowledge base use and, if suitable technology is available, a rapid and effective strategy.

Pathfinder projects will be explicitly chartered to contribute to knowledge base development. In addition, *all* IS development and maintenance projects should be encouraged to use and contribute to the contents of the knowledge base. This process can be encouraged if the "owners" of the knowledge base actively solicit participation by developers and actively market the benefits that a knowledge base can bring.

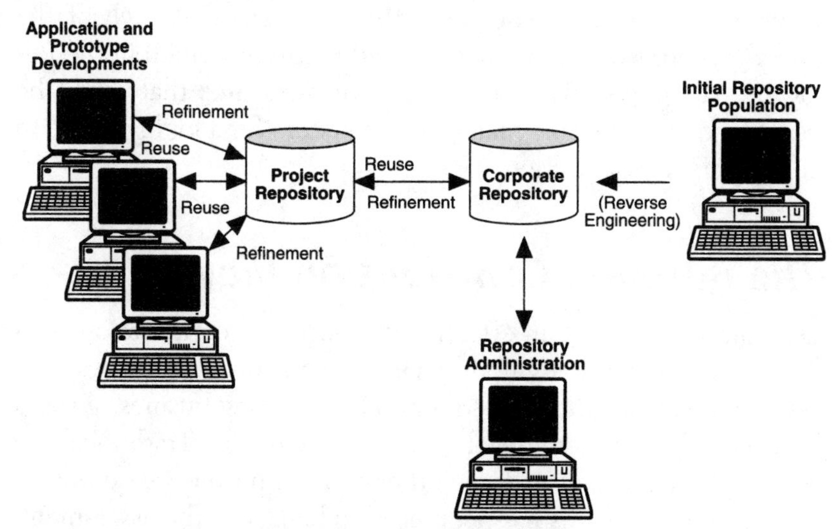

Figure 9.13 Populating the Knowledge Base

Effective Management of Change: Organize for Quality

One of the sadder aspects of the quality movement as it has been applied to the IS organization is the almost total failure of the basic principles of TQM to survive the translation into IS processes. In too many IS organizations, Quality Assurance is a standards compliance policing organization, not seen to add value to the development process and avoided if at all possible. This situation and its attendant behaviors must change. To be effective, the TQM process must be integrated with all other aspects of the future-state development process and the organization and culture that uses it. The enforced compliance behavior model discussed in Chapter 6 is inappropriate for this role.

Measurement of Development Effectiveness

The generic elements and questions of the IS Measurement Framework described earlier in this chapter take on life when they are applied to a specific situation, such as a Development Effectiveness program. Some of the measures that each of the four viewpoints of the framework lead to are described in the following paragraphs. The emphasis is on measures that might be developed as part of the management system for a highly effective development organization.

The Business Contribution View

One characteristic of an effective development organization is its ability to select the right projects to work on. Having ways to assess projects for their contribution to achieving business goals is critical to the ability to develop this characteristic. Traditionally, a return-on-investment or some other form of business case involving financial measures has been used to help with the assessment.

However, there is a growing movement to go beyond or, at least, to complement financial measures with other ways of looking at the value of an IT project.[9]

The key is to establish a process that allows projects to be reviewed, but not capriciously redirected or terminated. Nothing compromises the productivity of an application development group more than an environment of constant second-guessing and project redirection. Yet at the same time, no good can come from continuing a project that is no longer related to business needs or that has encountered obstacles that escalate the risk of poor implementation or payoff. We frequently see projects that have become monsters with lives of their own, consuming vast resources and yet unwanted by any business area.

Finally, an effective management system is one that incorporates learning from previous decisions. This means creating a mechanism to track the realization of benefits and the implementation experiences of completed projects. Well executed, such a mechanism can greatly increase learning about IT investment selection and implementation. The availability of reliable measures is important in achieving these results.

The User/Customer View

Also characteristic of an effective development organization are "customers" who think well of it and who are satisfied with the products and services it provides. The importance of having a customer focus, which has always been important, has received a recent boost as a result of the interest in quality improvement that has swept the world.

A number of techniques are used to learn about the needs, expectations, and satisfaction of customers. Organizations often track changes in customer perceptions. Such data can often signal that trouble exists before financial measures show changes. Analysis of perceptions can also help pinpoint specific problems that other measures have flagged, thus helping to guide corrective actions. Another common measure involves tracking the achievement of established service-level agreements, which is particularly important in tracking one of the issues Development Effectiveness is intended to address—unreliable performance.

Internal Performance Review

In addition to looking externally, it is usually appropriate to look inward at dimensions that are important to systems delivery, such as cost, cycle time, and quality. A change to any of these will often effect the others. It is necessary to "triangulate" the three metrics to ensure that unexpected tradeoffs are not being made and that the dynamics that exist between the three elements are understood.

Measurement can be applied to the processes that underlie the development, or to their outputs—whether products or services. Examples of process measures include work output delivered per developer month, elapsed time to deliver a given work output, or defects per given work output. Examples of product measures include total size of a given system and an analysis of such factors as the amount of new and changed code delivered.

Productivity

Productivity is measured in the development area as in any other production area—work output versus work effort (or cost). The common measure is Function Points (FP) per work-month.

Just as with other production measures, there can be variations depending on the investigation being conducted by the person doing the measurement. For example, does interest lie in the amount of function being delivered to the business, or in the amount of work the development team had to do? In either case, the function point is a reasonable "currency" to use; however, the "charts of account" will vary depending on which question is being investigated.

In the first case, the underlying question concerns the productivity of the development groups in delivering new function to the business. It is the kind of question that a senior business manager might ask. Only the actual function asked for and delivered to users would be counted.

In the second case, the question concerns the work done by the project team. This is the kind of question that a project manager, trying to understand how much effort it takes to do a particular task, might ask. All of the function delivered *and* all of the scaffolding, test, and other support functions that often accompany a project would be counted in this case.

These two instances illustrate that there can be a number of different, but valid, questions asked about productivity in the context of Development Effectiveness. Thus, it is always necessary to keep in mind the audience and the purpose of the question being answered. This point is true for other measurements as well.

Cycle Time

The measures of cycle time are similar to those used in determining productivity. The basic form is elapsed time to deliver a given amount of work output; for example, elapsed months to deliver 1,000 function points (FPs).

As with productivity measures, there are variations depending upon the question being asked. Two common variations are elapsed time *from project start to delivery* per 1,000 FPs and elapsed time *from known need to delivery* per 1,000 FPs. The latter can be substantially longer, for it includes the time spent waiting for management decisions to go ahead and waiting in application backlogs for project resources to be assigned. It also reflects the time that determines business management perceptions about the responsiveness of the development organization and is therefore an important Development Effectiveness measure. As this is the case, this is often an important Development Effectiveness measure.

The first measure is also of interest to the manager of a Development Effectiveness initiative. It reflects the time it takes to accomplish a project and may thus be a better measure when the need is to assess the effect of different tools and techniques on the project.

Product Quality Versus Process Quality

The first step toward process-quality improvement is to understand how the process actually works, how and where defects are introduced, and how they are identified. This understanding provides the knowledge and insight necessary to make changes to the process.

Starting a Measurement Program

Companies have a hard time starting measurement programs and a harder time keeping them going. We find two common problems.

First, there is a tendency to dwell too long on trying to identify the "right" things to measure. Not that answering this question is not important—it is. Some people, however, become frozen into inaction by looking for the one or two "right" measures and by asking all the wrong people what those measures should be. For example, anyone who has ever established any reputation in the metrics field is constantly being asked "What should we measure?" No metrics expert, however smart, can tell someone what to measure—each individual has first to identify his or her own measurement purpose and then ask key stakeholders and customers what is important to *them.* There are almost never just one or two right measures—there is a set, and that set will be different for every situation and will change as the situation changes.

The second measurement problem is that when it is eventually implemented, measurement is often performed in a vacuum, without the other elements necessary for a complete *measurement system.* We have seen IS measurement groups who tell us with pride about their metrics program. When we ask what happens to the data, we are usually shown impressive, colorful graphs on walls. When we probe further about *what actually happens* to the data beyond being charted and displayed, we get blank looks, as if charting and displaying data *is* the ultimate goal.

Our last probe is usually, "So what changes as a result of the measurement?" This usually turns on the lights. "Oh, so *that's* what you mean! Well, nothing actually *changes,* but at least we now know how we are doing." Measurement should not just tell you how you are doing. It should be part of a system that guides your efforts to *change* how you are doing; this is its value.

Continuing Synchronization of Development with the IS Plan

Developing, or having developed, an Information Systems Plan is not included as a part of the Development Effectiveness transition plan, but is an essential part of long-term effective development. The IS Plan provides an effective framework for medium-term to long-term strategic alignment with business partners and, as an essential component, develops the target technical and organizational architectures that developers can use to plan effective use of the new IS infrastructure.

The planning process is an excellent forum for the IS organization to demonstrate and implement an effective contribution to the creation and support of business value. It can also be used to spread IS influence into new areas of the enterprise and to create new opportunities to get improved levels of business sponsorship for IS. An active IS planning process and the continuing evaluation of the relevance of the plan extends the constituency of interest in IS priorities and improves the effectiveness of the IS plan itself. Be aware, however, that the theoretical perfection in IS planning often promised in the literature is seldom achievable in practice, and that it will take time for the IS organization to establish that it can add value to enterprise planning by its involvement in the wider planning process.

Also remember that, if appropriate, the development of an IS Plan can be a midterm Pathfinder project within the transition.

Working in Partnership with the Business

Setting up an effective partnership with the business requires special attention be paid to achieving the necessary changes in behavior from all participants. The typical expectations of both the information system developer and the business user/customer must be modified during the initial partnership formation process. This change can be painful for both parties. There is more than one possible model of partnership behavior, and different models may be appropriate for different stages of the transition process or for different situations during and after transition.

Techniques For Establishing Partnerships

One obvious opportunity for developing partnership relationships and behaviors is the program of Pathfinder projects. Ensure that each Pathfinder project establishes and builds on a partnership with the customer community. Use the education and training components of the transition to train both IS and business participants at the same sessions. Each group can thus discover that it has much in common with the other and recognize that both groups are embarking on a new process that is unfamiliar to all involved. This can be a powerful first step in discovering the benefits of working together. Other approaches include the following:

- **Service-Level Agreements.** More conventional service partnership models can also be used. If the IS organization has yet to implement service-level agreements with customers, transition management should encourage it to do so and should make sure that an effective means of measurement is in place to support this step. Focus attention on improvements in service levels where this is needed, and publicize both good service and areas where improvements are achieved. Focus in particular on business benefits derived from improved service levels achieved in partnership with business customers.

- **Joint Information Management.** Most data managed by the information systems that the IS organization develops and maintains is really owned by someone in the business. Encourage these people to accept ownership (or at least stewardship) of the data. Where there are multiple owners, get them together under the auspices of the IS organization. Involve customers for the data in setting and monitoring data quality and data management policies.
- **Whose Knowledge Base Is It Anyway?** In the end, the knowledge base is an enterprise-wide resource. Look for opportunities to support the wider business strategy and needs of the enterprise through the capabilities offered by a comprehensive knowledge base, and make sure that the enterprise knows that IS is willing to participate in and help with wider business issues.

Keep in mind, too, that an IS planning effort is a great focus for developing effective business partnerships.

Development for Development: The Training Model

Education does not stop with awareness building. Even in the unlikely event that everyone who will eventually be involved in the transition has participated in the awareness building elements of Development Effectiveness, new targets for education will arrive throughout the transition as the organizational structures and individuals within the enterprise change. In any case, education is an essential element of continuing communications and public relations surrounding the changes that will take place as transition proceeds.

In the readiness assessment activity, an initial assessment is made of the inventory of IS and business skills that can be drawn upon to support the transition to the future-state vision. In addition to this initial inventory, the transition must aim to reinforce existing skills and behaviors and create new ones as they are required by elements of the change process. For a large organization and its customers, this must be a well-planned and continuing effort. In particular:

- Education and training requirements must be matched to the needs of the future state vision, where these can be anticipated.
- Needed skills, both for the transition and, afterward, for the future state, must be identified and monitored.
- Existing skills must be certified or at least reviewed for appropriateness and effectiveness in use.

This assessment process allows the training program to build on an objective view of the existing skills base in the IS and business organizations, their strengths and weaknesses, and the effects that these will have on transition plans.

Curricula For The Future State

Once the transition has been achieved, two kinds of curricula will be required:

1. **Induction.** This curriculum focuses on the effective introduction of new staff into the culture, organization, infrastructure, and processes of the future-state IS organization. A transition-specific version of this curriculum should also be developed.
2. **Competency Development.** This set of curricula is focused on the various possible career development routes available to staff within the future-state vision. It is the basis for planning staff capabilities as needs and technology evolve.

Building from the experience of Pathfinder projects, an initial version of the curricula should be built, tested, and delivered.

Continuous improvement will then be required to keep the training in step with changes elsewhere in the process, organization, infrastructure, and business needs.

Establish a Performance Support Capability

Because reskilling will be a continuing challenge in the future state, the transition must create a fundamentally new capability to acquire cheaply and deploy easily a range of skills that changes over time. It must also create a capability to substitute for the depth of experience that has previously characterized technical competency. If the pace of change continues as expected, IS and business staff will no longer have the time to gain this depth of experience before being required to perform as expert practitioners.

Coping with these new pressures to perform is a necessary facet of the learning organization that forms a part of the future-state IS vision. We have chosen to call this capability "performance support," because it must embrace all aspects of conventional education and training, as well as facilitation, coaching, and mentoring. It must also provide "in the workplace" and Just-in-Time facilities, in as much as this is where and when the support will be needed.

Creating the Infrastructure Through "Real Work"

We conclude the discussion on infrastructure implementation with a short reminder of the basic principles discussed repeatedly throughout this chapter.

- Infrastructure is nothing if it is not in use.
- Pathfinder projects use and prove each iteration of the infrastructure.
- Each Pathfinder project creates improved infrastructure for the future.

- Infrastructure is never "finished." Infrastructure investment is the price of continuing innovation capability.

It is only by applying these principles and beginning the continuous improvement process right from the start of the transition that an effective infrastructure can be put in place as and when it is needed. Chapter 10 further describes the role of Pathfinder projects as a vehicle for achieving transition.

Notes

1. The authors are grateful to Ernst & Young's UK Consulting practice for permission to use this 1991 example.
2. The "burning platform" metaphor resulted from the reported experiences of survivors of the Piper-Alpha oil production platform disaster in the North Sea in 1990. It was first articulated by Daryl Conner, President of ODR Inc., an Atlanta-based change management consulting firm.
3. Stephen R. Covey, *The 7 Habits of Highly Effective People* (New York: Fireside, 1989).
4. See Robert B. Grady, *Practical Software Metrics for Project Management and Process Improvement* (New York: Prentice-Hall, 1992), for an excellent introduction to the implementation of a system of measurement.
5. The IS measurement framework resulted from, and continues to be developed by, participants in the IS Leadership Multi-Client Research Program facilitated by the Ernst & Young Center for Information Technology & Strategy[SM].
6. James McGee and Laurence Prusak, *Managing Information Strategically* (New York: John Wiley & Sons Inc. 1993).
7. There is no room (or need) here for a treatment of the statistical theory that underlies the law of large numbers and its applications in measurement. It is sufficient to say that *all* natural phenomena exhibit characteristics that follow this form of distribution.
8. Gerald M. Weinberg, *The Psychology of Computer Programming* (New York: Van Nostrand Reinhold, revised edition, 1974).
9. Marilyn Parker and Robert Benson, *Information Economics* (New York: Prentice-Hall, 1989).

10

Transition Through Action: The Pathfinder Process

The theory of Development Effectiveness is all very well, but if an IS organization cannot make the practice work, Development Effectiveness remains just an interesting theory. Therefore, a transition must contain an effective deployment process for the new infrastructure, a process that uses all of the changes and improvements to deliver real business benefits within a short time frame—usually sooner than the Information Systems (IS) organization feels is reasonable, given the level of the changes involved. That is where the Pathfinder process comes into play.

Pathfinder Projects

Because it is clear that infrastructure and processes that are not used cannot provide benefits, getting them into use quickly is essential. The selection of the first few projects, therefore, is critical. These projects must be seen as successes in order to fuel the organization's enthusiasm for continued rapid deployment of the new development approach and tools. Projects must have the potential to deliver something useful and must be provided with the resources and support necessary to maximize their chances of success. The approach to choosing such projects should therefore:

- Be based on realistic and required developments, rather than artificially created projects that will never deliver useful results and benefits, even if successful,
- Cover a range of project types so that the new infrastructure and processes can be seen to be widely applicable,

- Involve staff at all levels of skill and experience, avoiding the use of "experts only" teams that are not truly representative of the IS organization as a whole,

- Allow for the verification of the infrastructure support services and the technical services organization that will be developed in parallel with project activity,

- Encourage early population and use of the development knowledge base so that the leverage available from reusability is exploited at an early stage, and

- Deliver working information systems to business users within as short a period as possible so that measurable business benefits can be identified.

The program of Pathfinder projects should contain a number of projects that represent the range of development activities the IS function currently undertakes or plans to undertake during the transition period. It may also contain projects new to the IS function that are made possible by the new infrastructure or development process.

Management of the transition through a series of short, overlapping Pathfinder projects provides the means to ensure that the lessons of each project are carried forward to subsequent projects and that commitment accumulates with experience and success. As described earlier, this process is like building a bandwagon in support of a cause.

The process starts with the staff working on the first project, which must include people within the organization whose opinions are listened to with respect in informal conversation and who are seen as role models. These will be the key change agents in future projects and advocates when they are not working on transition activities. The first project team must also include ordinary staff—it is important that success should not be attributable to the fact that the "A team" was allocated to the project.

Selecting Pathfinder Projects

Given these objectives, it is perhaps unfortunate that most Development Effectiveness implementations start with a requirements analysis project. There is nothing really wrong with this—after all, requirements specification is one area in which the new partnership culture, process, and infrastructure are supposed to make a significant impact. It is also an area that most IS organizations feel they already know how to do, so that training effects can be minimized. Unfortunately, this is often a *bad* place to start from if the objective is a successful first Pathfinder, due to the following reasons:

- A well-defined requirements analysis process, which the Development Effectiveness transition needs to have in place, is often absent or, if present, used badly or not at all. Analysts do not understand how to use the new approaches and expected behaviors effectively because they do not really understand the techniques the process supports. In particular, data-analysis techniques are often inadequately understood and poorly executed, yet the deliverables from these techniques are essential to the production of a high-quality specification that can drive an automated development environment.

- Many of the architectural issues raised by using the process for the first time cannot be resolved if there is no Strategic Information Systems Plan in place, so early Pathfinder projects can get sidetracked into addressing these strategic issues and fail to deliver the required results to meet their original (tactical) objectives.

- Scoping an analysis project accurately is very difficult without corporate models for strategy, organization, data, and functions, so early Pathfinder projects may well have to be adjusted as they go along, thus adding control complications, distorting any comparisons that might be made, and potentially wasting scarce change resources on unproductive or irrelevant work in the early stages of the project.

- There is a significantly reduced opportunity for added value from the first Pathfinder project if the models built with the new infrastructure tools are limited to one business area and are not readily usable in others. This is especially important to remember when looking for opportunities to populate the development knowledge base with reusable components.
- Training is often hurried in the rush to get started, resulting in confusion and uncertainty in the project team and low morale during the project. This outcome is usually seen as a bad reflection on the change process rather than on the organization of the Pathfinder project.
- There is a severe danger of "the blind leading the blind" on the project. Recently trained or even untrained IS staff and business users have to become instant experts, and they usually cannot manage to do so. They make mistakes in their use and understanding of the new processes and tools, which can easily become working practice because there is no one to correct them.
- The deliverables from a requirements analysis project do not usually represent much of a benefit for the business—nothing is actually implemented as a result of all the effort. Although there should be benefits in terms of improved understanding between IS developers and their customers in the business, these will be less tangible than those, ideally, needed. Only implemented and working information systems can really prove the correctness of the Development Effectiveness thesis. Stopping a Pathfinder project after requirements analysis will not get the project to a point where such proof is available or believable.

In an ideal world, the best place to start a transition is with a proper information strategy planning exercise, with a major organizational division as its subject, so that the key corporate models (strategy, organization, data, and function) can be in place and agreed to, and the essential architectures (data, applications, technology, and organization) identified, planned, and understood. Subsequent development projects can then work from a common and consistent baseline, with assigned and agreed-upon priorities and high added value from the availability of the planning models in the knowledge base.

Moreover, the information strategy planning process is less dependent on existing skills (although it still requires the basic skills of enterprise-level data and function modeling to be available to the team), and planning teams usually consist of more experienced staff. The duration of the planning phase also allows time for sensible infrastructure deployment and training for the analyst and designers who will be involved in later projects.

Despite such a strong case for starting with an information strategy plan, many IS organizations actually start somewhere else. We have come to recognize a few specific and important reasons why this happens:

- The choices of infrastructure and tools that support the planning process are limited. There is a much wider range of support capability for requirements analysis and systems design and delivery, so it is safer to start with an analysis project and then move on to the design phase.
- A Strategic Information Systems Plan can simply take too long. If an IS organization is expecting to show some benefits from the transition process, it does not want to wait the several months such a project usually takes.
- Not everyone feels confident that such a plan is necessary or desirable—it may even show up other problems that IS management would rather not make visible. If this is the case, Development Effectiveness is going to

fail as well, because the transition will inevitably run into the same problems.

- The IS organization may already have, or claim to have, a strategic plan in place, and probably does not want to repeat the planning exercise just for the benefit of the transition program.

If a recently developed Strategic Information Systems Plan already exists, a good approach is to use the new infrastructure tools and processes to document it thoroughly and to construct the relevant corporate models. This helps validate the contents of the plan and gives any subsequent requirements-analysis projects a head start with a set of models in the knowledge base.

Characteristics of Pathfinder Projects

Every development project is somewhat different, so finding a relatively small number of representative project types can be difficult. Nevertheless, a few common project types can be identified and used. Plan to include Pathfinder projects that:

- Develop a medium-sized business-operations support application from requirements analysis to delivery of the working application. This is the most common kind of custom-development project, so it may be as well to include more than one in the overall program. Plan on trying out a number of rapid development approaches within this type of project.

- Develop an application that uses existing data resources for new purposes, such as decision support or analysis. This is also a fairly representative type of development with the greatest variability in the project, because of the quality of existing data and the sophistication of the software used to manage existing data structures. The IS organization may wish to consider adding some redevelopment engineering components to these projects to get rapid understanding of existing structures and to assist with the design of efficient interfaces to existing applications.

- Develop a specialized application in an area such as expert systems or geographical information systems, where new or unorthodox techniques and tools will be required. This may not be a large area of activity at present, but Pathfinder projects should test the capability of the selected tools to support future requirements as well.
- Develop some key elements of the enterprise information architecture. One or more projects can be set up to do various types of rapid planning for the definition of an enterprise data architecture, an enterprise applications architecture, and an enterprise technology architecture. All these will be needed sooner or later and are a good test for the knowledge base. If an information architecture is already in place, the project can act as a coordination exercise to validate the architecture as each Pathfinder project delivers a model of a new working application.
- Reverse-engineer an application as an aid to maintenance and as a demonstration of this approach to rapid population of the development knowledge base. Reverse-engineering technology will play an important role in the creation of a highly effective development and maintenance environment and should therefore be included as an early Pathfinder project.
- Develop a requirements model for which the solution will be implemented by a software package, or part of a package, supplied by a third party. This will be a significant test of the capability of selected infrastructure and process to support essential activity that results in a "design" from a source outside the IS organization but

which must still be integrated with custom software and maintained in the medium term.

- Develop a requirements model that can be implemented by end-user computing tools, paving the way for the wider inclusion of business users within the overall information systems development and evolution process.

The First Pathfinder Project

If an IS organization is one of the eight out of every ten installations for whom the preferred transition route is an initial Pathfinder project in requirements analysis, followed by design, construction, and implementation, then there are some important issues to consider in selecting a suitable first project. The following are among the key considerations:

1. The project should be one that is going to be done anyway, not something invented for the purpose of creating Pathfinder projects. This means that it is a "real" project, the outcome of which matters to both the IS organization and the business. Given that there is actually some risk in introducing Development Effectiveness, the project should probably not be a strategically vital development, although the selection and scoping criteria given earlier, and in the following paragraphs, will tend to rule such projects out of consideration. The initial project should, however, be a nontrivial development that will be implemented on completion and for which the IS organization has made delivery commitments to business users.

2. The project should be one that has already been scoped and sized so that, at worst, some comparison can be made between what was expected and what actually happens, provided there is a suitable measurement program in place.

3. The project should be the right "size." If it is too big, there may be problems in training and coordination for an inexperienced team using new approaches and tools. If the project is too small, the results, although achieved rapidly, will be dismissed as trivial and unrepresentative of most development requirements. The project should require a team of reasonable size and a representative mix of skills, so that a group of staff can be trained economically, and can form a core group of experienced developers for future Pathfinder projects. The development should last long enough to get the project team over the worst of the learning-curve effects, but not so long that the benefits realization, assessment and evaluation are delayed.

4. A good guideline is to use a team of between 6 and 10 people for between 3 to 6 elapsed months, with an absolute upper limit of 9 months. The maximum team size is less critical but should be kept below 15. The team should be led by an IS project manager, but at least one third of its members should be users from the business area under investigation.

5. The project should be in an area that is already well understood by both the business and the IS department. Try to avoid areas that are changing for other reasons, or that have serious organizational or managerial problems that will blur the effect of the tools on development progress, productivity, and quality.

6. The area to be investigated should not be associated with the introduction or use of too much new or unfamiliar technology or new business processes. Once again, the idea is to minimize the number of variables that the project team has to cope with, and to simplify the assessment of benefits.

7. If possible, the project should provide opportunities to

add value to the knowledge base by reusing work or deliverables in subsequent projects. This potential is difficult to assess without the corporate models and architectures developed by a strategic planning project, but some estimates should be made of the usefulness of the deliverables to other teams within and beyond the Pathfinder program.

In selecting a set of Pathfinder projects, it is a good idea to use a type of weighted scoring scheme. An example is shown in Table 10.1. The weights used here are derived from a number of real Pathfinder programs, but they should be assessed in the light of each organization's objectives and capabilities.

Most medium- and large-scale installations will have a project that fits the majority of these criteria, although selection may pose a problem in smaller departments. Where no obvious

Criterion	*Weight*	*Scores*									
		Project 1		***Project 2***		***Project 3***		***Project 4***		***Project 5***	
Relevance	5	3	15	6	30	1	5	9	45	6	30
Sponsorship	8	7	56	2	16	8	64	7	56	5	40
Size	7	5	35	2	14	3	21	1	7	5	35
Scope	8	5	40	2	16	4	32	9	72	5	40
Target Area Familiarity	4	2	8	8	32	8	32	7	28	1	4
Target Change Index	5	5	25	1	5	7	35	3	15	5	25
Added Value Potential	8	3	24	4	32	7	56	9	72	8	64
Support Capability	5	4	20	3	15	3	15	6	30	1	5
Skills Required	8	4	32	1	8	5	40	6	48	1	8
Cost of Support	4	6	24	6	24	5	20	3	12	3	12
User Involvement	7	1	7	6	42	5	35	9	63	1	7
Total			286		234		355		448		270

Table 10.1 *Weighted Selection Scores for Pathfinder Projects*

candidate can be found, developers should consider exactly why they are introducing Development Effectiveness and select a project that will best allow the performance of the products selected to be matched against these objectives of the transition program.

To prove that all of the preceding criteria are only guidelines, we offer our experience of a successful installation at a merchant bank. Here, virtually everything in the IS organization was changed all at once (hardware vendor, operating system, software package, DBMS, development language, and departmental location) and still managed a successful first implementation project in a strategically critical business area. It was a painful process, yet it worked for this organization, and took relatively little time to achieve. The approach certainly focused the minds of all involved on the commitment to succeed.

Remember, the first Pathfinder project must be successful, and must be seen to be successful. An IS organization is only allowed one good shot at Development Effectiveness, so it must make sure it gets a good first project and does it right.

Planning Pathfinder Projects

How Many?

Most organizations should plan on between 6 and 10 Pathfinder projects spread over a selection of categories. A good reason for planning on a number of projects, beyond the need to cover different types of development, is to minimize the "Hawthorne Effect"—the phenomenon, referenced in Chapter 7, whereby almost any change in an environment provides a short-term improvement in some aspects of worker performance. A program containing a number of projects will help to distinguish between the desired fundamental changes and the more transitory effects.

The Climate of Consent

If everyone in the IS organization is aware that the "platform is burning," then all will buy into the change quickly, and the main constraint on the number of Pathfinder projects will be expertise. If only members of top management have really seen the need for change, then the Pathfinder process has to win friends and influence people—step by step, project by project.

The Starting Point

A baseline will have been established in the readiness assessment. If the new methods and concepts represent a major break with the past, then take the first Pathfinder project slowly; if there is already an appreciation of the principles of an engineered development process and some of the techniques are widely used, then plan to introduce several Pathfinder projects in parallel before very long (subject to availability of coaching resources). Always start with a single project to kick off the various elements of the transition.

Resource Constraints: Selecting the Project Team

Another key area for consideration is the composition of the team for the first few projects. It is important to select a team that will have a good chance of being successful, but not one that's so unlike the usual project teams that everyone else knows that the results are not typical.[1] It is also an advantage if team members can be used as the nuclei of future Pathfinder project teams, so as to spread experience and confidence as rapidly as possible. In practice, it is very difficult to satisfy both criteria. The main considerations for selecting initial project team members are as follows:

- Team members should be enthusiastic about the transition, but not to the point of unreasoning fanaticism. They must be: (1) prepared to be positive in the face of the difficulties and problems that will inevitably arise in the first few projects, and to work to solve them rather than give up too easily, and (2) objective in their assessment of the contributions of infrastructure and process to the success of the project in contrast with other sources of improvement.
- Team members should be people whose views and abilities are trusted and respected by colleagues in the IS

and user departments, so that they can act as advocates for the transition process and the Pathfinder approach once it has been proven by Pathfinder projects. However, avoid using only "star" developers and users. The average developer or user will be someone with less than 2 years' experience in his or her current job, and the future-state processes must therefore be useful to someone at this level. If the new processes can be used only by real experts, they will not be used effectively by 80% or more of those who really need them.

- At the same time, avoid using people who are very inexperienced and will require constant supervision and help from other team members who may themselves be uncertain as to what they should be doing. Nor is it wise to include those who are strongly against the future-state vision for any reason. They will spend their time on the project trying to prove that the vision cannot work, rather than finding out what can actually be done and then doing it.

- *At least one-third of the team should be business-users.* Pick people who are keen on "systems" and pro-technology. If the project creates a favorable impression with users and generates a great deal of positive interest outside the IS organization, it will be difficult for IS staff not to accept the changes, simply in order to stay ahead of their customers.

- Select a really good project manager, assuming one is available. If not, hire one. Project management skills are one of the main determinants of success for any development project, and ensuring that the project will be managed effectively is of vital importance. Once the project manager is selected, be prepared to give him or her a great deal of encouragement and support during the Pathfinder project itself, and plan a reward to follow. Remember: doing the same thing again immediately—

managing another difficult Pathfinder project—may not be seen as much of a reward.

- Make sure the project team has plenty of support and "comfort." This support will almost certainly have to come, in part, from external sources who have the practical experience that the team lacks. Consider a support program that: (1) includes an experienced external change consultant as a team member—one is usually enough, as the team should be small, (2) holds a regular "clinic" to which problems and issues can be brought and where expertise that is not justified full-time on the project can be made available, and (3) has an escalation process that ensures that any serious issues can be addressed quickly if they are identified by the team itself or at one of the clinics.
- Be sure to get help from an organization that really knows how to use the new processes and infrastructure effectively and is experienced at working in an advisory or coaching role. Avoid those who want to do everything for you, or people who cannot explain to others what they are doing or have only theoretical knowledge of the transition process. This tends to rule out many conventional training organizations as sources of help. It is a lot better, therefore, to get help on the basis that the helpers work as coaches, *with,* rather than *for,* the initial project teams. Distributing support among current IS staff and users helps with the skills-transfer process and, over time, broadens the available range of support capabilities. It also improves the chances that there will be a helper on hand when the inevitable problems and difficulties arise.

Skimping on this kind of support is tempting because of the expense, but is actually a very unwise economy. The first projects will be the IS organization's main chance to learn how to use the new tools and approaches correctly, so investing in some help to ensure that this happens is money well spent.

Provided that the first Pathfinder project has sufficient management commitment, the kind of staff member needed can usually be made available, even though they will probably be busy on other things. Once the team members have been selected, it is a good idea to train them as a team in the use of the new process so that they get used to working together and understand each other's strengths and weaknesses. This familiarization process also makes life a lot easier for the project manager, who will then know what to expect from each team member and can adjust the project roles and responsibilities accordingly.

It is also a good idea to budget for additional review and presentation time to allow IS staff other than team members to be briefed on progress during the course of the project. A monthly seminar, given by the project team to groups of colleagues, will stop the project from being seen as "special" or "for only the privileged few." Right from the beginning, participation in the transition program should be seen neither as being elitist nor difficult, and keeping as many people as possible informed about what is going on is one way to prevent this from happening.

Do not forget that, even when things are going well, everyone in the transition process is using up assimilation energy. Make sure that transition management keeps an eye out for dysfunctional behaviors and adjusts the pace of the program accordingly. Data collection instruments can be used to monitor the health of the change processes as the transition proceeds, and these should always be used with the participants in the Pathfinder projects who are at the leading edge of the change.

Integrating with the Infrastructure Programs

In putting the new infrastructure to use it is useful to review the principles of infrastructure implementation that have already been discussed.

- Infrastructure is nothing if it is not in use.

- Pathfinder projects use and prove each iteration of the infrastructure.
- Each Pathfinder project creates improved infrastructure for the future.
- Infrastructure is never "finished;" infrastructure investment is the price of continuing innovation capability.

Each Pathfinder project must apply these principles and contribute to the continuous improvement process right from the start of the transition, so that an effective and improving infrastructure can be put in place as and when it is needed.

Supporting the Pathfinder Projects

It is the developers and business users who are making the change who must take charge of the projects and carry the change through; this is not an occasion to have the transition consultants take over the management of the project, however urgent the need for change.

Just as in medical training, "See one; do one; teach one" must be the guiding principle for the transition from introduction to internalization of the change process.

Build on the principle "I teach and I remember," and use staff from each Pathfinder project to coach subsequent project teams, thus building the commitment bandwagon. Have staff from infrastructure support work on Pathfinder projects as developers. Have developers work with the infrastructure team. Have customers work with everyone. This allows all sorts of profitable cross-fertilization between Pathfinder and infrastructure projects and keeps the continuous improvement initiative going. And make sure that the "experts" act in support of the change process, not in charge of it.

The quality of the "product" of the development process is clearly critical. However, the focus in a transition is shifted to the process itself—by improving the process, the products of information-systems development will be improved fundamentally and will go on improving.

Closing the Pathfinder Effort

In many ways, change in even the relatively small group of people represented by an IS organization and its customers is unpredictable. If new techniques, tools, or methods are simply introduced among the general mass of IS development staff, it is difficult to know where they will be taken up with enthusiasm, where they will be misdirected, or where they will be set aside without a proper trial. By mounting development projects onto the bandwagon one or two at a time, the process of change will be more visible and easier to direct.

The Pathfinder effort and the transition that it implements, is "over" when the principles of the effective development process are spread so widely in the development shop that the majority of projects are applying them. This may happen as a result of the Pathfinder process expanding to include more and more projects, or as a result of "mass" education through Pathfinder projects and the dissemination of Pathfinder-trained staff.

It is misleading, however, to talk of the *end* of a transition. A transition takes the development organization to the point where continuous improvement becomes a way of life. Thus, a transition is not an event, but a process. Moreover, the process of improving the development process may change after the transition, but will remain a permanent feature of organizational life. The final chapter of this book discusses the implications of internalizing continuous improvement and constant change.

Notes

1. This is somewhat contrary to conventional thinking that suggests using only the best staff for the initial projects. Nevertheless, we have seen many deployment failures after an initially successful effort by the "A" team, resulting from an inability among other staff to leverage the initial experience.

11

Living with the Future: Internalizing Continuous Improvement

Development Effectiveness does not end, per se. To remain effective, IS must embrace continuous improvement and learning. This chapter looks at the consequences of internalizing continuous learning and suggests a future-state information systems (IS) vision, using the five dimensions of the Diamond Model: Mission, Power, Structure, Resources, and Culture.

The Need for Continuous Change

It is wrong to think of the change to a high-performance development organization as an event. The end goal of Development Effectiveness is an organization that seeks out change—not for its own sake, but for the sake of continuous growth and learning for both the organization and its members.

This is the notion at the heart of the Japanese ethic of *Kaizen,* the never-ending quest for perfection. *Kaizen* leads to continuous improvement for every strategy, product, and process throughout an organization.

Although *Kaizen* does not emphasize innovation, a more radical approach to improvement, it does not preclude it. In many ways, facility with continuous learning is a prerequisite for harnessing successful innovation, and IS professionals must learn to master both incremental and radical approaches to change.

In theory, IS professionals ought to be very comfortable with change, inasmuch as the mission of the IS organization and the role of information technology (IT) have been in continuous flux since the beginning of commercial data processing. IS has long been an agent of change for those enterprises that it serves. In practice, however, IS has often been overconservative and reactive to change in its own use of information technology.

As the cycles of business change shorten, IS must respond more quickly and become *proactive* in embracing and facilitating change. Consistent with the evolving definition of quality, IS must anticipate the needs of its customers—must excite and delight them with its products and services and with its positive impact on the business.

Today IT is taking an increasingly strategic place in business, through information-based strategies, technology-enabled products and services, and business process innovation. With this shift in role, the primary goal for IT has changed from cost reduction to business value added. In response to the shift in IT's role, the mission for the IS organization is changing. IS must increasingly focus its energies on infrastructure-related activities—providing shareable IT resources for the businesses and ensuring that those resources are optimally used.

In many respects, this has always been the role of IT. However, back in the 1960s, fulfilling this role meant that IS professionals had to handle all IT aspects on behalf of the business; that is, they had to analyze systems requirements and design, develop, test, and maintain applications systems and data bases. Business professionals were cast in the role of "users." Like other groups to whom this label has been attached, "users" were dependent on the IT "pushers," coming to them for "fixes."

Today IT is becoming an increasingly dispersed and distributed resource, available to the masses. The notion of an information system as monolithic, inflexible sets of programs and files, designed for specific functions and used by specific clerical groups, is changing to a more organic model. The information system of the future will comprise many small components, each of them constantly evolving and metamorphosing, used directly by business professionals rather than by clerical intermediaries.

With this shift in the nature of an information system, the nature of systems development is also changing. Alvin Toffler, in his book *The Third Wave,*[1] coined the term *prosumer* to describe the merging of production and consumption. In the spirit of "prosumption," large, slow, monolithic development projects, run by IS professionals, are giving way to small, incremental, iterative projects, run by business units. With this shift, IS must increasingly hand over responsibility to business units, while retaining control over those IT components best shared, and enabling their sharing.

Planning for Continuous Change and Its Consequences

It is all well and good to describe a future state for IS development, but people will not readily follow a desired set of behaviors if these are inconsistent with their beliefs. No matter how much classroom education and training people have in project management, for example, if they do not believe in the underlying rationale for project management disciplines, they will not use them effectively.

Unfortunately, most people believe that the changes involved in upgrading the software development process will, at some point, be finished. In reality, the changes do not stop—change itself must become institutionalized. In the terms of the Lewin Model, introduced in Chapter 6, organizations move from the Beginning State to a Desired State, where the Desired State is one of continuous change—institutionalized learning. It is therefore important that people's belief systems are reset to expect this.

In Chapter 6, we discussed the ambiguity of the transition state. For people to feel comfortable with continuous change, they must have a clear mission and clear values. Even if the specifics of the future are fuzzy, a well-articulated set of shared values helps people to make the right daily decisions in the midst of uncertainty, and gives them a better sense of their overall mission and purpose.

From "What" to "Why"

Much of this book has approached things from a process perspective. Processes focus on how things are done and the ways in which people interact. Process skills include the recognition that results can be improved by improving processes that produce them.

In the deliverables-focused world of IS, and the results-driven mentality of contemporary management, it is easy to lose balance between processes and results. One of the key challenges in moving to a continuous improvement culture is to restore the balance by emphasizing process skills.

Process skills require a climate in which challenging the way things are done is not only accepted, but is expected, and problems are approached by multidisciplinary teams who value diversity, are skilled at reaching consensus, and find creative new ways to solve problems. Process skills thrive in a culture in which people feel ownership in results because they have ownership in the processes.

Process skills should be included in skills training curricula and practiced at every opportunity. In larger organizations it may be possible to identify particular individuals who already possess strong process skills, or can be trained in these skills, and position them as coaches or mentors to other groups. Unfortunately, however, it is recursive that coaching and mentoring programs work best in organizations that already have good process skills and a participative climate. Therefore, in a culture that is less participative, it is well to be prepared for an uphill battle in introducing these kinds of skills and to give the mentoring programs every incentive and opportunity to be effective.

The Transition Framework—Iterate, Iterate, Iterate!

We cannot overemphasize that although the Development Effectiveness transition framework may appear to be linear and sequential, with a beginning and an end, it is an iterative process. In fact, each element of the framework can be thought of as a "mini-process" that needs to be implemented, having its own feedback and control mechanisms. Awareness building, for example, is an ongoing activity. In most organizations, this already happens. We are suggesting that it be formalized and measured. One of the reasons so many business executives are challenging the value of IT is that they have little awareness of the nature of IT or of the IS function. IS must be more proactive in "marketing" IT through continuous awareness-building campaigns. In this sense, "marketing" includes careful analysis of market segmentation needs, positioning to market solutions, and creating an environment in which those solutions will be acquired.

Furthermore, one of the reasons IS has accepted a status quo that business finds unacceptable is that IS staff have often been disconnected from the day-to-day problems of business—they have lacked *awareness* of the cost of the status quo. Consider the proverbial frog who will jump out of boiling water if thrown into it, but will boil to death if it is already in the water before it is brought to a boil: the water around IS has been heating up for years.

Vision setting, similarly, should be institutionalized. The IS vision must be constantly refined and updated. It should be a living document, not one that is the focus of attention for a week or so every couple of years. Readiness assessment, transition planning, transition management, infrastructure implementation, and Pathfinder projects—all require ongoing attention.

Continuous Change—Innovative Change

We mentioned in Chapter 4 that change can be either incremental or radical. Although incremental change may be motivated and led from the top, it usually happens from the bottom up. People closest to a process identify ways to improve it. Radical change, or innovation, involves step-function improvement. It is nearly always led from the top and implemented from the top down. Those closest to a process may lack the insight, perspective, or motivation to radically change it. In fact, radical change may involve eliminating the process or combining it with another process. As such, discontinuous change must be driven from the top down.

IS must be skilled in both types of change, for use both within IS and within the broader enterprise. With the current popularity of business-process reengineering, IS has an important role to play. Where is its credibility in fulfilling this role if it has not taken the medicine itself?

We have used an exercise in workshop training settings to help people experience the differences between continuous and discontinuous change. The exercise, called the "ball toss," involves two teams passing three numbered tennis balls in a predetermined sequence among members of each team. The teams compete with each other to complete the sequence in the shortest possible time.

The trainees are shown the exercise and the sequence in which the balls must pass from person to person. The facilitator instructs the trainees to use creativity and team techniques to improve the "cycle time" of the process of completing the sequence. Once they have been instructed, the group is split into two teams. Each team works independently in a separate room.

Each team practices the sequence of ball tossing and is timed with a stopwatch. The facilitator gives specific improvement goals. For example, if the initial attempt to complete the sequence takes 17 seconds, the team is urged to reduce the time to 15 seconds. The facilitator moves between the two rooms, encouraging and motivating each team with the other team's performance. (A little "license" is taken by the facilitator in order to play one team against the other.) For example, one team is told, "The other team has got the sequence down to 13 seconds, so you have to do better than 12 seconds!" Several improvement cycles are allowed, and typically the teams are able to respond to the urgings for incremental improvement.

Then the facilitator drops the bombshell. Returning from one team's room, he says, "The other team has achieved a remarkable result. They have the sequence down to 2 seconds! You now have to better a 2-second sequence." Invariably, although the team struggled with the incremental change approach to get the sequence down from 17 seconds, to 15 seconds, to 12 seconds, and so on, they are quickly able to get the sequence down to less than 1 second.

The point of the exercise is that the teams' *approach* to improvement changes dramatically once the goal they are given becomes a "stretch" goal. The team members know, having spent 15 minutes or so, and several incremental improvement cycles, that they are not going to get down to less than 2 seconds by using the same incremental improvement techniques they used to get from 17 seconds to 12. They have to challenge their assumptions and rethink the problem they are trying to solve. Important also to this exercise is the fact that they have a benchmark—the other team. The facilitator is not just saying, "Do this in less than 2 seconds," but rather, "The other team has found a way to do this in 2 seconds."

Stretching goals, using different problem-solving approaches, challenging all assumptions, and rethinking the process from a high-level vision of the future state—what needs to be accomplished, rather than improving what has already been achieved—are the hallmarks of discontinuous change.

Being proactive in both continuous and discontinuous change and taking advantage of emerging technologies and methods requires organizations to become more effective at learning. In his book *The Fifth Discipline: The Art and Practice of the Learning Organization*,[2] Peter Senge, director of the Systems Thinking and Organizational Learning Program at MIT's Sloan School of Management, describes five disciplines as prerequisites for organizational learning: Systems Thinking, Personal Mastery, Mental Models, Shared Vision, and Team Learning. We have touched on each of these, from an IS development perspective although with different labels, within this book.

Infrastructure as Organizational Memory

For a systems-development organization, there is another important dimension of the learning process, which may be found in infrastructure, thought of as *organizational memory*. As an organization learns how to do something and makes it repeatable and predictable, that knowledge becomes a shared resource by being made part of the IT infrastructure.

A problem with infrastructure, however, as discussed earlier, is that it is often viewed as overhead rather than as an investment that enables IT solutions to business needs. In order for it to be positioned correctly, infrastructure must be linked to the IS mission, which in turn must be linked to the business mission.

To show how the Diamond Model, first discussed in Chapter 8, can be used to evaluate and plan continuous change necessary to keep IT aligned with shifting business needs, we map in Table 11.1 the five dimensions of the Diamond Model—Mission, Power,

	Data Processing 1950s–1970s	***Information Processing 1970s–1980s***	***Personal Computing 1980s–1990s***	***Information Engineering 1990s–2000s***	***Knowledge Engineering 2000–***
IS Mission	Support corporate functions. Administrative and clerical applications. Custom develop medium and large isolated systems. Provide hardware, software, and support.	Support departmental functions. Information analysis applications. Support small and medium systems. Interface applications through data. Provide data extracts and technical support.	Support personal needs. Information management applications. Enable small systems. Interface applications through "look and feel." Provide micro-mainframe linkage.	Strategic systems planning and analysis. Enterprise systems. Value-enhancing applications. Automate development and maintenance. Integrate applications through information. Provide models, facilitation and development. Provide infrastructure.	Interenterprise systems. Innovate business processes. Preempt development and maintenance. Integrate applications through knowledge architecture. Provide objects and coaches. Enhance infrastructure.
Source of IS Power	Potential cost savings. Need for DP experts. Handle DP volumes. DP owns systems. Taylor "Scientific Management."	Department needs. Need for corporate data. Need for technical support. User capability.	User needs. Access to corporate systems. Local budget. Technical infrastructure. User empowerment.	Strategic alignment. Joint development. Information engineering expertise. Information infrastructure. Participative management.	Business value added. User ownership. Object engineering expertise. Credible leadership. IT infrastructure. Self-managed team.

Table 11.1 *The Diamond Model Dimensions by Stages of Automation* *(continued)*

	Data Processing 1950s–1970s	***Information Processing 1970s–1980s***	***Personal Computing 1980s–1990s***	***Information Engineering 1990s–2000s***	***Knowledge Engineering 2000–***
IS Structure	Centralized DP. Program standards. Program libraries. Project management. Change control. Hierarchical reporting. Manage technology. Separate infrastructure for each project.	Information Center. Terminal networks. Data standards. Data dictionaries. Configuration management. Iterative development. Manage data.	Support desk. OA and PC standards. Software packages. Data methods. Manage end-user computing.	Development Center. Information architecture and standards. Repositories. Formal process. Structured and IE methods. Measurement. Flat hierarchy. Reduce and manage conflicts.	Hybrid IT structure. IT architecture and standards. Knowledge base of reusable parts. Incremental development. OO methods. Semantic modeling- Network/matrix. Manage reuse.
IS Resources	Mainframe data center. Utilities. DP specialists.	Time-sharing. 4GLs. Hierarchical DBMS. Query and reporting tools. Packages. Para-programmers. Consultants.	Stand-alone PCs. Personal tools. Applications and templates. End users.	Workstations and LANs. CASE tools. Relational DBMS. Application models. Joint user/developer design teams. Outsourcers.	Clients and servers. LANs and WANs. OO tools. OO DBMS. Architects and coaches. Software "chips." User partnerships. Vendor alliances.

	Data Processing 1950s–1970s	***Information Processing 1970s–1980s***	***Personal Computing 1980s–1990s***	***Information Engineering 1990s–2000s***	***Knowledge Engineering 2000–***
IS Culture	Applications can be prespecified. Users know nothing. Software is a craft. Hardware is an asset. Focus on reliability, availability, security. Value "superstars." Focus on project completion. Project success measured by technical correctness. "Take it or leave it" quality attitude. Every project is unique. Infrastructure resisted.	Applications evolve. Start-it-yourself. Users can do the simple stuff. Focus on programming speed. Defined process. Conform to specifications. Deliver when promised. Detect defects. Build interfaces. Information can be common.	Applications are one-offs. Do-it-yourself. Users can do the small stuff. Focus on user efficiency. Data is an asset. Conform to requirements. Deliver when needed. Prevent defects. Tools can be common.	Models are reusable. Build from stock. Users participate. Software is engineering. Focus on development effectiveness. Manage process. Information is an asset. Emphasize training and skills development. Team orientation. User as customer. Project success measured by customer satisfaction. Deploy on time. Continuous quality improvement. Models are common.	Objects are reusable. Mass customization. Users should own it. Software is manufactured. Focus on application effectiveness. Zero defects. People are an asset. Objects are an asset. Cross-function teams. Anticipate requirements. User as partner. Project success measured by business contribution. Deploy "just-in time." Optimizing proccess. Objects are common.

Table 11.1 *(continued)*

Structure, Resources, and Culture—against five "Stages of Automation." We then use the fifth stage, Knowledge Engineering, as an example of a future-state vision for Development Effectiveness and discuss each Diamond Model dimension in detail.

Stage 1: Data Processing

The first automation stage, which lasted from the early 1950s through the early 1970s, we refer to as "Data Processing." The primary IS mission was to support central business administration and operations, usually by delivering functionally oriented systems. Applications such as payroll, accounts receivable, and order processing were the "meat and potatoes" of this era, implemented as batch, and later, on-line systems. Throughout the Data Processing Stage, systems development was almost entirely performed by data processing professionals, using second generation programming languages (e.g., assembler), eventually moving to third generation languages (e.g., COBOL). Methods and techniques were highly variable and usually informal. Processes were poorly defined, if at all. Systems analysis was typically achieved through interviews, often with unwilling or ill-informed end users. System designs, if documented, were described through voluminous narrative specifications. One cynic insightfully referred to systems analysis during this era as "a resting place before programming," and to design as "an activity that takes place during maintenance"!

Stage 2: Information Processing

The second automation stage, starting in the mid-1970s and lasting until the early 1980s, we call the "Information Processing Stage." This stage was catalyzed by fourth generation languages (4GLs) and information-reporting tools, which did not so much replace traditional programming as supplement it. Fourth generation languages were primarily used in departmental and tactical applications, frequently working with data extracted from operational transaction processing systems. These applications were motivated by information value, as opposed to cost reduction, and were typically viewed initially as "one-offs." The information they generated was the primary object of interest, rather than the routines that generated it.

Stage 3: Personal Computing

The third automation stage, occurring during the early 1980s, we refer to as "Personal Computing." The IS mission accepted personal computers (PCs) for their potential to improve personal productivity and to support office automation. PCs helped users mechanize their own clerical activities, communicate with each other, and manage information. Some small business applications were developed for PC platforms, and IS provided linkages to mainframe applications in support of personal computing.

Stage 4: Information Engineering

In the mid-1980s, PCs, particularly because of their graphic capabilities, provided an ideal platform for the automation of structured analysis and design, and thus CASE technology was born. In turn, CASE enabled the creation of rigorous enterprise models, automatic data base and program generation from graphical models, and the structured methods of the mid- to late 1970s evolved into "Information Engineering." In the Information Engineering Stage, the IS mission shifted to emphasize strategic information systems planning and analysis, and automating the redevelopment of large enterprise applications. With CASE, the end product of development has changed from application programs as the primary deliverable of interest, to information models and the end user's ability to participate in rigorous analysis and design.

Stage 5: Knowledge Engineering

What does the next decade hold for IS? Stan Davis and Bill Davidson have described the evolution of IT as first based on data, then information, then knowledge and, ultimately, wisdom.[3] The next major computing era, following this evolution, will focus on knowledge engineering. Knowledge engineering will build upon the disciplines of information engineering, the techniques associated with CASE, and the methods and technologies associated with object orientation. Although object-oriented (OO) programming has been around for years, it has yet to reach the commercial mainstream, where OO tools and methods will need to scale up for industrial strength applications. Many predict that OO approaches will represent the greatest single revolution in systems development ever, although similar predictions have accompanied other innovations and have failed to materialize.

Mission

The Knowledge Engineering Stage will play an important role in supporting strategic and interenterprise systems, with object-oriented technology enabling business process innovation.

Although information engineering could be said to focus on automating systems development and maintenance, knowledge engineering will focus on preempting it, enabling systems to be constructed from prebuilt "objects," or subassemblies of program code.

Ultimately, knowledge engineering will allow end users to take a far more proactive role in systems delivery, and the mission of IS will shift to object provisioning and coaching end users in analysis, process redesign, and object-oriented development.

Power

Business value added will replace strategic alignment as the main source of organizational power in the Knowledge Engineering Stage. For IS, the need for corporate objects and object engineering expertise will be a major power source, whereas end-user ownership of application development will be an important source of power for the business. Self-managed teams will represent the prevalent approach to tapping the power of human resources.

Structure

Knowledge engineering will require several important structural changes. Incremental development and OO methods will replace the waterfall life cycle and extend information engineering. Entity-relationship techniques will be supplemented by higher forms of modeling, and relational data base structures supplemented by object-oriented data base management.

Hierarchical organization structures will almost entirely give way to loose networks, virtual teams, and matrix structures.

Managing reuse will become the focal point for the Knowledge Engineering Stage. Whereas the vendor community has been less than successful in agreeing on CASE standards, the object community is organizing itself around standards from the outset, facilitating object reuse and better tool integration.

Although in the Information Engineering Stage information models became the primary element for integration, objects will evolve to be the point of integration.

Resources

Client-server technology and other forms of distributed computing will dominate the hardware scene, and local area and wide area networks will dominate communications technology. CASE technology will evolve into OO tools and integrated object development environments. IS will become a source of object architects and end-user coaches.

Grady Booch was the first to coin the term *software chips*,[4] picking up the term for integrated circuits and implying the ability to build working systems from available supplies of objects, thereby achieving reuse.

Partnerships of various kinds will be important to knowledge engineering. User-developer partnerships will be the primary source of analysis and design effort. Industry partnerships will be an important source of ready objects. Vendor partnerships will sometimes be formed to provide object libraries where there are shortages.

Culture

The key cultural shift of this era will center on reusability. Today, developers believe their job is to develop software. Time or energy spent on nonprogramming activities is considered to be "loafing." The heroes are those who produce the most software code or the most complex and intricate programs. For software reuse to become a reality, this culture has to change. Producing new code will be viewed almost as a failure. The heroes will be those who achieve the greatest reuse.

With reuse, the paradigm for software manufacturing will shift to resemble the highest form of manufacturing known in industry today—mass customization. Eloquently described by John Naisbitt in *Megatrends,*[5] mass customization takes "manufacture from stock" to its ultimate form, where stock is reduced to zero through "just-in-time" availability of material and flexible production lines. With such approaches, which require sophistication with Total Quality Management, the benefits of mass production become available to production lots of "one."

In the Knowledge Engineering Stage, the concept that users should be heavily involved in the development process will shift even further, to the extreme that users own their systems, together with the responsibility for building, maintaining, and supporting them.

Systems will be viewed as a manufacturing process as a result of the previous era's realization that information systems are an engineering discipline.

The improvement culture institutionalized in the Information Engineering Stage will shift its emphasis from Development Effectiveness to Application Effectiveness.

The quality culture will have moved from defect prevention to a goal of "zero defects,"[6] and from meeting or exceeding customer requirements to one of anticipating customer requirements. Software process maturity will move toward an "optimizing process."[7]

The team culture will evolve into one where cross-functional and virtual teams—where team members are not co-located either geographically or organizationally—are commonplace and where the end user is viewed as a partner to IS.

Conclusion

Business needs and expectations for IT are evolving at an accelerating pace, requiring rapid response from the IS organization. As IS itself turns to information technology to help meet maturing business requirements, it must ensure that its mission fully supports business needs and directions and must align its changing mission with the infrastructure necessary to support its own automation. It must also re-skill its resources and evolve its culture so as to be compatible with that automation.

This also requires that IS management maintain a solid grasp of the business goals for IT and the resulting mission for the IS organization, and then support that mission with an appropriate infrastructure and resources that are resilient to the inevitable changes in IT purpose and IS mission.

In our discussion of Development Effectiveness, we have tried to lay out a structure for managing the enterprise's transition to a high-performance development organization. We have grouped activities into seven components: awareness building, vision setting, readiness assessment, transition planning, transition management, infrastructure implementation, and Pathfinder programs. We have emphasized that these components should not be approached sequentially, or in isolation. They are iterative and interrelated. Certain steps are repeated over and over, with different audiences, and with different aspects of an overall change initiative. Depending upon an organization's situation, the "middle" of the Transition Framework may be the starting point for working forward (toward program implementation) and backward (toward more awareness building) concurrently.

The Cliff Analogy

We have chosen to summarize this book with an analogy that we have found to be particularly useful in helping people understand the kind of change that is involved in moving to a high performance development organization, and explaining the Development Effectiveness approach to achieving that change. The "Cliff Analogy" addresses the nature of change as perceived by change targets, and the role of change agents and sponsors.

As we discussed in Chapter 6, organizational change negatively affects people's "Three C's"—their comfort, competence, and confidence. An objective of Development Effectiveness is to help sponsors, change agents, and target groups recognize this fact and create strategies to effectively rebuild target's comfort, competence, and confidence in the new future state.

Prior Ways of Viewing the Change Process

We use the Cliff Analogy during sessions designed to raise awareness about change. We begin by drawing a bridge, as in Figure 11.1. We explain that change agents have historically been viewed

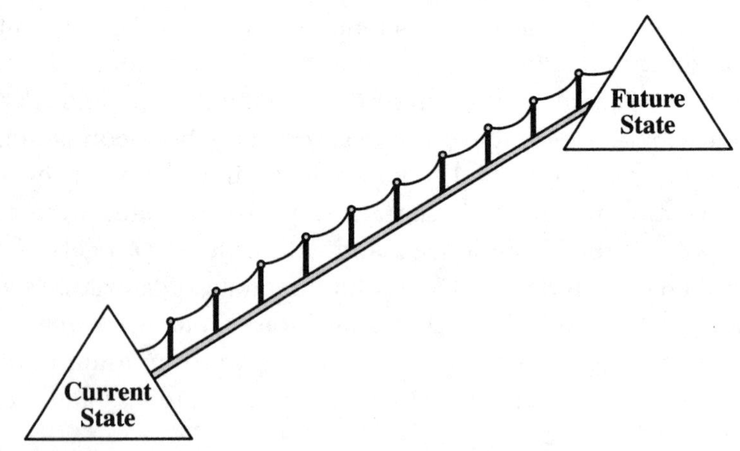

Figure 11.1 *The Change Agent as Bridge Builder*

as bridge builders—they were expected to complete the bridge from the current state to the future state relatively quickly, with the least possible interference with the organization's daily operations. While people might recognize that there is a slight incline to the bridge (moving from the current state to the future state is an uphill journey), there is a common perception that once the bridge is completed, most staff can simply walk across it to the other side.

A More Accurate View

Traditional ways of viewing the change process do not accurately describe reality, particularly from the perspective of those who are being asked to change their skills, knowledge, attitude, or behavior. A new analogy is called for.

We then draw the cliff, as in Figure 11.2, depicting how the change really looks to most change targets. The distance between the current and future states is so great that it is impossible to just throw a line over or build a bridge. Change targets must first descend one cliff, then ascend the other. Yet everyone affected by the change is being asked to walk to the edge of the cliff and jump!

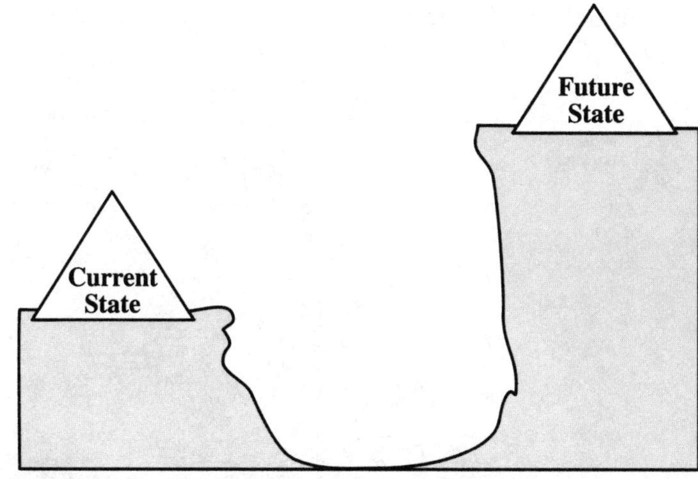

Figure 11.2 *The Cliff Analogy*

The cliff's depth affects the "Three Cs." It represents the degree of incompetence, discomfort, and lack of confidence that every individual in the target group will face. Imagine how the target group would feel if told, "Congratulations! We're implementing this new high performance development environment today, so you get to be incompetent, feel uncomfortable, and have your confidence threatened. We expect you to do more work, or at least not skip a beat." As ridiculous as this sounds, it is what organizations typically expect.

Role of the Change Agent and Sponsor

We then add the change target, the fire, landing pads, rope, and so on (see Figure 11.3) and discuss how the role of the sponsors, working in conjunction with the change agents, is to:

- Get people to move from the current state (i.e., "to jump"),
- Provide a variety of "safety nets" and "landing pads" at the bottom of the cliff so that no one "dies" as a result of taking on the change (i.e., "deciding to jump"), and
- Devise and implement ways to climb the cliff to the future state so that everyone becomes competent, comfortable, and confident *in doing things the new way.*

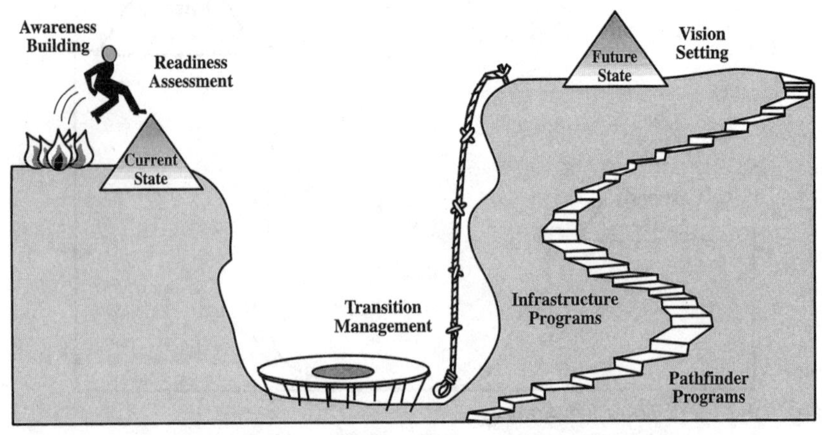

Figure 11.3 *Development Effectiveness and the Cliff Analogy*

Moving People from the Current State

We first described the need for Awareness Building to create incentives to make people jump. These are typically associated with the cost of the status quo—the cost of "not jumping," and the possibilities of the future state. Some of these are factors that "push" people over the edge (e.g., a "moving wall" or "burning platform"). Others "pull" people toward the other side (e.g., a clear, compelling vision of the future state).

We explain that this does not mean it is necessary (or even desirable) for everyone to jump at the same time. What is necessary is that everyone, without exception, be expected to jump at some specified time. No one will be permitted to hide in the current state. The sponsor's job is to stay focused on the change process by stripping away all hiding places.

We note that what is important to each individual (and so, will influence their behavior most strongly) is the *individual's* perception of the cliff's "depth," not the sponsor's perception. Two people can look at the exact same change and differ widely in their perceptions of how difficult it will be to achieve.

Helping People Come Down Safely

Sponsors and change agents can remove some of the fear of "making the jump." One way is to set and manage expectations so that individuals believe it is acceptable to be vulnerable (i.e., temporarily incompetent, uncomfortable, and unconfident). This can be done in terms of various "landing pads," such as sufficient learning curve time, sanctioned risk-taking, and recognition of the personal issues involved in change.

For example, it is unrealistic to expect individuals to make a significant change and still look and act the same to all customers and co-workers. Productivity will slip; mistakes will be made. Individuals need to vent their feelings and frustrations. And sponsors must expect and accept this if they do not want change target groups to revert to their previous, comfortable way of doing things.

Another way to encourage individuals to "make the jump" is to assure them that others have jumped successfully, and that, if need be, you will jump right along with them. The sponsor or change agent must stress that they are not the only ones making the change, nor do they face this change alone. They will have guides every step of the way.

Building Ways to Climb Back Up

Achieving a state of competence, comfort, and confidence in the new state takes time. We discuss techniques that can help this, including formal training, documentation, success stories from others that have jumped before (e.g., testimonials from individuals involved in Pathfinder programs). We describe the roles of coaches and mentors, and the need for opportunities to practice and make mistakes. Development Effectiveness provides a phased change process so that some individuals are already on the way up while others are facing their first jump off the cliff.

We discuss the importance of a clear future-state vision (the far cliff), and how a readiness assessment can be used to find out how deep the cliff is for each individual, and how ready people are to make the jump. Transition planning, infrastructure programs, and Pathfinder projects help create the steps for climbing the cliff. (Transition planning involves deciding how to bring everyone up to the future state, with the Infrastructure and Pathfinder programs providing the means for making the climb in manageable steps.)

The Development Effectiveness approach has been used successfully by a number of organizations, of varying sizes, in different industries, and in different countries. While it does not pretend to provide easy solutions, it does restore the balance of focus from purely technological and methodological perspectives, to a more process- and organizational-change perspective.

If it sounds like a great deal of work, your instinct is correct. Some of the root causes of today's systems development problems are deep seated, and have been compounded by wave after wave of purported instant "silver bullet" solutions, that have all largely missed their mark. Only through significant attention to IT process improvement and innovation, and organizational and culture change within the IS function, can substantial, lasting solutions be implemented.

As mentioned earlier, there are no easy answers. Every organization is unique and will approach change in its own way. We hope, however, that this book has provided food for thought, a way to structure thinking about the challenges facing the IS professional today and how best to respond to those challenges.

Notes

1. Toffler, Alvin, *The Third Wave* (London: William Collins Sons & Co., Ltd., 1980).

2. Senge, Peter M., *The Fifth Discipline: The Art & Practice of The Learning Organization* (New York, NY: Doubleday, 1990).

3. Stan Davis and Bill Davidson, *2020 Vision* (New York: Simon & Schuster, 1991).

4. Grady Booch, *Object-Oriented Design with Applications* (Redwood City, CA: The Benjamin-Cummings Publishing Co., 1991).

5. John Naisbitt, *Megatrends* (New York: Warner Books, 1982).

6. Armand V. Feigenbaum, *Total Quality Control* (New York: McGraw-Hill, 1991).

7. Watts S. Humphrey, *Managing the Software Process* (Reading, MA: Addison-Wesley Publishing Co., 1989).

References and Bibliography

Most IS professionals read, on average, less than one technical book a year, although the IS industry publishes well over 1,000 new titles each year. Everyone is busy, but we all need to keep current with the key concepts and trends in the industry if we are to cope with change. Here is a list of useful reference material and background reading on the various aspects of implementing a Development Effectiveness program covered in this book. We have taken the liberty of marking a few of these (*) as "essential reading" for those who are going to be transition program managers. This is our personal view—for which we make no apologies—but with which you are free to disagree after reading.

*Albrecht, A. J. "Measuring Application Development Productivity." In *Proceedings of the Joint SHARE/GUIDE/IBM Application Development Symposium*. Guide International Corporation, 1979.

Allen, Brandt. "Making Information Services Pay Its Way." *Harvard Business Review* 65:1 (January-February 1987).

Andrews, Dorine C., and Naomi S. Leventhal. *Fusion*. Englewood Cliffs, NJ: Yourdon Press, 1993.

Arthur, L. J. *Measuring Programmer Productivity and Software Quality*. New York: John Wiley & Sons, 1985.

August, Judy H. *Joint Application Design*. Englewood Cliffs, NJ: Yourdon Press, 1991.

Bailey, J.W., and V.R. Basili. "A Meta-Model for Software Development and Resource Expenditures." In *Proceedings of the 5th International Conference on Software Engineering*. New York: IEEE Computer Society Press, 1981.

*Barker, Joel A. *Future Edge: Discovering the New Paradigms of Success*. New York: William Morrow & Co., 1992.

*Beckhard, Richard, and Reuben Harris. *Organizational Transitions*. Reading, MA: Addison-Wesley Publishing Co., 1987.

*Boehm, B. *Software Engineering Economics*. Englewood Cliffs, NJ: Prentice-Hall, 1981.

*Bridgers, William. *Managing Transitions*. Reading, MA: Addison-Wesley Publishing Co., 1991.

*Brooks, Frederick P., Jr. *The Mythical Man-Month: Essays on Software Engineering*. Reading, MA: Addison-Wesley Publishing Co., 1982.

Byham, William C., and Jeff Cox. *Zapp!: The Lightning of Empowerment*. New York: Fawcett, 1992.

Chen, E. T. "Program Complexity and Programmer Productivity." *IEEE Transaction Software Engineering* SE-4 No. 3 (May 1978).

Chin-Kuei, Cho. *An Introduction to Software Quality Control*. New York: Wiley Interscience, 1987.

*Conner, Daryl R. *Managing at the Speed of Change*. New York: Villard Books, 1993.

Cusumano, Michael A., *Japan's Software Factories: A Challenge to U.S. Management* (Oxford, England: Oxford University Press, 1991).

*Davenport, Thomas H. *Process Innovation: Reengineering Work Through Information Technology*. Boston: Harvard Business School Press, 1992.

*DeMarco, Tom, and Timothy Lister. *Peopleware: Productive Projects and Teams*. New York: Dorset House Publishing, 1987.

Egan, Gerald. *Change Agent Skills: A. Stressing and Designing*

Excellence; B. *Managing Innovation and Change*. San Diego: University Associates, Inc. 1988.

Gilb, Tom. *Software Metrics*. Winthrop Publishers, 1977.

Gilb, Tom. *Principles of Software Engineering Management*. Reading, MA: Addison-Wesley Publishing Co., 1988.

Glass, Robert L. *Building Quality Software*. Englewood Cliffs, NJ: Prentice-Hall, 1992.

Goldratt, Eliyahu M., and Jeff Cox. *The Goal: A Process of Ongoing Improvement*. Croton-on-Hudson, NY: North River Press Inc., 1984.

*Grady, Robert B. *Practical Software Metrics for Project Management and Process Improvement.* Englewood Cliffs, NJ: Prentice-Hall, 1992.

*Grady, Robert B., and Deborah L. Caswell. *Software Metrics: Establishing a Company-Wide Program*. Englewood Cliffs, NJ: Prentice-Hall, 1987.

Hammer, Michael, and James Champy. *Reengineering the Corporation: A Manifesto for Business Revolution*. New York: HarperBusiness, 1993.

Jones, T.C. *Programming Productivity: Issues for the Eighties*. No. EHO 186-7, New York: IEEE Computer Society Press, 1981.

Jones, T.C. *Programming Productivity*. New York: McGraw-Hill, 1986.

*Katzenbach, Jon R., and Douglas K. Smith. *The Wisdom of Teams: Creating the High-Performance Organization*. Boston: Harvard Business School Press, 1993.

Longworth, G. *Realistic User Requirements.* Manchester: NCC Publications, 1987.

*McGee, James V., and Laurence Prusak. *Managing Information Strategically*. New York: John Wiley & Sons, 1993.

Myers, Glenford J. *The Art of Software Testing*. New York: John Wiley & Sons, 1979.

Parker, Marilyn M., and Robert J. Benson. *Information Economics*. Englewood Cliffs, NJ: Prentice-Hall, 1988.

Parkinson, John. *Making CASE Work*. Cambridge, MA: NCC Blackwell, 1991.

Prahalad, C. K., and Gary Hamel. "The Core Competence of the Corporation." *Harvard Business Review* (May-June 1990).

Putnam, L. H. *Software Cost Estimating and Life-Cycle Control: Getting the Software Numbers*. No. EHO 165-1. New York: IEEE Computer Society Press, 1980.

Schaefer, Robert H. *The Breakthrough Strategy*. New York: HarperBusiness, 1988.

Schein, Edgar H. "Planning and Managing Change." Management in the 1990s Working Paper, Sloan School of Management. Cambridge, MA: Massachusetts Institute of Technology, August 1988.

*Senge, Peter M. *The Fifth Discipline: The Art and Practice of the Learning Organization*. New York: Doubleday, 1990.

*Tuttle, T., and D. Sink. "Taking the Threat Out of Productivity Measurement." *National Productivity Review* (Winter 1984-85).

Weinberg, Gerald M. *Quality Software Management. Vol. 1, Systems Thinking*. New York: Dorset House Publishing, 1992.

Weinberg, Gerald M. *Quality Software Management. Vol. 2, First Order Measurement*. New York: Dorset House Publishing, 1993.

Yourdon, Edward, *Decline & Fall of the American Programmer.* Englewood Cliffs, NJ: Yourdon Press, 1992.

Zachman, John. *A Framework for Information Systems Architecture.* G320-2785. IBM Corporation, 1986.

Index